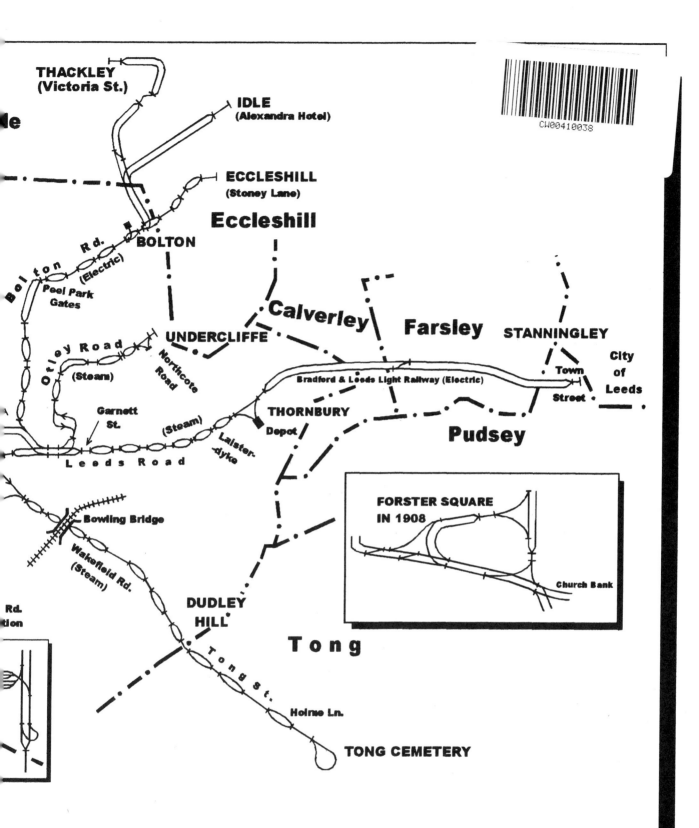

BRADFORD CITY TRAMWAYS, January 1902

THORNBURY --- destination name

Wibsey --- placename

T o n g --- exsisting or pre - 1899 Urban District

▬ • ▬ • ▬ boundary

(JSK/WEW,1998)

BRADFORD CORPORATION TRAMWAYS

by

Stanley King

Dedicated to the memory of
Mr Frank Hartley
of Eccleshill, Bradford, (1905-1999)
whose long memory, powers of observation, genial humour and endless patience,
inspired the writing of this book.

CONTENTS

The end of the line for the Shelf trams came in 1935.
Three summers previously 'Greengates' car No. 90
had been photographed at the terminus with the
narrow-gauge Halifax tracks in the foreground and a
competing Hebble bus approaching.

FOREWORD

By Mr H. Cooke

B.Sc., A.M.I.C.E., A.M.I.M.E.

retired Bradford City Engineer

I am very pleased to be asked to write a short Foreword to Mr King's book on the Bradford Trams. I am reminded of a little piece of doggerel from many years ago which goes as follows:

> *'A creature of habit I am,*
> *For change I could not give a damn;*
> *A creature who moves in predestined grooves–*
> *In fact, not a bus, but a tram'*

That, to me, epitomises a way of life which has gone for ever, when people had more patience and were prepared to sit in a passing loop without grumbling for a tram to come in the opposite direction.

We did not expect routes to be changed at the whim of some bureaucrat: we lived on established routes which involved track laying, overhead equipment and the rest. Most authorities had their own tramway system. In many cases the Permanent Way was laid down by a Permanent Way Engineer, but in many cases the Local Authority Engineering Department, City Engineer or Borough Engineer looked after the track as was the case in Hull and in Bradford where I worked. We had our own Permanent Way Assistant. Trackwork was very interesting – it meant that the track had to be designed within the confines of the street layout, with sharp curves and, in many cases, highly complex junctions. This work was mostly complicated and employed a staff of draughtsmen and designers, pattern makers and steel workers, so that eventually the whole layout was erected in the works of these firms before being installed in the towns or cities for which it was required.

This was a fascinating subject and, as I say, employed many people, something which is to be regretted in these days when accountants run everything and have no idea what an Engineering Department is like.

Mr King, I know, is a tram enthusiast: he can not only write about them, he can actually drive trams and has done so, to my knowledge, in Bradford, Stockport and Dundee. His knowledge is encyclopaedic and I wish him well in this book.

Sadly, Mr Cooke died in his 90th year on 9th June, 1999, only a few weeks before the publication of this book.

PREFACE

by Mr Michael Wharton ('Peter Simple')

Anybody who grew up, as I did, in what is now called 'Greater Bradford' in the 'twenties must think of the Bradford tramway system as one of the wonders and glories of what was then a unique city (as, no doubt, it still is, even though so much has irrevocably changed). I think of those double-decker trams proceeding so majestically along the hilly streets, with their clanging bells, their overhead conductor-arms occasionally producing showers of beautiful blue sparks.

I think of the tramwaymen in their blue uniforms, wielding their old-fashioned ticket-punches and dispensing tickets variously coloured for the differently-numbered values, or operating the old-fashioned destination indicators, some referring to parts of the district ('Shelf', 'Odsal', Drighlington') I had never visited and therefore, as a child, thought infinitely mysterious.

I remember my daily journeys, later on, from Nab Wood (then part of Shipley), where we lived (that tram-route started at far-off Crossflatts, on the very edge of Ilkley Moor), along Manningham Lane to the grim old Grammar School at the top of Cheapside, opposite the Yorkshire Penny Bank. As the trams began their steep descent to Forster Square, a great meeting-place of trams, they seemed to groan with particular anguish. As we schoolboys sat in our classroom not far away, one of our teachers, a much-mimicked man, noting hesitation over some passage of translation, would invariably make the same remark: "Speak up, speak up! Remember, we have the whole of the Bradford tramway system to contend against", then wait, teacher-like , for the expected laugh.

Romantic in memory even now, the trams provided for me a whole mythological realm, so that when I became a writer I made my fictional figure of a majestic alderman the 'perpetual chairman of the Bradford City Tramways and Fine Arts Committee', while in my satirical fantasy *Sheldrake*, where Bradford declares its unilateral independence, the tramwaymen become the elite of its armed forces.

Fantasy apart, the real-life story of the Bradford tramways, as told by Councillor Stanley King, is a fascinating, even exciting one, full of stirring incidents like to Great Fire Disaster of November 1926 at Thornbury Depot and the Great Snowstorm of February 1933, which proved, if proof were needed, the superiority of the tram over other vehicles in extreme weather conditions.

Nothing, however, not even the Bradford tramways, can stay the same for ever. The original old open-top trams – it was (or seems now) a real delight to ride on those in fine weather, as they surged and swayed so proudly through the streets and the smoky vistas of the city stretched away on every side! – soon disappeared, giving way to ever more convenient and comfortable models. We did not realise then what an immense amount of engineering skill, hard work and dedication went into this service of which the City Council was so justly proud.

But for the true tram-lover the story is still a sad one. It is the story of a long, hard-fought but eventually hopeless battle against change, and against rival, new-fangled forms of public transport. Even in the 'twenties motor buses were beginning to appear in Bradford streets, vulgar, parvenu vehicles hooting and belching fumes as they crawled insolently in the very shadow of the majestic tram-galleons.

Not that these interlopers had things all their own way. The tramways, which had their determined partisans, fought back bravely. Even towards the end, though some tram-routes were abandoned, others were still being extended. A new single-decker tram, less imposing than double-deckers but still *trams*, was flung into the battle, luxuriously furnished, smooth-running, and capable, when driven flat out by elite crews, of reaching unprecedented speeds.

But it was all in vain. Soon came the challenge of the trolley-buses, as strongly supported by their modernising advocates as the trams were defended by theirs, and fated in the nature of things to gain the victory. The deciding factor, of course, was simply that trolley-buses, free of fixed lines, were better able than trams to manoeuvre among the ever-increasing motor-traffic which swiftly came to rule the roads in Bradford as it did everywhere else.

With the all-conquering car, the noble trams, which had served the city so well and contributed so much to its peculiar and individual character among English cities, were doomed, like so many other much-loved things, to disappear at last.

Will they ever return? It may be that with the growing movement against what has become the tyranny of the motor car and the demand for more and better public transport, some new kinds of tramcars, 'environmentally and ecologically acceptable', will appear in the wholly transformed streets of a future Bradford. But one thing is certain. Whatever such vehicles may look like and whatever they may be called, they will be no more than a pale travesty of the mighty trams of old.

AUTHOR'S ACKNOWLEDGEMENTS

This book, the final instalment in the Bradford Corporation transport trilogy of trolleybuses, motor buses and tramcars, is the culmination of countless years of study, research, discussion and friendship.

Without the expert knowledge and encouragement of Mr Frank Hartley, Mr James Copland, Mr Eric Thornton, Mr Herbert Cheetham and our late friends Mr John A. Pitts and Mr Maurice Peck, no worthwhile history of the tramways would have been possible.

Valuable information has been unstintingly contributed by Messrs J. Breeze Bentley, Harold Smith (who remembered the horse and steam trams), H. Brearley, A. Feather, N. Hinchliffe, J.H. Price, F.P. Groves, R. Brook, G.M. Baxter, B.M. Robinson, J. Pollard, Dr P. Excell, F.D. Richardson, A.K. Terry, J. Soper, E. Turner, Messrs M. Boyes and S. Holmes (Blackburn), and my parents. Similarly the Bradford press (Telegraph and Argus and its predecessors), the Yorkshire Post, Keighley News and Halifax Courier, the public libraries of Bradford, Halifax, Leeds, Manchester and Sheffield, the British Library, West Yorkshire Archives, the National Tramway Museum (Crich), Messrs R. McHugh and E. Nicholson of Bradford Industrial Museum, and the late esteemed Bradford Corporation Transport Department (Messrs C.R. Tattam, C.T. Humpidge, N.A. Scurrah, K.E. Griffiths, E. Oughtibridge, H. Lightowler, J. Elam, T.M. Franks, J. Moorhouse, W. Northrop, H. Lincoln, my grandfather J.E. Hornsby and many others).

Grateful thanks also to Messes H. Cooke and M. Wharton for the Foreword and Preface, Mrs. J.B. Ball. Mr. and Mrs. W.E. Wakefield, the J.L. Langtry - Langton Partnership, and Venture Publications for their patience and thoroughness.

J.S. King
Heaton
Bradford

TOWN HALL & MARKET ST
BRADFORD

1 - NARROW IS THE WAY

"Broad is the way that leadeth to destruction, and many there be which go in thereat .... narrow is the way that leadeth unto life"

(Matthew 7, v.13-14)

Tramways, like marriage, are not to be entered into 'inadvisedly, lightly or wantonly'.

Prudent municipalities always felt a need to ensure that the costly enterprise of laying tracks and launching tramcar services would fulfil a known public need, pay its way and promote the development of their town.

Such was the view of the Mayor and Corporation of the Borough of Bradford in the West Riding of Yorkshire when first approached by promoters eager to woo them with schemes for tramways linking the fast-growing town with its outskirts.

A borough since 1847 and owing its meteoric rise and prosperity to wool, worsted combing, spinning and weaving as well as iron, sandstone and coal, it remained a collection of villages and suburbs until the present century. Railways, first introduced in 1846, were restricted by the challenging terrain of the Pennine foothills, although Clayton station had a thriving clientele until the 1920s, and Frizinghall once boasted the busiest suburban station on the Midland Railway.

The Corporation's caution did not stem from ignorance of the subject, as the question of tramways had often been aired by the local press.

As early as 22nd January 1857, the 'Bradford Observer' had brought to the notice of townsfolk the then novel idea of 'tramroads' or 'horse railways' in the highway. The old mail-coaches having succumbed to competition from the railways, many villages were without any regular means of communication. Mineral tramways had long been a familiar feature in and around the local ironworks, and what was now proposed was 'the old trams with a new face and new-fashioned flanged wheels – smart, roomy omnibuses for 50 people', which would be readily patronised. 'Horse railways are found popular in America – why not in England?'

The question remained unanswered until April 1862, when the *Observer* discussed 'Mr G. F. Train and his Tramways', together with a plea for 'tram ways' or smooth iron plates to be laid in the ill-paved Bradford streets to ease the burden of cart-horses. Details of a novel 'tram' or street railway in Marylebone, London, were followed in June by a plea for a 'tram railway' from Bradford to Denholme, a 5¾-mile ascent over country roads.

Even more imaginatively *Hortonian* in November 1871 published ideas for four circular horse-tram services, viz,

(1) To and from Midland Station via Thornton Road, Whetley Lane and Manningham Lane (4 tramcars);

To and from Peel Place via (2) Bankfoot, Dudley Hill and Laisterdyke – 2 cars; (3) Manchester Road, Park Road, Little Horton and Great Horton – 1 car, and (4) East Parade, Undercliffe and Laisterdyke - 2 cars.

Cheap fares and a track gauge of approximately 4ft 7¾ ins were envisaged, with dividends optimistically forecast at 15% on a capital of £40,000. However, teams of quadrupeds would have been needed to drag the laden cars up the unrelenting gradients, and the sparse service proposed did not justify the outlay.

More soberly the Bradford District Tramways Company (Messrs J.F. Easby, G. Newby, J.S. Muir, William Turton and Joseph Speight) in November 1872, advertised a parliamentary Bill for tramways to Thornton, Bankfoot, Eccleshill, Saltaire and Thornbury, all of which (except Bankfoot) lay beyond the borough boundary. Obliquely referring to G.F. Train's 'street railways' which had hindered the progress of tramways through 'being brought before the public in an immature form', the promoters claimed that 'the Tram Car' was 'loftier, better ventilated, easier of access' and wider than other public conveyances, and being able to carry as many passengers as ten cabs or carriages, would occupy less space on the highway, especially as the track gauge was to be a sensible four feet. Always suspicious of private tracks laid in public highways, Bradford Corporation insisted on financial guarantees which the company deemed unreasonable, and the project was abandoned in 1874.

A like fate befell the Bradford Tramways Company (promoters Messrs W. Page, H.W. White, W.E. Wynne, Mason and others) who proposed 4ft 8½ins gauge lines to Manchester Road (St. Stephen's Road) and Lister Park Gates, using horse, steam, atmospheric, hydraulic or other authorised power (although afterwards the promoters revealed that they had intended to use San Francisco-type cable haulage).

Public attitudes changed greatly with the passing of the 'Act for the Use of Mechanical Power on Tramways' in August 1879. At a special Town Council meeting on 14th October Alderman

Horse tramcar No. 2 at the Victor Road terminus of the Rawson Square-Park Gates route.

Edward West successfully moved the adoption of tramways in the borough, with 4ft gauge lines from Rawson Square to Lister Park, from Peel Place to the borough boundary in Leeds Road and from Bridge Street to Four Lane Ends. With the addition of a link line between Peel Place and Bridge Street the proposal gained Parliamentary approval as the Bradford Corporation Tramways Order, 1880. The tramways were to be constructed by the Corporation but must then be leased to an operating company.

Yorkshire tramway operators were criticised as early as 1900 for their apparently random selection of track gauges, the inference being that the 4ft 8½ins width should rank as 'standard', even though major centres such as Birmingham, Glasgow, Dublin and Portsmouth thought otherwise. It must therefore be stressed that in the early years the Yorkshire municipalities, not being part of a conurbation in the Lancashire sense, had little reason to expect that their lines would one day meet. Inter-town traffic was handled by the railways, and horse-trams or steam cars could never have struggled over the hills between Bradford, Halifax and Huddersfield. Each town therefore used the gauge which suited its own circumstances. Bradford chose 'the narrow way' – the 4ft gauge – partly because of the narrowness of many of its streets (Manchester Road was actually deemed impassable) and partly because they had been advised that in Leeds the broader-gauge tracks suffered obstruction and excessive wear from the hooves and tyres of horse-drawn carts and waggons whose wheels conveniently fitted the rails.

Following its first meeting on 12th November 1880, the Corporation Tramways Committee inspected tram rails at Liverpool and Manchester and sampled steam trams at Dewsbury and Leeds, as steam traction was needed for all the routes except the fairly level Manningham Lane (Lister Park) line.

In July 1881 a tender for the operation of the tramways by Messrs William Turton, William Mason and Daniel Busby was accepted and a 21-year lease granted with a rental per mile of single track of £290 per annum for the first ten years and £300 thereafter. The three gentlemen were lessees of the Leeds and Liverpool tramways, Mr Busby being a resident of the latter city and Messrs Turton and Mason having been promoters of the 1872 and 1878 schemes respectively.

Manningham Lane, 'a sea of mud' until the Corporation experimented with granite sett paving in 1879, was first visited by track-laying gangs on 8th September 1881. When the Corporation had prepared a concrete foundation, the contractors laid the grooved steel rails, after which the entire carriageway was re-paved with new setts. Like all Bradford tramways laid before 1900, the track was single with strategically-placed passing places (loops), extending from Rawson Square to Lister Park Gates with an extended turning-circle via Oak Lane, St. Mary's Road and North Park Road and a terminus at the foot of Victor Road.

Watched by interested crowds the first tramcar was placed on the rails at the junction of Manningham Lane and North Parade on 15th January 1882. From there it was pulled by horses to the Company's depot in Oak Lane in preparation for an inspection of the line next day by the Town Clerk, Borough Surveyor, Chief Constable and Mr Turton.

Five more cars arrived in the next few days; all had been built by the Ashbury Railway Carriage Company of Manchester, and were painted in a pleasing nut-brown and yellow livery. They were double-deckers with 18 longitudinal (inwards-facing) seats inside and 20 'knifeboard' (outwards-facing longitudinal) seats on the open upper deck. In order to spare the horses, the cars were lightly-built and single-ended, with only one staircase, on the Eades principle whereby the body could be swivelled round each time the tram reached the end of the line.

Before being opened to the public, all British tramways were required to undergo a Board of Trade inspection. Accordingly Major-General C.S. Hutchinson met Corporation and Company officials on 31st January in Rawson Square, whence they travelled by tram, driven by Robert Lawson, to Victor Road. The inspector then returned on foot, inspecting the track as he did so. He warmly approved of all that he saw – the well-laid Mountsorrel granite paving, the 60lb per yard rails and the spring-operated points (an unusual refinement in the early days) at all loops.

Next day two triumphal tramcars suitably bedecked with banners conveyed the Tramways Committee to a celebratory luncheon – a very late one at 5pm, which, as Yorkshiremen, they doubtless classed as 'high tea'. On 2nd February the Company commenced a half-hourly service from 8am to 11pm at a flat twopenny fare, and when the stables were completed on 6th February the frequency was doubled. The Bradford tramway era had begun.

Rawson Square, at the heart of Bradford's fashionable shopping area, was the terminus of the Manningham Lane horse trams. Two well-dressed ladies are climbing on board car No. 5, about 1895.

The stud of 60 horses, working as pairs in five relays, were well cared-for by the Company and appreciated by the passengers, who often alighted before their usual stop to relieve the steeds of the strain of starting the car unnecessarily. Many regular users had their own special favourites, such as two grey mares, Violet and Fairy who worked as a pair; a bay mare, Maggie, and a light grey called Daisy were always popular, as were Tom and Doctor, who often took waggonette parties on Sunday excursions into Wharfedale.

An extra 'trace' horse was attached for the ascent of Oak Lane and, at busy times, for the slight gradient past Belle Vue. Riding along 'The Lane' – Bradford's premier thoroughfare – in the 'eighties and 'nineties was a pleasant and fashionable practice for those who could afford the high fare.

The Leeds Road and Four Lane Ends lines served densely-populated workaday areas whose modest gradients called for steam trams. By the time that the permanent way had been completed on 22nd May the company (now styled 'The Bradford Tramways and Omnibus Co' having apparently bought out the horse-bus operating Bradford Livery Stables Company) had acquired seven cars (Nos. 7-13) for the service, the vehicles differing from Nos. 1-6 in having a glazed canopy fitted to the leading end of the top deck to protect passengers from ash, grit and steam emitted by the engines.

As the engines themselves were not available in time for the inspection of the Leeds Road line on 7th June, 'four fine grey horses' had to be borrowed from the Manningham tramway. A

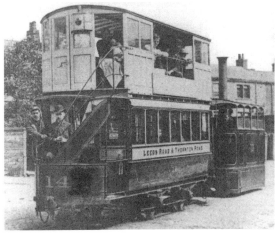

Bradford carthorses look askance as a Kitson engine and car steam down Leeds Road early in 1882. The exact location seems to be in the vicinity of Garnett Street.   *Photo: the late F. C. Cork*

Car No. 14, one of the 'rocking-boats', awaits departure time at Four Lane Ends behind a Green engine, c.1885.

month later the first locomotive was delivered to the new depot at Lee Row, the outer terminus, from where it made successful trial runs as far as the top of Sunbridge Road on the Four Lane Ends line. Engines Nos. 1-3 were tested in Leeds Road on 2nd August, commencing a 20-minute service to Peel Place next day.

Following an experimental run to Four Lane Ends on 12th September with engine No. 5 and Car No. 11 one steam tram commenced an hourly service from Sunbridge Road (Godwin Street), probably on 21st September, and with the arrival of engines 4/6 a 20-minute through service from Lee Row to Four Lane Ends was instituted on 30th October.

The engines, built by Kitsons of Leeds, were of that firm's early design with 7¼ins bore 12ins stroke cylinders, 28½ins diameter wheels and 4ft 6ins wheelbase, the machinery being totally enclosed for the peace of mind of passing horses. Waste steam was condensed via banks of roof-mounted air-cooled copper tubes which returned the condensate to the water tank, and as a precaution against locomotive thirst a water-hydrant was installed at Four Lane Ends. The engines could be driven from either end, being uncoupled from the car at each terminus and then reversed by means of the passing loop for re-coupling at the opposite end. While this ritual was being enacted, the conductor swivelled the car body around to face the new direction, as the cars were single-ended like the horse trams.

This quaint practice led to a ludicrous mishap at Four Lane Ends in March 1887, while conductor John Oughtibridge was turning the body of car No. 10 before the engine entered the loop. Waiting until the body was at right-angles to the truck, a mischievous breeze swept down from Thornton and blew the car halfway to Bradford with resultant harm to two horse-drawn drays. Triangular reversers were therefore laid at all the Company's steam tram termini so that the cars did not need to be uncoupled from the engines.

An extension of the borough boundaries in 1882 to include the districts of Heaton and Allerton and the hamlets of Thornbury and Tyersal provided new territory for the tramcars, commencing with an extension of the Manningham Lane tramway to Frizinghall which opened on 26th January 1885. The four trams bought for the new service, Nos. 16-19, were again of the Eades reversible type but with light top-deck covers to protect passengers from overhanging trees in Keighley Road. A 15-minute service was provided, which, together with the Park Gates (Victor Road) service, gave a 7½-minute frequency between Rawson Square and Oak Lane, all fares being 2d.

Two double-ended cars for the Leeds Road – Four Lane Ends steam service (14-15) had been acquired a few months previously, with glazed end vestibules and an overall roof, thus allowing the Company to respond to a petition from Thornbury residents. The Corporation laid a 356-yard extension of the Leeds Road line across the old borough boundary, with a reversing triangle at the foot of Upper Rushton Road, to which point the Leeds Road – now Thornbury – cars began to run in July (probably 17th or 18th), 1885.

In order to accommodate the growing steam tram fleet a larger depot was opened at the new Thornbury terminus in late 1887. At the depot entrance the tracks were arranged in triangular fashion, superseding the Upper Rushton Road triangular reverser. The small Lee Row depot was sold, and many years later its site was occupied by Crofts' Engineering Works, where the old locomotive inspection pits remained visible until 1945.

Larger cars and more powerful engines were now needed for the steadily increasing traffic. Tramcars 20-23 represented a distinct improvement on the earlier rolling-stock, as they were large enclosed bogie cars seating 54. Engine No. 8 was an advanced Kitson product with 8½ins diameter cylinders, whilst Nos. 7(ii) and 9-11 were Thomas Green and Sons locomotives with 9ins diameter cylinders. Number 7(ii) replaced an earlier Wilkinson-patent engine loaned by Greens in 1883. The five new locomotives were the only ones capable of hauling the bogie cars; all entered service in 1885 and were joined by a further Green engine, No. 12, two years later.

Competition from horse-buses and waggonettes on Manningham Lane compelled the tramway company to halve its 2d fare, and the Corporation agreed to double much of the track on all three routes, so that by April 1887, a continuous double line extended from North Parade to Park Gates. In September turning-circles were laid at the Rawson Square and Frizinghall termini to obviate the need for the horses to mount the pavement when turning the car bodies on their pivots.

Working conditions of the tramway staff were typical of their day. In a four-week period the men worked 15 hours a day for three weeks and 12 hours a day in the fourth week. Sunday was almost a day of rest, as they worked only ten hours! In return for these demanding duties, exposed to all weathers, the drivers received a guinea (21 shillings) per week, and meals had to be taken at the termini between journeys.

Reminiscing 64 years later, Mr John Noble recalled that the 15-minute journey time from Park Gates (and 25 minutes from

Frizinghall) provided a social occasion – and chance to exchange gossip – for Bradford's elite who used the services.

During 1887 a semi-rural extension from Four Lane Ends to the village of Allerton was laid on a maximum gradient of 1 in 19½. From the triangular terminus at the Druid's Arms a half-hourly cross-town service to Thornbury opened on 19th November.

In 1884 the Bradford Tramways and Omnibus Company (BTOC) had committed an error of judgement which no doubt they rued many times. Offered the 'first refusal' by the Corporation of proposed tramways in Bolton Road and Manchester Road, they failed to display sufficient interest, whereupon the Corporation invited tenders. The thinly-populated Bolton line attracted no worthwhile interest, but the Manchester Road tender was won by a new, locally-based company calling itself 'The Bradford and Shelf Tramways Company' and offering either 9% of its profits or £400 per single track mile per annum. On that basis a 19-year lease was granted so that the leases of both companies would expire simultaneously on 31st January 1903.

As its title implied, the Bradford and Shelf Co. (BST) had the long-term ambition of operating as far as Shelf, an isolated village midway between Bradford and Halifax. Initially, however, they were to operate as far as the borough boundary at Bank Foot (correctly Wibsey Bank Foot and later simply Bankfoot), a distance of nearly two miles on an average gradient of 1 in 28.

Firmly declining to run their cars along Market Street to a central terminus near the Midland Station, which would have involved a right-angled crossing of the BTOC's Allerton-Thornbury tracks in Bridge Street, they opted for a terminus outside Bradford Town Hall, with a turning circle around the statue of Sir Titus Salt, founder of the village of Saltaire. The company's depot and offices were to be located at Rathmell Street near the Bank Foot terminus and turning-circle at the 'Red Lion'.

The permanent way, which comprised double track as far as Hope Street and from Tudor Street to the terminus with an intervening section of single line and passing loops, was inspected and opened on 6th September 1884. The inspector disliked the points, which had no tongues and relied on a straight 'run in' by the engines and cars. Only a few days after the opening an engine and car took different roads when negotiating the points, and the Corporation agreed to provide sprung points, but not until the original units wore out!

Five Thomas Green engines constituted the original BST motive power, Nos. 1-4 being Wilkinson's patent with vertical boilers and 7¼ins diameter cylinders, whilst No. 5 (delivered in January 1885) was the first locomotive-type engine built by Greens, with 9ins cylinders. The tramcars were large 58-seat double-deck bogie units with padded seats – a rare refinement – in the lower saloon. Numbered 1-6, they were built by Starbuck and painted Prussian blue and ivory.

With a maximum fare of 2d and a penny stage at Ryan Street (later Ripley Street) the service was an instant success, and pending delivery of No. 5 a hired Burrell compound engine, No. 6, helped to provide a 10-minute frequency. The rival horse-buses soon withdrew from the unequal contest.

Purchases of further passenger cars enabled the company to provide an even more frequent service, as from the outset every BST engine and tram had been needed at busy times, leaving only the night-hours for maintenance. Five 18-seat single-deck four-wheel cars, 7 to 11, were bought, probably from Starbuck, in the Spring of 1885, followed by identical Nos. 13-14 in the Autumn. Only one extra engine was needed – No. 7 from Thomas Green – as the Company planned to attach the little single-deckers to the double-deckers at busy times, albeit in contravention of Board of Trade regulations.

To the displeasure of the Corporation the Company duly carried out their plan, and soon trains of tramcars could be seen labouring up Manchester Road. With a full load the engines proved unequal to the task, and on 27th July 1885, two engines hauling fully-laden cars came to a standstill on the long gradient, having run out of steam, and the whole cavalcade remained immobile until a third engine also pulling two cars (or, more correctly, one and a half!) drew up behind and gave them a push.

Warning the Company against this unauthorised practice, the Town Clerk wrote on 4th January 1886 that 'at this moment one of your engines is passing the Town Hall with **three** cars attached'. Following a similar missive from the Board of Trade, the convoys reduced to two cars only, but after a fatality in which a passenger intent on evading payment of his fare jumped off the leading car and was run over by the trailer, the Board prohibited the practice altogether. One single-decker fell into disuse, while the other six were spliced together into three 40-seat bogie single-deckers numbered 8, 9 and 13.

The BST company suffered its only other serious accident on 12th September 1885, when engine No. 5 managed to escape

Viewed from Bradford Mechanics' Institute around 1894, Shelf car No. 3 stands on the turning-circle around the Salt Monument, with Leeds Road (centre) and Bridge Street (left to right) in the background. Engine No. 12 (centre) has efficient Burrell condensers, whereas the older engine (bottom) advertising Rhodes' Lump Butter has to rely on copper-tube condensers.

from the depot and run down into the town centre. Attempting to repair the engine's mudhole joint the driver, whose responsibility it was to undertake routine maintenance, had disconnected the brake lever, regulating valve and reversing lever. Then he had raised 30lb of steam pressure before dismounting to check the joint.

Without warning the engine moved out of the depot. The driver leaped aboard but, devoid of braking power, was unable to halt the runaway until it collided with a horse-drawn trap whose driver was catapulted with fatal results into the engine. Sister engine No. 1 which had been sent in pursuit was quickly attached to No. 5, but when the chain snapped, No. 5 resumed its escapade. Warned by telegraph of its approach, the police cleared Town Hall Square in time for crowds to witness the errant engine pass the Town Hall, derail at the turning-circle and come to rest within inches of a shop window.

To prevent the recurrence of such calamities the Corporation installed a catch-point in the depot yard which led to a sharp (26ft radius) curve into the outward-bound track in the street, and the Company equipped all its cars with Vacuum Brake Co. automatic brakes capable of halting any car which might become detached from its engine – an improvement which remained unique in British tramway operation although widely adopted by railways.

Meanwhile the Bradford Tramways & Omnibus Company (BTOC) had extended its sphere of operation – not altogether willingly, as Messrs Busby and Turton and their company secretary, J. C. Chaplin, were cautious men who avoided ventures of dubious value.

Thus, when offered the lease of a proposed Otley Road tramway they declined in January 1887, on the grounds that it would not pay its way, and that the proposed junction of the Otley Road and Leeds Road lines at Harris Street would be dangerous, as both lines were to be single track. After protracted negotiations the Corporation agreed to (i) double the Leeds Road track from Well Street to Harris Street and allow the Company £100 per annum to pay for a pointsman at the junction, (ii) consent to a 2d fare, and (iii) lay a new double-track tramway from Leeds Road to Manningham Lane via Well Street and Cheapside, thus facilitating a cross-town service from Undercliffe to Frizinghall.

Accordingly on 2nd October 1888, the first of ten additional Green engines (13-22) and ten new Milnes bogie cars (24-33) conveyed the Mayor, Tramways Committee, Borough Surveyor and Company directors up the new Cheapside and Manor Row tracks as far as the Grammar School, where they reversed for a journey up the Otley Road line to the borough boundary at Undercliffe. From Well Street to the terminus the run occupied only fifteen minutes despite the continuous gradients in Leeds Road, Harris Street and Otley Road culminating in a 1 in 15 drag from the 'Cock and Bottle' to Airedale Square and 1 in 14 above Idle Road. The terminus included a reversing triangle on spare land which later became Northcote Road, and at Peel Park a crossover was provided for holiday traffic. Inward-bound cars travelled via East Parade and Humboldt Street, rejoining Harris Street about 100 yards above Leeds Road. The Undercliffe service opened on 10th October 1888, at a 2d fare for lower-deck passengers, whilst upper-deck patrons had the privilege of a 1d stage at Tennyson Place (outward journey) and St. Augustine's Terrace (inward).

A cross-town service of steam trams between Undercliffe and Frizinghall began on 6th December, replacing the Rawson Square-Frizinghall horse cars.. A friendly rivalry sprang up between the new 'steamers' and the remaining Rawson Square – Park Gates – Victor Road horse cars whose drivers derived quiet satisfaction from entering Manningham Lane at either North Parade or Oak

Engine No. 24 and car No. 28 passing Heaton Grove on their way from Frizinghall to Undercliffe, about 1890.

Lane just ahead of a steam tram, thereby compelling the more powerful vehicle to moderate its pace. The influential householders of Oak Lane, St. Mary's Road and North Park Road were relieved to learn that they were to retain their friendly and dignified horse-trams, as they did not relish any contact with the noisy, smoky 'Puffing Billies'.

In the town centre a newly-cleared area bounded by Kirkgate, Well Street and Bolton Road had been transformed into Forster Square during 1887, and was immediately earmarked for a tramways centre. Many and varied were the track layouts prepared by the Corporation, including (as indicated above) a turning-circle for the Manchester Road cars, but all that materialised in the steam era was the Undercliffe – Frizinghall line and a reversing triangle opposite the end of Canal Road which could be used in either direction and was long enough to serve as a siding.

Observing that the BTOC steam trams were now regularly negotiating steep gradients, the Board of Trade recommended that they be equipped with screw-applied slipper brakes acting on the track, and that the braking-power of the older engines be improved. The Corporation Hackney Carriage Committee threatened to withhold licences unless the Company adopted vacuum brakes like the BST Company, but as the Undercliffe-Frizinghall cars were already receiving slipper brakes, the Company declined to go further until the Board of Trade inspector next visited Bradford, which he did on 30th September 1889. Before his report was received, however, the BTOC suffered its most serious accident – a runaway.

The 6.30pm departure for Allerton on 4th December comprised one of the new Green engines, No. 16, and bogie car 21 carrying 17 or 18 passengers. On the ascent of Allerton Road above Crow Tree Lane the rhythmical jolting over rail-joints and points caused the pin which secured the drawbar to work loose. The car became detached from the engine, imperceptibly glided to a halt and then rolled with increasing velocity back down the gradient to Four Lane Ends, where it smashed sidelong into a corn merchant's shop, wrecking the car and causing serious injuries, one of them fatal.

A sorry tale of carelessness emerged at the ensuing inquiry. At first the workshop logbook 'could not be found', and great was the Inspector's wrath when it was eventually produced with the vital page missing. The slipper brake had been removed for repair and not replaced; the handbrake, which relied on a chain attached to the engine's brake cylinder naturally did not work when the car parted from the engine (and even when properly secured it had already broken twice that day), and the pin securing the drawbar lacked a cotter-pin.

A new brake designed by the BTOC manager and engineer (Mr Walter Vaux) was approved by the Board of Trade in

September 1890. A pair of wooden shoes mounted beneath each car bogie pressed down on the rail, being applied by a chain and a horizontal hand-wheel on the car platform as well as by a chain fixed to the engine brake-lever. If the car broke free, the sudden tension on the chain lowered the shoes and halted the car. The fitting of screw-couplings between BTOC engines and cars in 1892 finally dispelled the spectre of runaways.

Other forms of mishap naturally occurred from time to time. When a carelessly-driven butcher's cart collided with a horse tram in North Park Road, the tram horses took fright and bolted. Pausing only to apply the brakes, the driver, conductor and passengers 'baled out'; the horses stumbled and fell, breaking the trace-pole, allowing the tram to run past and halt. One of the horses sensibly galloped back to the stable, and the other, when extricated from its harness, was found to be unhurt.

Steam tram accidents were inevitably more serious. When the mudhole joint of BST engine No. 6 blew out at the Salt monument one day in 1888 the badly-scalded driver had to escape through the window. In the following year a boiler tube exploded as BTOC engine 5 and car 7 were mounting Leeds Road. Fatally scalded, driver James Jarratt, aged 24, leaped out and fell on his back while the vehicles ran back downhill until halted by the conductor. In the absence of a damper the driver had had to regulate the draught by opening the firebox door, thus admitting blasts of cold air to the hot tubes and corroding them to paper-thinness.

The BTOC fleet was augmented in 1889 by two Green compound engines (23/24) with high and low pressure cylinders of 9¼ins x 14ins and 14½ins x 14ins diameter respectively; G.F. Milnes supplied two large bogie cars (34/35) similar to 24-33 but with reversible 'garden' seats arranged 2 and 1 along the upper deck, an improvement which became standard for all future purchases.

Meanwhile the BST Company had achieved its original objective of reaching the village of Shelf, 2 miles 5 furlongs 6 chains from Bank Foot terminus, of which 4 chains (90 yards) lay within the borough boundary, 5 furlongs 8 chains in Shelf and the remainder (1 mile 7 furlongs 4 chains, of course!) within North Bierley, whose Local Board insisted on owning the permanent way and leasing it to the Company. Consequently the Bradford and Shelf Tramways Order as confirmed in 1885 stipulated a lease to expire simultaneously with the Bradford Corporation lease.

At the outer end of the line the rural Shelf Local Board had no ambitions for tramway ownership, and so on 20th January 1886 a locally-based Shelf Tramway Company was registered with an authorised share capital of £5,000, of which shares to the modest value of £3,468 were issued for the construction of the permanent way in the Local Board district.

The entire line from Bank Foot to Shelf ('Bottomley's Arms') was laid as single track with only two passing-places, as the route lay within open country with small settlements, mills, public houses and small foundries; a broad-gauge colliery line was encountered near Buttershaw. With the commencement of a half-hourly service as far as Buttershaw Mills immediately after the inspection on 11th June 1886, every third car from Bradford operated to the new terminus.

As on the North Bierley section, Gowan's girder rails and Mountsorrel granite setts were used by the little Shelf Tramway Company's contractor (James Biggs of Birmingham) for their own extension to the 'Bottomley Arms', which was inspected and opened on 27th July with an hourly service and at a 4d fare with 1d stages. For a brief period cars worked between Bank Foot and Shelf only, possibly pending the arrival of three additional Green engines (8-10) and a replacement No. 3 for the Wilkinson engine.

It could be argued that the BST Company cared more about their passengers' welfare than did the BTOC management; not content with fitting the safe and reliable vacuum brake to all their cars, they installed steam heating in at least one of the cars in 1887 – a rare luxury in those Spartan days.

Working conditions were improving too. From 1889 the Shelf drivers received 32/- (£1-12s-0d) and conductors 21/- (£1.1s.0d) per week for an average 11-hour day with one free day in nine. For extra journeys drivers received 4½d and conductors 3d, and 50 minutes per day were allowed for meal breaks.

Anxious to serve more fully the district through which their route passed, the BST Company surveyed lines from Odsal to the nearby hilltop village of Wibsey and the more distant settlement of Wyke on the southern slopes of North Bierley Local Board District. Although the Wibsey project was thwarted by the narrowness and awkward layout of Holroyd Hill and High Street, the Wyke plan progressed via the medium of a subsidiary Bradford and Wyke Tramway Company (chairman J. H. Breaks) set up by the BST Company to construct the line. The Local Board then purchased the completed line and granted the BST Company a ten years' lease from 1892 at a yearly rent of £240 per single-track mile.

Laid as a single line with passing-places, various level crossings near the famous Low Moor Iron Company works and a reversing triangle at the junction of Town Gate with Huddersfield Road, the Wyke tramway was inspected on 23rd January 1893, and opened for traffic next day at a 2d fare from Bank Foot with a 1d stage at Low Moor. Service frequencies were hourly except on Saturday,

Engine No. 13 of the BST fleet, fitted with Burrell condensers, simmers gently at Shelf terminus around 1893 while local youths lean delightedly out of the tram windows.
Courtesy the late R. B. Parr

Sunday, Monday and Thursday afternoons when the service was doubled. Wyke soon acquired the reputation of being 'the place where they blackleaded the tramlines' – a wry compliment shared by other houseproud Northern villages.

Calmly ignoring protests from Bradford Corporation that the Manchester Road tramway had not been designed to carry so much traffic, the Company operated the Wyke trams in addition to the Shelf and Bank Foot cars from the Salt monument, purchasing three Green engines – 12 to 14 – and four Milnes bogie cars – 14, 7(iii), 12(ii) and 13(ii) to cater for the extra loadings.

Meanwhile four miles north of Bradford independent horse tramways had been operating with indifferent success in the Shipley Local Board District. Mr Joseph Speight of Eccleston Park, Lancashire, had launched a short (6 furlongs 4 chains) 4ft gauge line from Shipley town centre via Commercial Street and Saltaire Road to the Rosse Hotel, Saltaire on 3rd August 1882. A stud of ten horses and two tramcars – Oldbury Carriage Company products comprising an 18-seat single-decker and a double-decker seating sixteen on each deck – were housed in a tiny two-road depot in Moorhead Lane, behind the Rosse Hotel. Lack of passengers caused a suspension of the service – temporarily from 18th-22nd February, 1883, and permanently on 2nd May. 'Small wonder', the press recalled later, 'when a shower of rain was frequently sufficient to stop the service for the day'. The cars and horses were sold by auction.

Under the auspices of Mr Maurice Jones of Liverpool the service re-commenced on 7th March 1884, with two light 16-seat one-man-operated cars, but within five months only one car and driver were licensed, and operation ceased again on 13th February 1885, with fitful forays in 1886, 1887 (the year of the Saltaire Exhibition) and about June 1890. The derelict rails were removed in 1896.

Mr Jones sold his interests in July 1885, to the Bradford and District Steam Tramway Company which despite its title never operated in Bradford or owned a steam tram. Its ambitions included a route from the Branch Hotel via Shipley town centre to Charlestown (New Inn) and an 8-mile line from Shipley via Saltaire, Bingley and Keighley to Low Utley. Apart from a local horse tramway laid in 1889 by the startled Keighley Town Council as a defensive measure, the only outcome of these plans was a line from Saltaire to Frizinghall, along which a 20-minute public service began on 26th August 1888, at a 2d fare.

The company's initial fleet of two 18-seat horse cars was augmented by two double-ended 40-seat double-deckers early in 1889, and, apparently, by a fifth car for the Saltaire Road line. Unfortunately, although the cars met the BTOC horse trams at Frizinghall, the larger company declined to allow through-running, and unhelpfully introduced an Undercliffe-Frizinghall steam tram service instead (see above) in 1888. Having consistently operated at a loss like its two predecessors, the Bradford and District Steam Tramway Company went into liquidation in September 1887, its assets being bought six months later by the optimistic Bradford and District Tramways Company who in turn ceased operation on 9th October 1891, leaving Shipley tramless once again.

Single-deck horse car No. 40, purchased by the BTOC from the Shipley tramways, enters Rawson Square from North Parade about 1896.

Courtesy: J. Copland

2 - POWER FROM ABOVE

(Luke Ch 24 v 49)

The inventiveness of 19th Century intellect knew no bounds. On 12th October, 1837, a few months after Queen Victoria ascended the throne, the Bradford press announced that an unnamed Bradford operative had invented a machine which enabled him 'to produce a rotatory movement by means of battery-powered electromagnets'. In other words, he had devised an early electric motor, but lacking a source of constant power was unable to put his discovery to practical use, and a whole lifetime passed before electricity became commercially available.

In 1889, the year in which Bradford became an all-purpose County Borough, the progressive Corporation opened the world's first municipal power station to provide a public supply, and when in the following year the residents of Wakefield Road petitioned for a tramway, Councillor William Lister urged (August 1890) that 'towns be visited where electric trams are running.' Delegations were therefore despatched far and wide to sample not only the electric conduit tramway at Blackpool but also battery traction at Birmingham and cable haulage at Edinburgh and Frankfurt.

Encouragingly, the Tramways Institute of Great Britain and Ireland descended on the Alexandra Hotel, Bradford, on 7th January 1892 to hear Mr J.H. Cox, the Borough Engineer, declare his desire to be rid of the noise, dirt and track wear caused by the heavy steam engines. After Mr Vaux (BTOC) had voiced a similar wish, the assembly adjourned to Leeds to inspect the American electric trams which had been working on the overhead electric wire system since the previous October.

However, having viewed the overhead wires with disfavour, the Bradford representatives approached Mr Michael Holroyd Smith who had designed and constructed the pioneer Blackpool line six years earlier. Mr Holroyd Smith produced coloured drawings of a Blackpool-style double-deck tramcar numbered 8, and the Corporation voted £500 for a practical trial. 'Great interest was aroused in the town', the press noted, and Dr J. T. Riley promptly delivered a lecture on 'Electric Traction' to the Bradford Scientific Association.

Amicable agreement was reached between the Corporation, BTOC and Messrs Easton and Anderson of 3, Whitehall Place, London, for whom Mr Holroyd Smith was to act as Electrical Engineer in charge of an experiment whereby an electric tramcar was to be operated over the Cheapside tramway. Conduits being ruled out by the temporary nature of the trials, Mr Holroyd Smith also furnished drawings of the despised overhead wire system from which he suggested the current should be drawn.

Much thought was given to the method of current collection from the wires. A preliminary sketch depicted 20ft-high roadside lattice poles with elaborate 3ft 6ins long brackets supporting a live wire along which ran a small carriage attached by a flexible cable to a 14ft 6ins-high (and 6ft 6ins wide) tramcar.

The actual installations were simpler and more practical. Wherever possible, the live wires were suspended from cross-street span wires attached to buildings at a height of 21ft above ground level. Elsewhere the spans were fastened to tapered light blue painted wooden poles 29ft long, of which 5ft was sunk into the ground; 3ft high fluted iron bases protected the lower part of the poles from damp and decay. The weight of the $^3/_8$ins diameter copper live wires caused the poles to flex and the wires to droop visibly.

Presumably on its first day of operation with a trolleyboom (the boom at the leading end has not yet been fitted), the experimental car is turning Cheapside corner alongside the Midland Hotel. The driver's outstretched left arm is manipulating the "ship's telegraph"-type controller behind the stairs, and the gentleman on the rear platform appears to be Mr Michael Holroyd Smith, designer of the tram. *Bridges & Smith*

The current collector itself comprised a horizontal brass bar mounted upon twin galvanised stanchions at each end of the tramcar upper deck, with small indiarubber springs to keep the bars in regular contact with the wire, and an insulated cable in a tube to convey the current to the driver's controls.

Unlike the Leeds cars, Mr Holroyd Smith's tramcar was unquestionably English, and reflected great credit on its designer. Despite the fact that electric traction was still in its infancy, the design was so advanced that it embodied features which were hailed as new more than three decades later (see Fleet List). Built to his specification by the Lancaster Carriage and Wagon Company (who had built some of the original Blackpool cars), the body resembled a dark green and white horse-tram described as 'comfortable and tasteful', seating eighteen inside, twelve on reversible 'garden' seats on the upper deck and three on each of the short balconies above the end platforms.

The neat four-wheel motor-truck on which the car body rested had been built at Easton and Anderson's Erith works to Holroyd Smith's design, and incorporated a form of differential worm drive to minimise friction on the 35ft radius curve at the foot of Cheapside. The twin 'electromotors' produced a total of 35hp, more than ample for a car weighing only 6½ tons.

The test route, from the reversing triangle in Forster Square to the Grammar School at the junction of Manor Row and North Parade, was 660 yards long, with gradients of 1 in 150 in Lower Kirkgate, 1 in 13¼ in Cheapside and 1 in 90 in Manor Row. Current at 305 volts dc was fed from the two smaller 36hp dynamos at the Canal Road power station.

Originally intended for Tuesday, 8th March 1892, the first trial runs were made early on Saturday 12th March, while the steam trams were still slumbering. 'On the whole they proved satisfactory', the press reported. 'With a fair number of gentlemen in the car, it ran smoothly up the hill, and on coming down the incline was stopped several times in a ready manner by the ordinary and slipper brakes'.

Minor adjustments having been made to the 'wires and appliances', a public demonstration was arranged for Corporation and BTOC representatives on 16th March. Unfortunately when they boarded the tram at a few minutes after midnight snow was falling heavily, the cold was intense and no power was available. When the overhead wires eventually became live three hours later it was found that one of them 'was in contact with the uprights' (i.e. the stanchions supporting the current collector bar), causing another postponement for a day or two.

It was soon realised that the rigidly-mounted current-collectors on the tram were incompatible with the flexible overhead wires which sagged between the cross-spans and expanded or contracted with temperature fluctuations. They were therefore replaced by American-style trolley booms referred to as 'fishing rods' and comprising 'long ash rods attached to the front of the roof of the car and held in position by strong springs' thereby keeping a 'grooved pulley' – a fixed (non-swivelling) rotating trolley wheel – in contact with the underside of the wire; an insulated cable conveyed the current to the driver's controls and the motors. The curve of the live wires around the Cheapside corner had to be realigned to conform to the path of the trolley wheel.

Cheapside, 1892: 'the electrical car' climbs the 1 in 13 gradient on the wrong track, having demonstrated its ability to negotiate the sharp 35ft radius curve from Lower Kirkgate. The wooden traction pole is bending under the heavy burden of the overhead wires.

Following three successful trials with a full complement of passengers on 12th April, representatives of the technical press were treated to lunch at the Midland Hotel by the Corporation and contractors on 2nd May prior to a journey 'at a considerable speed' on 'the electrical car'. Next day the Board of Trade in the persons of Major-General Hutchinson and Major Cardew formally inspected the car and installations. Before the inspection could begin, an exhausted steam tram had to be removed from Cheapside, but then the electric tram steadily and effortlessly conveyed its august cargo up to Piper's Grave through the agency of the most permanent source of power in the Universe.

On the descent the car was stopped and restarted at will, though the military gentlemen unimaginatively declined to allow Mr Holroyd Smith to control the momentum by the sole means of the rheostatic brake, insisting on the additional security of the wheel and track brakes.

A trial period of public service began on 16th May. On the first day the tramcar made sixteen return journeys between 11am and 4pm 'and on every journey it was accompanied by a considerable crowd of boys and others who ran beside it', the press noted. Indeed, the public seemed a little distrustful of the novelty (or, more likely, unwilling to pay the 1d fare!), as on the opening day only 238 persons rode on the car, and of those only 187 were paying passengers (who therefore produced a modest revenue of 15/7d!). Already, however, the cost of the current was causing concern and the trials ended on 9th June.

Reporting to the Corporation on 16th June the Borough Surveyor noted that a few faults had developed during the trials, 'but nothing to raise much doubt as to the ultimate success of the experiment'. The motors were 'amply powerful'; indeed, although the inspectors had stipulated a maximum 4mph speed limit, the tram was capable of three times that unexciting velocity, and had run smoothly, with little noise or nuisance. Messrs Easton and Anderson had offered a guarantee for the motors and gearing, and were willing to leave the car and installations in place until mid-July for inspection by interested parties. Mr Holroyd Smith submitted a formal bid for a lease of the proposed Wakefield Road line on 15th July.

At its meetings on 25th June and 13th September the Corporation discussed the comparative merits of steam, conduit and overhead wire. Erring on the side of caution the Borough Engineer forecast a low service frequency (fifteen minutes) for Wakefield Road, insisting nevertheless that a fleet of seven cars would be needed, even though only four would be in daily use. He was not to know that ten years later a three minute frequency would be required to meet popular demand. Not surprisingly, his estimates revealed that whereas steam operation would be profitable, electric traction would produce deficits of £399 per annum with the overhead system or £682 with conduit.

Should the Corporation lease the line to the BTOC for steam working and receive a rental of about £700 per annum or subsidise an electric service? With an eye to the future Councillor Priestman boldly advocated the latter, but his colleagues supported Councillor Cowgill's view that as an isolated electric line was bound to be a drain on finances, steam was the only practical alternative. The press, however, forecast that before long electric traction and municipal operation would be universally favoured.

The Cheapside installations were dismantled shortly afterwards and the ingenious tram returned to its makers; its subsequent fate is unknown. The Borough Treasurer recorded the cost of the 'Electric Motive Power Experiment, Cheapside', as £518-7s-8d less £43 refunded by Easton and Anderson for labour and materials supplied by the Corporation.

The Wakefield Road lease was duly granted to the BTOC, and the line to the boundary at Dudley Hill (Mulcott Road) was completed by 22nd July 1893; farsightedly the rails were copper-bonded in the expectation of electric operation at a future date. The track was single with passing-places and a reversing-triangle into Sticker Lane. In the town centre a clockwise loop was formed by Croft Street, Nelson Street, Norfolk Street and Bridge Street with connections to the Allerton-Thornbury tramway. Public service began on 31st July at a 2d fare and (as on the Undercliffe service) 1d stages for top-deck passengers only.

The extension beyond Dudley Hill into the Tong Local Board District was delayed by the attitude of the BTOC, who would have preferred to run to Rook Lane only, so as to entice the railway passengers who used Dudley Hill station. The Tong Tramways Committee sensibly insisted that the line should serve their district properly. "If they won't come all the way, we won't let 'em into Tong at all" they decreed. Construction of the line as far as Holme Lane was complete by mid-September 1893, and after much persuasion the BTOC began a service. The final extension to Tong Cemetery opened on 2nd March 1894, the terminus being a large turning circle at the junction of Westgate Hill and Heckmondwike Road. The fare was 3d.

No further expansion of the steam network was envisaged, as the leases were due to expire within nine years. The Corporation concentrated on doubling and improving the permanent way as the traffic increased, and in 1892 the Oak Lane/North Park Road junction was altered to allow the horse cars to work anti-clockwise and thus take advantage of the easier ascent of North Park Road, a practice which was followed until the mid-1940s by horse-drawn tower-waggons.

In 1893 Michael Booth, a member of Halifax Town Council and Northowram Local Board proposed the laying of a tramway from Halifax to Shelf to enable the BST cars to operate into Halifax. However, in view of the sparseness of population along the proposed route and the daunting gradients at Stump Cross and New Bank the company declared the proposal to be 'hardly worth while', and Halifax were therefore obliged to wait for their own electric trams five years later.

Shipley Local Board, meanwhile, had taken steps to overcome the three-year absence of horse-trams from their streets by acquiring the disused Saltaire-Frizinghall permanent way for a mere £600 and discussing terms with the BTOC for a through service from Bradford. The Shipley and Bradford tracks were linked up for an exploratory steam tram expedition to Saltaire on 10th March 1893, and, agreement having been reached, the Undercliffe-Frizinghall service was extended to Saltaire (Rosse Hotel) on Good Friday, 31st March.

The success of the venture was startling – on the first day the trams were crowded, and on Easter Monday every horse-bus that the BTOC could muster had to be sent to assist the 'steamers'. On 13th April engine 26 and car 29 were used for the Board of Trade inspection, and by the end of the year the little Moorhead Lane depot had been bought by Shipley and resold to the BTOC. The disused Shipley horse trams had already been sold, and the single-deckers had apparently become Nos. 39 and 40 in the BTOC fleet serving the Park Gates route.

Moorhead Lane depot and its steep approach road were the scene of two unusual events. In July 1883, the Shipley tramway manager, Harvey Watkins, had been fined 5s. 0d. for being 'drunk and riotous' in the stables, whilst eleven years later BTOC car 42 was virtually wrecked when its conductor, who was illicitly reversing the car and engine 20, mistakenly opened the steam valve and caused the cortege to race down Moorhead Lane and across Bingley Road. The engine fell into an allotment while the car capsized with a splintering crash.

By 1894 both the BTOC and BST were prosperous companies paying handsome dividends – particularly the BST Company.

A scene outside Thornbury depot circa 1890. Car No. 38, attached to engine No. 12, was rebuilt from two of the former Frizinghall horse trams.

Copyright: Yorkshire Post

Legend tells of an aged couple who withdrew their life's savings from under their mattress and invested in the BST Company. At the end of the first year their dividend was so large that they thought their capital had been refunded!

Unfortunately the Corporation were realising that the rentals agreed with the operators no longer covered the cost of track repairs. Heavier cars and more frequent services were wearing out the original light Winby and Levic rails, and all renewals had to be carried out with 108½lb per yard Gowans' girder rails. Stronger fishplates were needed also, as rail-joints were working loose, with resultant damage to paving and the ears of passers-by. In Leeds Road an experimental length was relaid with patent rails supplied by the Belgian firm of V. Demerbe and Company of Jenappes; weighing only 70½lb per yard, it comprised an inverted steel trough 5ins deep and filled with concrete.

Postboxes on tramcars were introduced on the Saltaire-Undercliffe service in 1894. Red-painted boxes measuring 1ft 8ins x 8ins were hung on the rear dashplate of each car from early morning until late evening (Sundays and holidays excepted) and were cleared every time the cars passed through Forster Square. A penny charge was made if a car was stopped specially for the purpose of posting a letter, and the practice was retained on most Corporation routes until September 1939, albeit limited to 9pm (or thereabouts) departures from outer termini.

The BTOC fleet was reaching its maximum strength with seven new engines and four new bogie cars, the total stock being 33 and 41 respectively. Two one-horse toastrack cars (called 'chars-a-banc cars' by the press and recalled as 'very nice in summer' half a century later) were introduced on the Manningham Lane service; equipped with light awnings after a few months, they lasted until the end of horse operation. Less loved were the 'rocking-boats' used on the Thornbury-Allerton service; these

were the original four-wheel steam-hauled cars of 1882, and the Company improved them by fitting doors to the upper saloon and converting them to six-wheelers with a bogie at one end.

Uproarious gales in December 1894 overturned six BTOC and two BST cars and blew a startled horse-tram bodily across Manningham Lane, whilst the entire top deck of BTOC car 33 was wrenched off and blown 100 yards into a field at Saltaire. Services were suspended for half a day until the winds abated. A few years later, in March 1897 BTOC car 35 hauled by engine 34 capsized in a gale as it halted at Idle Road, Undercliffe, to allow two ladies to alight, but although 21 passengers were on board and the roof was smashed to pieces, no serious injuries were sustained. The cause of the instability was the high centre of gravity, as the cars were merely trailers with no heavy mechanism underneath. In May 1896, a horse-car being prepared for service but unable to face the monotonous sameness of its humdrum wanderings, managed to escape unnoticed from Oak Lane Depot, gliding quietly downhill, derailing at the curve into St. Mary's Road and demolishing a garden wall.

The South African ('Boer') War touched the tramways briefly when some of the horses were requisitioned for duties far more exciting than their normal daily jog. Shortly afterwards a steam tram leaving Frizinghall was boarded by a gentleman bearing glad tidings of the relief of besieged Mafeking, whereupon the passengers leaped to their feet and cheered lustily, and a city alderman requested the conductor to halt the car at the 'Spotted House' where it stood simmering gently for about seven minutes while he provided refreshments for passengers and crew.

The end of the companies' leases was now approaching, and expenditure was reduced to a minimum, second-hand engines and cars being reputedly purchased to replace worn-out stock. Standards were not allowed to suffer, however; allegations of neglect of horses and engines made decades later were hotly refuted by former drivers. No fuel other than good coke was ever used, they insisted, and claims that engine smoke had blackened Titus Salt's monument were indignantly denied.

When the BTOC secretary, Mr Chaplin, died at the early age of 30, his duties were assumed by Mr Vaux, the engineer and manager, a no-nonsense man who one night dashed from Exchange Station intent on catching the last Thornbury tram, only to see its tail-light receding into the distance, three minutes before the appointed time. His cab fare was deducted from the crew's wages next day. Mr Turton, chairman of the BTOC since its inception, died in August 1900, and was succeeded by Mr Mason, last of the three promoters.

A brief foretaste of the 20th Century was glimpsed about 1896 when a Shelf tram hauled by engine No. 5 was captured on an early, flickering ciné film as it steamed across Town Hall Square. An even stronger link with the coming heyday of tramways was forged when Mr Arthur R. Fearnley, later the renowned and respected Sheffield tramways manager, was appointed by No. 5's owners as their secretary and general manager.

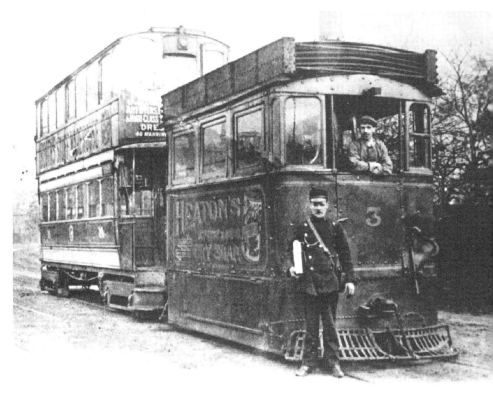

Towards the end of the steam era Green engine No. 3 and Milnes tram No. 14 pose with their cheerful crew outside the 'Bottomley's Arms' at Shelf.

Horse-drawn 'toastrack' No. 16, accompanied by a dog, trots past the 'Royal Standard', the Theatre Royal and the 'Theatre Tavern' about 1895. In the distance a steam tram is passing the 'Penny Bank' on its journey to Forster Square.

3 – BRIGHT CONFIDENT MORNING

Renewed interest in the long-term future of the tramways was aroused in 1896 by the passing of an Act of Parliament which allowed local authorities to operate tram services instead of merely owning the tracks and leasing them to companies. Within three months agitation for electric tramways was being raised in Great Horton, a suburb hitherto inaccessible to trams until the construction of Morley Street a few months earlier; indeed, Hortonians agitating for trams had been jocularly advised to remove nearer to town!

The following year, 1897, was a significant milestone in the history of Bradford. Already a County Borough, the municipality was granted the status of City in honour of Queen Victoria's Diamond Jubilee. Then in October a large new electricity generating works was opened in Valley Road, being capable of supplying dc power for traction purposes at an economic price of 1d per unit. The stage was now set for Bradford City Tramways.

Visits to electric tramways at Birmingham, Bristol, Brixton and Leeds resulted in the Bradford Tramways and Improvement Act, 1897, which sanctioned electric lines to Bolton and Horton Bank Top, and the full process of municipal planning was then brought into play.

Under the supervision of the City Surveyor, City Electrical Engineer and Town Clerk contracts for the supply of materials, vehicles and electrical equipment for the two routes were soon awarded. Steel girder rail was purchased for both routes except for the length between Bolton Church and the terminus, where Demerbe rail was used as in Leeds Road and Well Street a few years earlier. The tracks were laid by the City Surveyor's staff, all rails being copper-bonded at joints and also cross-bonded every 80 yards for electrical continuity.

For the tramcars and electrical equipment a contract was awarded to the Westinghouse Electric Company, who supplied the traction motors and power controllers but subcontracted the other items. The car bodies were manufactured by the Brush Electrical Engineering Company of Loughborough, the 4-wheel motor trucks by Peckham and the trolley equipment by R. W. Blackwell.

Messrs Blackwell also supplied the overhead equipment and elegant tram standards (or poles). The latter were of wrought lap-welded steel in three sections telescoped into each other for 18ins, with cast-iron collars to cover the joints. Ball-and-spike finials kept out rainwater, and 4ft-high cast-iron tapered and fluted bases displaying the civic arms protected the lower part of the poles from corrosion. Each pole was 31ft long, of which 6ft were embedded in the ground – dimensions which applied to almost all subsequent purchases.

The overhead electric wires, of .325 inches diameter hard-drawn copper, were suspended 22ft above the ground from bracket arms comprising 2ins diameter steam pipe clamped to the pole and supported by wrought-iron tie rods. Along various sections of both routes the poles were planted between the tram tracks, in the centre of the road, but for the most part they were sited on the pavement at one side of the road, with bracket arms usually about 16ft long. Power was supplied from Valley Road at 550 volts dc by underground cables, with feeder cables attached to the overhead wires at half-mile intervals and negative cables fixed to the rails.

The appointment of a manager for the Corporation's tramways posed a problem, as the few men who had experience of electric trams were in great demand. Possibly not without misgivings the Tramways, Baths and Team Labour Committee on 21st March 1898, resolved that 'Christopher John Spencer of Walsall be appointed as Manager of the new Tramways to Bolton and Great Horton at a salary of £150 per annum', and by May he was taking instructions from the Committee. The misgivings were understandable, as Mr Spencer was only 22 years old, but in fact no better appointment could have been made.

Despite his youth he had gained sound, practical experience of electric operation with two of the principal pioneer lines. Apprenticed to Mr Holroyd Smith's Blackpool undertaking in 1889, he had become electrician to the new South Staffordshire Tramways in the year of the Cheapside experiment under his father, Mr Fred Spencer, the resident engineer. In January 1898 he succeeded his father when the latter was appointed manager of the nascent Halifax tramways, only to migrate to neighbouring Bradford himself two months later. In the rapidly developing tramway industry meteoric rises were not uncommon, but 'Chris Spencer' displayed abilities above the normal.

The first seven tramcars to arrive from the Brush Works at Loughborough were delivered to Thornbury steam-tram depot where, by courtesy of Mr Vaux, they were stored and then assembled by their future drivers with the aid of BTOC facilities.

Observing that car No. 3 on which George Seniour was working was likely to be the first tram ready for use, Mr Spencer asked whether Mr Seniour would care to work late in order to finish the job. Agreement was quickly reached, and as soon as the car was complete, it was hauled down to Forster Square and placed beneath the overhead wires. Shortly after midnight the electric current was switched on, and thus in the early hours of Wednesday 20th July 1898, 'Alderman Cowgill ran his trial trip' in the company of Corporation officials and contractors'

Bradford Corporation's first operational tramcar, No. 3, driven by George Seniour, poses proudly at Bolton terminus on 20th July, 1898, carrying a hastily-assembled Tramways Committee. Mr Spencer, wearing a straw 'boater', is seated in front of the trolley mast, and the tall gentleman standing alongside the car is Mr Requier, the Westinghouse representative. *Photo: Albert Sachs*

representatives. When Mr Spencer arrived by train at 8am he found car No. 3 waiting for him in Forster Square, and Major Cardew also used it in the afternoon when inspecting the overhead equipment. And so 'the wheels of a great municipal enterprise began to turn' on that bright, confident late-Victorian summer day.

In their gleaming Prussian blue and ivory paintwork the new tramcars were a splendid sight. The blue panels were lined in gold and white with the city arms in the centre, whilst the ivory rocker panels were lined in brown and bright red; a fine red line also outlined each window-post, and the four corner-posts were embellished in vermilion with gold and white transfers. The fleet numbers and name were in gold, shaded with rich red and white. The trucks, lifeguards and railings were in red oxide, with beadings, fenders and trolley (and later, axleboxes) in black.

The car bodies were of oak with a light interior polish and longitudinal slatted saloon seats and ceilings of stripwood stained alternately to resemble mahogany and pine. Lighting was provided by 10 to 16 candle-power carbon filament electric lamps – six in the saloon and one at each end of the top deck, two of the interior lamps being arranged to shine through a red or green glass disc in the upper part of the bulkhead to indicate the direction of travel at night. At first the headlamp comprised an oil-lantern hung on the dashplate.

The 6ft wheelbase Peckham trucks supported the car bodies on twelve coiled and four elliptical springs. Motive power was provided by two 25hp Westinghouse motors geared directly to the axles; unlike the ingenious Cheapside car, chilled-iron (later steel) flanged tyres were shrunk on to the wheel centres which in turn were shrunk on to solid axles with no thought of differential gearing. Power was fed to the motors via Westinghouse controllers embodying 4 series and 3 parallel power notches with 5 notches of rheostatic braking for emergency purposes, normal braking being effected via cast-iron brake-blocks acting on the tyres and applied by a brass handle and ratchet mounted outside the platform dashplate. Depots were built at Bolton Junction and Horton Bank Top terminus, as both routes were isolated from each other, even though the Bolton tracks were physically joined to the BTOC metals in Forster Square where the overhead wires ended. The city terminus of the Great Horton line was in Victoria Square where Little Horton Lane, Morley Street and Great Horton Road converged, a short distance from the BST lines.

As soon as the Bolton drivers had become acquainted with their new duties and Sir Francis Marindin had viewed the track, notice was given that the route 'will be OPENED for Traffic TODAY (SATURDAY), the 30th instant,' with a five minutes

With pleased smiles and admiring glances passengers leave car No. 7 to attend a 'Grand Gala' in Peel Park during the weekend of 30th-31st July 1898.

service from 12.30pm onwards, and the Committee travelled in state on two special cars, the first (No. 2) being driven by the Chairman, Alderman Cowgill, in place of the Mayor who had not been invited.

'From many houses along the route flags were displayed; as the cars passed cheering was frequent and the bells of Bolton Church were rung; spectators gathered in the gardens and fields of Upper Bolton, and, in short, indications were general that the institution of the tram system was being warmly welcomed.' The pleased smiles and admiring backward glances of holidaymakers travelling to and from Peel Park at the weekend were sufficient evidence of the instant popularity of the electric cars. Not everyone was happy, however. A disapproving alderman conducted a private traffic survey and concluded that the tramway would never pay its way. He was reminded of his pessimism when the trams came of age twenty-one years later.

At Horton Bank Top the trial trip out of the depot at 11.30pm on Sunday 21st August, demonstrated that although electricity was indeed wonderful, it should be treated with respect. A violent thunderstorm erupted as the tramcar moved out of the depot, and after it had been driven only a few yards, to the Reservoir Hotel, there was a hasty retreat to the depot – a corrugated iron structure! Emerging unscathed, the Committee and contractors traversed the Horton line next day in twenty minutes, including stops, and Major Cardew duly gave approval.

A gala day greeted the inauguration of the Horton section on 27th August, when two brass bands provided entertainment and dancing until late evening, the afternoon revelries being fittingly concluded with the galop 'Electricity'. A quarter-hourly service was then provided by newly-arrived cars Nos 8-16, which were identical to Nos. 1-7 apart from roller-bearings.

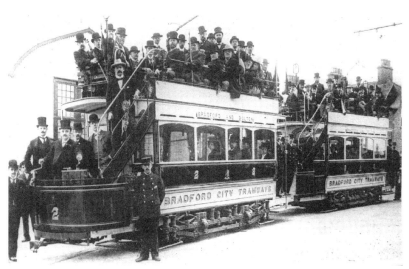

Top hats were required for the official opening on 30th July 1898, when Alderman Cowgill drove car No. 2, followed by No. 3, from Bolton depot to Forster Square. Mr Spencer and Driver Seniour in his new uniform are standing in the road.

Photo: Albert Sachs

Public confidence was briefly shaken on 19th September when car No. 16 returning to City was unable to halt at Grange Road; entering the sharp curve into All Saints Road at considerable speed, it overturned, ejecting the top-deck passengers into the road, with two fatalities. Ironically, only a fortnight previously the Committee had decided to equip the cars with screw-applied slipper brakes for use on steep gradients; designed by C. J. Spencer, they used two 18ins x 2ins hardwood shoes, and were quickly fitted to the whole fleet to prevent future mishaps.

The loop line via Laisteridge Lane and Park Avenue, opened on 19th November, was used throughout its existence for holiday traffic to Horton Park and 'sports specials' to the adjoining Park Avenue cricket and football grounds. In later years Little Horton and Wibsey cars used Laisteridge Lane for access to Little Horton Lane, but regular services used the northern part of Park Avenue only when track renewals elsewhere necessitated service diversions.

The popularity of the tramways encouraged the Committee to institute workmen's return fares between midday and 2.0pm, and the resulting practice of 'going home for dinner' became a feature of Bradford life for the next half-century. Provision of an intermediate crossover at Southfield Lane in October/November 1899, enabled the Department to provide a more effective service, with a five-minute service to the crossover and a twenty-minute frequency to Horton Bank Top. Facilities for intending passengers were provided also, in the form of a lean-to "ladies' waiting room" outside Bank Top depot and a neat stone, slate and glass waiting room opposite Peel Park gates.

Extra trams were called for also, and in October 1898, a Westinghouse tender was accepted for eight cars (17-24) similar to Nos. 8-16 but with higher dashes. Experimentally, four double-deck trailer cars (Nos. 25-28) were bought from Brush, being shorter and lighter than their predecessors and sporting comfortable rattan sprung seating in the saloon, a luxury regrettably never repeated. Cars No. 17-24 were sent to Horton Bank Top depot, which was enlarged to house 24 cars, but the Board of Trade having forbidden the use of trailers on the long Horton gradients, Nos. 25-28 went to Bolton. Unfortunately the 2 x 25hp motors of the Bolton cars (Nos. 1-7) proved unequal to their added burden, and in July 1899, the Committee accepted a Westinghouse tender to equip the trailers with Westinghouse motors and controllers and Blackwell trolley fittings.

In preparation for large-scale expansion of the Corporation network, tracks were laid in Tyrrel Street early in 1899 and brought into use on 19th December as a central terminus for the Horton cars, a largely single-line connection from Victoria Square having been laid in such a way as to avoid contact with the BST tracks, though a junction was made with the BTOC tracks in Bridge Street to allow electric cars to be transferred between Horton and Bolton Depots by courtesy of BTOC whose engines hauled them across the city centre.

Little could be done to provide a comprehensive tramway system until the company leases expired in 1903, but gaps could be filled and outlying areas reached. A major opportunity arose with the enlargement of the City in 1899, when the Urban Districts of Eccleshill, Idle, Thornton, Tong and most of North Bierley accepted incorporation on condition that they should benefit from electric tramways as soon as possible. Indeed, Eccleshill UDC were so eager that they obtained their own Tramways Order thereby allowing the Bolton route to be extended to Eccleshill (Stoney Lane top) on 21st February 1899. With the boundary extension on 9th November the Corporation inherited also the Tong Street and Wyke steam tramways as well as the Shelf line as far as Blackshaw Mills.

The pace of planning, legislation and construction then began to accelerate so rapidly that in 1900 four new routes opened in quick succession. The first, to Lidget Green, passed along lower Thornton Road which for years was so narrow that the span-wires were attached direct to the buildings. The trolley wires, of heavier gauge than previously, were suspended over the track centres to minimise trolley dewirements, unlike the line up Horton Bank where the inward wire was so far from the track that the trolley boom of City-bound trams stretched over the heads of upper-deck passengers aboard outward-bound cars. The terminus was in Cemetery Road outside the 'Second West Hotel' named after the West Riding (Duke of Wellington) Regiment 2nd Volunteer Battalion, and the cars shared the Tyrrel Street departure point and the Horton Bank Top depot facilities with the Horton trams.

Hundreds gathered to welcome the first tram, No. 34, late in the evening of 20th August, and the public service commenced eleven days later. Car 34 was one of 25 trams (29-53) ordered from Brush, and embodied various design improvements, notably extended balconies over the platforms and reversed stairs for greater safety. On the underside of the balcony a deep white-painted cornice (which gave rise to the name of 'white board cars') gave the driver some protection from the weather and incorporated a small destination box. Peckham trucks were used again, this time with plain bearings and 30hp Dulait 'Electricité et Hydraulique' motors supplied by Witting Eborall of London (hence the usual reference to 'Witting motors'). Mechanical slipper brakes made by Messrs C. Whitaker of Bradford ensured safe descents of long gradients.

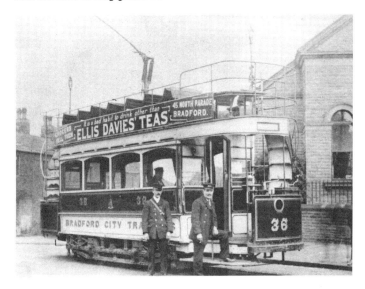

Soon after the Lidget Green route opened in August 1900, 'White Board' car No. 36 was photographed at the terminus alongside the Wesleyan Chapel. The conductor has swung the trolley for the return journey, but the cigarette-smoking driver has not yet found time to carry the detachable headlamp to the leading end of the car. *Courtesy: F. Hartley*

The next route was built to serve the densely-populated White Abbey area, the villas of Toller Lane and the suburbs of Girlington and Duckworth Lane. The city terminus was to have been in Forster Square, but as that would have involved the widening of Kirkgate, a temporary terminus was provided in Westgate opposite Grattan road. At Duckworth Lane the construction of a depot was so long delayed by disputes with the landowner that when three new 'White Board' cars (?45-47) arrived by rail and

The rural nature of Toller Lane before the construction of the 'Boulevard' is shown in this view of 'White Board' car No. 53, now with partly-enclosed balcony and permanent headlamps. A gas street-lamp stands alongside the McCartney, McElroy tram standard. *Courtesy: the late R. B. Parr*

The first extra-steep gradient encountered by the Corporation trams was Whetley Hill, left, where 'White Board' car No. 48 confidently halted on a trial run. *Courtesy: the late R. B. Parr*

were hauled off by traction engines, they had to be assembled on 12th/13th October 1900 in the road outside the temporary wooden shed which was being hastily erected to house them.

As soon as one car had been completed, on 13th October, Mr Spencer drove it citywards as far as Sedgwick Street, effortlessly descending and reascending Whetley Hill, the first extra-steep gradient encountered by the electric trams. First to board the inaugural tram on 2nd November was 'Duke', an Irish wolfhound, followed by his owner, Councillor Burke, and officials. Mr Spencer confidently halted and restarted the car at the steepest part (1 in 9.7) of Whetley Hill at Arnold Place, whereupon a partial service was begun with five vehicles pending further deliveries. 'In the evening twilight the lighted tram with the then new electricity seemed to skim down Whetley Hill like a magic fairy barge' a spectator recalled years later. The children cheered but old folk doubted. "It won't work", they prophesied. "People will be killed!" But it did work – spectacularly – with receipts of 18.42d per car mile compared with Lidget Green at 11.19d. The first of BCT's 'money-spinners' had been born.

Major Marindin on his tour of inspection on 1st November had also visited a third route, a 2-mile double track line from Thornbury steam tram terminus through the outskirts of Calverley and Farsley Urban Districts to Town Street, Stanningley, in Pudsey UD.

Passengers from Stanningley alight from tramcar No. 31 at Thornbury to board 'one of the ugly great steam trams' which will complete their journey to Bradford.

The Stanningley route originated in an application made in November 1897 by the Power and Traction Company Ltd to build a 5½-mile light railway in the highway between Thornbury and the nearest terminus of the Leeds steam trams at Branch Road, Armley. In the light of their not-always-cordial relations with their tramway companies, Bradford and Leeds Corporations opposed the plan, especially as it envisaged compulsory running powers over Corporation tracks. Consequently the promoters agreed to sell their rights to one of the two cities, and the House of Commons favoured Bradford because the city lay nearer to the proposed 'railway'. For a sum of £1,500 paid to the company on 23rd November, 1899, the Corporation became owners of the grandly-named 'Bradford and Leeds Light Railway, owned and operated by Bradford Corporation'.

The line lay across open country along a dusty road as far as Dawson's Corner where the outskirts of Stanningley were reached, and Demerbe rail and span-wire construction were used almost exclusively. Farsley UDC having requested a branch line through the village as far as Bryan Street, a track curve was laid into Farsley Old Road, but surprisingly in view of the population waiting to be served, the branch was never completed or used. Following a trial run to Stanningley on 23rd October 1900, the formal opening was held on 16th November, when the Committee rode to Thornbury on 'one of the ugly great steam trams' before boarding new 'White Board' car No. 31 driven by a new Chairman, Councillor (later Sir) James Hill.

Pending construction of a new Corporation depot and works alongside the BTOC depot at Thornbury, cars 29-33 were housed in a timber shed which was removed to Lidget Green (Scholemoor Road) for use as a 'dormitory' tram shed as soon as part of the new Thornbury depot opened on 26th June 1901.

The two-mile line from Four Lane Ends to Thornton (Ashfield Road), last of the four 1900 extensions, was equally as rural as the Stanningley route and much more scenic. Between Fairweather Green and the entrance to Thornton village the tramway lay firstly alongside a winding, splashing beck and then up a long, gentle ascent between fields, with the beckoning spire of Thornton Church always in view.

A trial run was completed on 13th December, and five days later car No. 41 conveyed the Committee to a lunch at the Great Northern Hotel adjoining the terminus. Afterwards cars No. 41-44 commenced a service to and from Four Lane Ends (where the existing steam-tram tracks to the City centre had already been

electrically bonded for future use), retiring at night to a tiny timber depot at Fairweather Green.

On all the routes built in 1900 the overhead equipment was suspended from elegant McCartney McElroy poles embellished with 4ft 9ins-high Italianate cast-iron bases bearing the city arms, and (where span-wires were used) short bracket arms. These gave rise to complaints from Blackwells that the Corporation had rejected their tender in favour of inferior goods. While the McCartney poles – light, medium and heavy (A, B, and C) – appeared more robust and did not flex as visibly as the slender Blackwell poles, they embodied thinner metal, and within fifteen years a dewired trolley boom in Toller Lane had wrenched one of them askew, exposing chronic corrosion. All the 1901 routes were therefore equipped by Blackwells with poles of McCartney dimensions but with thicker steel and manufactured by British Mannesmann Tube Company instead of Stewart and Menzies as in 1898/9. Always devoid of any ornamentation except finials, some still survive.

In February 1897, the Clayton and Queensbury UDCs had requested that the Horton Bank Top tramway, when built, should be extended into their areas, and agreement was reached that if the councils built the tramway the Corporation would lease it and provide a service. The Clayton and Queensbury Tramway Orders, 1899, duly authorised a long 4ft-gauge line via Clayton Heights and Queensbury to the Northowram UD boundary at Catherine Slack. By this time, however, Halifax Corporation were planning a 3ft 6ins-gauge line to Queensbury from the opposite direction, and Queensbury sensibly decided that the two systems should meet in the village centre, each Corporation to construct its own permanent way.

As the Halifax line comprised long stretches of single track with few loops, their tracklayers made rapid progress, and the first Halifax tram reached Queensbury (Church) on 25th April 1901. Bradford's wholly double-track line was not ready for inspection until 2nd August by Mr Trotter, who with an excess of caution stipulated an 8mph maximum speed. Immediately afterwards the Mayor of Bradford drove the official first car to Horton Bank Top, where the Queensbury contingent boarded and were driven by their chairman, Col. H.A. Foster of Black Dyke Mills, to the new terminus at the Granby Inn, a few yards from the Halifax line. A ten minutes service was then opened by new car No. 56, although the Horton depot's quota of cars now comprised 'White Board' cars Nos.34-40 as well as lower-

powered cars Nos. 17-24 which normally served the undemanding Lidget Green section.

The rapidly-expanding network required permanent headquarters. Originally based at Bolton depot, Mr Spencer and his growing staff operated from Horton Bank Top until offices at No. 5 Forster Square, were leased in January 1901 for £75 a year.

The Victorian virtue of good timekeeping was carried into the new Edwardian era when, in March 1901, BCT ordered twelve Spencer Patent Time Recorders for use at termini; when each car commenced its cityward journey its trolleywheel passed under a 'skate' (contact) on the overhead wire, which via an electrical impulse recorded the time on a paper cylinder. A shortage of stonemasons delayed until early 1902 the completion of the new Duckworth Lane depot; the temporary wooden shed was then removed to Bankfoot, alongside the BST steam depot, in preparation for electrification.

At the Whitsuntide weekend 53 cars were in use to deal with record demand, and the seven cars in use on the Eccleshill section had to be augmented by nine borrowed from Horton.

By August the Department had received further Brush cars, Nos. 54-68, generally similar to the previous delivery but with a complete balcony protected by continuous 'tins' (decency panels), sturdier corner posts, single-line destination indicators on the top rails and no 'White Boards'. The next Brush products (Nos. 69-128) delivered during the following twelve months had flat ceilings adorned with birdseye maple veneer panels (instead of the traditional turtle-back ceilings) and two half-lights for ventilation purposes over each side window.

Meanwhile extensive road-widening had been carried out in the recently-incorporated Idle district, where many 'hills and valleys' had to be levelled before tram tracks could be laid. As there was no direct road to Bradford, a line was laid from Bolton Junction to Five Lane Ends, whence separate branches led to Idle (Alexandra Hotel) and Thackley (Victoria Street); both were built as double-track except for the terminal stubs and a short length of single line at the top of Town Gate where the highway squeezed through the gap left by a 17th-century chapel. Following a trial journey to Thackley on 26th August 1901 both routes opened on 10th September.

The scattered nature of residential development at Idle before the 1920s was indicated by the identity of the area's first tramcar accident victim – a cow – and by the end of the year the Tramways Department were so perturbed at the loss being incurred by the two services that they arranged for them to operate from Bolton Junction only, all passengers to and from City being required to use the Eccleshill cars. Predictably, the first day of the inconvenient arrangement, a rainy 2nd January 1902, was also the last.

The Corporation's use of the Belgian-made Demerbe rail had not gone unchallenged. Councillor Croft had thought it suspicious that despite its availability in Britain for ten years, Bradford had been its sole customer, and that although it weighed only 70lb per yard it cost more than 105lb girder rail. When tests proved that some of the rails were deficient in concrete and others totally devoid of it, Salford-type girder rail with $1\frac{1}{8}$ins groove was adapted as standard. Nevertheless, even though many sections of Demerbe track were short-lived (the Dirkhill Road-All Saints Road curve wore out in four years), the Idle and Thackley rails lasted a full lifespan.

Ever since the introduction of electric traction the maintenance of the overhead equipment had been performed with the aid of horse-drawn extensible 'tower-waggons', but the increasing size of the network and the taxing gradients of all routes except Stanningley made mechanisation necessary. Accordingly a 6hp 2-cylinder Milnes-Daimler tower-waggon registered AK49 was bought from G.F. Milnes in October 1902, and Mr Spencer was awarded a motor-car in place of his pony and trap. The pace of change was quickening, and 1902 was to see a dramatic transformation.

Idle terminus about 1910. Car No. 5 rebuilt with extended balconies and reversed stairs, is standing outside the Alexandra Hotel (invisible, on the right) with Idle Baptist Chapel on the left
Courtesy Mr F. Hartley

A quiet scene at Great Horton, about 1905. 'White Board' car No. 33 is following a newer Brush tram towards the city centre, possibly having reversed at the Southfield Lane crossover (bottom left).

4 - AND CORPORATION TRAMCARS CLANG

(John Betjeman – 'Christmas Day')

Having recently obtained statutory powers to terminate the Company leases before their expiry date in 1903, the Corporation served the BTOC and BST directors with one month's notice of their intention of taking full control of the leased lines on 1st February 1902.

The Leeds Road and Manchester Road tracks had already been relaid and local labour was hired to connect the Four Lane Ends rails with the Thornton electric tramway, to lay new connecting lines in Town Hall Square, and to extend the Duckworth Lane metals down Godwin Street to meet the Sunbridge Road line. Gangs of men toiled day and night in three shifts to erect overhead standards (purchased as in every subsequent year until 1913 from James Russell of Wednesbury) and miles of overhead wire, and to lay the underground feeder cables. The old order collided with the new on 30th January 1902 when a steam tram ran into a tower-waggon; the horses bolted and the men were slightly injured.

Next evening the ever-popular Manningham Lane horse-trams trundled back to Oak Lane depot for the last time after twenty years of faithful service. A new era was at hand: a few hours earlier Major Pringle, by permission of the companies on their final day of operation, had used an electric tram to inspect the reconstructed Bankfoot and Four Lane Ends lines.

The Bradford Tramways and Omnibus Company, owners of 38 engines and cars, agreed to let the Corporation use ten engines and cars without charge and hire others at £5 per unit per month in return for free storage of surplus stock at Thornbury until 30th April. The Bradford and Shelf Tramway Company consented to hire out fourteen engines and cars for a total of £70 per month, and the Corporation bought the BTOC waiting-rooms and coke sheds at Allerton, Harris Street, Saltaire and Tong Street.

Half an hour after the company leases expired, the Tramways Chairman and Corporation representatives assembled at the Mechanics' Institute for a journey by electric tram to Four Lane Ends and Bankfoot, to the cheers of the residents, who perhaps felt less cheerful when they realised that for driver-training purposes the tramcars were to run all night in preparation for public services at 5am!

Before daybreak the Thornton cars had commenced to run into the city centre (Sunbridge Road), and new Brush cars had opened a Town Hall Square-Bankfoot service, leaving one lone steam car to provide a Town Hall-Shelf working and two further steam units to work a Bankfoot-Wyke shuttle service. For the first time an ex-BST 'steamer' from Bankfoot depot ventured up Thornton Road to ply between Four Lane Ends and Allerton.

The other ex-BTOC steam routes continued as usual, viz:

9 cars worked a 15 minutes service from Saltaire to Undercliffe; 5 cars worked a 15 minutes service from Norfolk Street to Tong Cemetery; 5 cars worked a 10 minutes service from Mechanics' to Thornbury, a total of 23 steam cars being thus utilised.

At the BST auction at Bankfoot on 19th March Mr Spencer bought three engines and cars for £137-12s-6d for the Allerton, Wyke and Shelf services. The new Godwin Street link was used initially to allow the Thornton cars access to their new parent depot at Duckworth Lane, but from 13th March the Duckworth Lane service was extended inwards to the foot of Sunbridge Road.

Now in full control of the tramways, the Manager and the City Surveyor co-operated energetically in the formidable task of electrifying and in many cases reconstructing and doubling the steam-worked lines, and for the rest of the year a kaleidoscope of temporary services was arranged while the new superseded the old.

On 27th February the electrification of the City-Thornbury section not only enabled the Stanningley cars to work into the City centre but also provided general access to the workshops at Thornbury depot. After their visit to the new facilities the Committee enjoyed a cross-city run from Stanningley to Thornton, the longest tramcar journey made so far. Within a week even longer journeys became possible when Leeds steam trams also reached Stanningley and were replaced by electric cars a month later.

Meanwhile the Undercliffe-Saltaire steam service had been split on 3rd February to allow the relaying of the Cheapside track; the Saltaire 'steamers' then operated from Rawson Square, the first time they had ventured to the old horse-car terminus. A month later (8th March) they were supplemented by a Manningham Lane (Drewton Street-Park Gates) electric service, but with the inauguration of the Forster Square-Frizinghall electric trams twenty days later the steam trams were confined to a Frizinghall-Saltaire shuttle service only, being totally overwhelmed by the holiday crowds transferred to them from the electric tramcars at Easter.

Persistent legends of a fabled ciné film taken in 1902 with the aid of a camera mounted on the front platform of a tram were verified in 1996 when the film was

Car No. 86, one of the 60 elegant Brush trams bought in 1902, is displayed in the yard of the new Thornbury depot. *Photo: BCT*

miraculously unearthed and transferred to a video. On its smooth, steady-riding progress from Forster Square the tramcar was seen to pass an Undercliffe steam car, several sparkling new Brush trams returning from Frizinghall, and a track gang laying a new junction into Oak Lane. As in 1892, crowds of boys and youths ran alongside, delighted by the novelty.

On 13th April the remaining Frizinghall-Saltaire steam trams were withdrawn and sent to Thornbury for disposal while the tracks which they had been using were reconstructed by Shipley UDC, with junctions at the Branch and at the top of Saltaire Road for future lines being planned by the UDC.

Heavy tram poles with massive ornamental bases and pear-shaped finials were made by Lowdon Brothers of Dundee, and power was obtained from Shipley's small generating station at Dockfield Road. A 30-year lease was granted to Bradford.

As soon as one set of rails was completed, on 29th April, the Committee rode out to Saltaire on shiny new car No. 118 to share a celebratory lunch at the Rosse Hotel with their Shipley counterparts and Mr R. C. Quinn, Shipley's electrical contractor. The Frizinghall service was progressively extended to the 'Branch' on 3rd May and to Saltaire twelve days later. With the reconstruction of the abandoned horse-car tracks in Oak Lane and St. Mary's Road a Forster Square (Midland Station) to North Park Road (Victor Road bottom) service was opened on 28th May with a view to a possible extension to Heaton. In Forster Square the old steam tram reversing-triangle was extended round to the North side of the central island to provide a loading-point for Saltaire cars.

During April new track was laid from Bankfoot to Odsal, but the 9-year old steam-tram tracks to Wyke were retained for three more years and copper bonded for the electric service which began on 3rd May with a generous 10-minute frequency. At Wyke terminus two legs of the reversing triangle, in Town Gate and Huddersfield Road, were retained and wired up. At Low Moor the cars traversed a mixed gauge (4ft 8½ins and 3ft 10³/₈ins) level crossing used by Low Moor Ironworks waggons. As in the lower part of Manchester Road, the Odsal-Wyke tram poles were plain apart from finials.

The conversion of the Wakefield Road route presented few problems, as the track had been bonded when laid nine years previously, but underground cables and overhead equipment had to be installed, and the work was executed in four stages. On 14th May Alderman W. Lister who had advocated electricity in 1890 but had nevertheless ridden on the line's first steam tram in 1893, drove the last passenger steam tram from Tong Cemetery to City (Norfolk Street). Next day an electric service was operated as far as Dudley Hill, though for three weeks inward-bound cars had to coast across Croft Street bridge because the L&Y railway company were reluctant to allow the erection of poles and wires.

A forlorn steam tram worked between Dudley Hill and Tong Cemetery until 20th May, after which the service was suspended for track renewal. On 3rd July an electric cross-city route from Dudley Hill to Thornton was launched, being extended two days later to the Fairfield Street crossover in Tong Street. However, when the full electric service to Tong Cemetery (bottom of

When the Bradford 'city fathers' ventured to Saltaire on the first expeditionary tram No. 118, on 29th April 1902, they donned their smartest hats and overcoats. The Shipley UD councillors (centre) are less formally attired, while the contractors (in front of the tower waggon) are not concerned with fashion.

Westgate Hill) opened on 2nd August, all cars operated to City only, as Norfolk Street provided a more convenient loading point than the temporary facilities in narrow Bridge Street.

Simultaneously Otley Road had been enjoying the benefits of modernisation. The last Undercliffe steam car ran on May 21st and for the next five days a shuttle service was provided between Forster Square and the 'Cock and Bottle', but when an electric tram began to perform the same function on 27th May the patronage was so poor that no further facilities were provided until 10th June when a Forster Square-Peel Park electric service was inaugurated pending its extension to Undercliffe on 28th June.

Other track gangs had been at work in the city centre in May, removing the now-redundant steam-car track in front of the Town Hall and laying a new double track with a double junction into Bridge Street, thereby enabling the Horton cars to circumnavigate the Mechanics' Institute and reduce conflict with Lidget Green cars reversing in Tyrrel Street. With the electrification of Well Street and additional crossovers in Forster Square, revised schedules became possible – Forster Square to Saltaire, Forster Square to North Park Road and Rawson Square to Frizinghall on 15th July, then Undercliffe to North Park Road on 29th October.

On the last day of July Major Druitt inspected the Little Horton route whose construction, although authorised in 1899, had had to be delayed until the BST lease of the nearby Manchester Road line terminated. The tram service to the new terminus at the 'Black Horse' commenced on 1st August traversing the Laisteridge Lane tracks which were thus brought into full-time service for the first time. Possibly for purposes of standardisation, the route equipment was identical with the adjacent Great Horton installations, ie Blackwell poles and Demerbe rails.

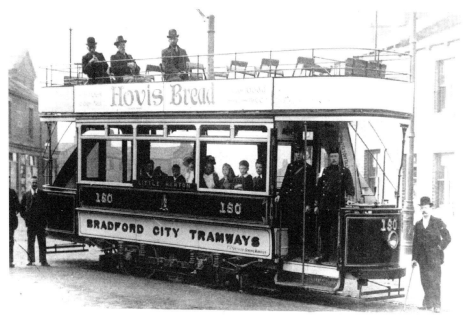

The children of Little Horton inspected new Milnes car No. 150 on its arrival at the terminus in 1902. In its later guise as No. 120, the tram was one of the last 'open-toppers' in the fleet.   *Courtesy Mr F. Hartley*

For the expanding services no fewer than 100 tramcars had been ordered. Between September 1901 and January 1902, the Corporation had accepted tenders from Witting Eborall (car bodies and electrical equipment), Brush (car trucks), and Hurst Nelson of Motherwell (Munro and Rogers patent trolleys and trolley masts), the cost being £507 per car. The bodies were sub-contracted to Messrs G. F. Milnes and Company, the controllers to BTH and the motors to Électricité et Hydraulique.

The first two cars, Nos 129/130, differed from the rest in having square-cornered saloon windows and Peckham B9 trucks, whereas Nos. 131-228, on Brush 'A' trucks, had radiused corners at the top of the window posts. With their large windows (three per side), clean lines and direct stairs they were more handsome than any of the Brush cars; inside the saloon carpet seat-runners and bevelled mirrors in the nearside upper bulkhead imparted an air of elegance, while their 35hp motors provided a distinct speed advantage.

As most of the surviving steam trams were due to be auctioned in early July, including the solitary unit which still trundled from Bankfoot depot each morning to provide the Four Lane Ends-Allerton shuttle service, overhead equipment was erected in Allerton Road, but as the rails had not yet been renewed or even copper-bonded, one of the twin overhead wires was temporarily used for the negative return. In this unique way the last of the ex-BTOC steam services, albeit maintained by ex-BST stock, passed into history on 5th June 1902. Next morning the first of the new Milnes-bodied cars, No. 129 temporarily fitted with twin trolley masts and booms, provided a 20-minute shuttle service until about 19th July, when the tracklaying gangs moved in. A partial service of conventional trams began using the new rails about 14th/15th August, with a full service from City (Mechanics' Institute) on 16th August.

In anticipation of holiday crowds travelling to and from Halifax at the Easter weekend the Corporation towed one of the redundant steam trams up to Queensbury terminus for use as a cash office, and left it there from Good Friday until the following Wednesday. This unsightly obstruction of their highway did not go unnoticed by Queensbury UDC, with the result that the 'Mayor, Aldermen and Citizens of Bradford' were fined 10s. 0d. at Halifax West Riding Court.

Arriving at Exchange Station very late one night, tired but triumphant following a successful tour, the Black Dyke Mills Band were dismayed to learn that not only had the last Queensbury tram departed, but also that the power had been switched off for the night. Somehow (legend tells) an unsuspecting steam tram was roused from its slumbers and induced to pant and struggle up to Queensbury, a unique and epic journey indeed, there being no 'coaling' facilities en route.

When appendicitis compelled the new King, Edward VII, to postpone his Coronation, the Corporation arranged a thanksgiving procession for his recovery, providing 50 trams as grandstands and thereby recouping a profit of £120. One of the Brush trams, probably No. 100, was specially decorated with bunting and coloured bulbs proclaiming the loyal motto, 'God save the King', and its appearances excited 'as much commotion as Halley's comet' as it progressed from terminus to terminus.

An extension of the Allerton tramway from the old steam car terminus at the foot of the village street to Ivy Lane at the top of the hill saw its first trial car on 17th October. A week later (24th October) Major Pringle visited the extension with the Committee, who fixed the fare at 2d before leaving the tram to stroll through Chellow Woods to the residence of the Deputy Chairman, where the luncheon awaiting them must have been satisfactory, as the Inspector authorised the service to begin immediately.

New byelaws prohibiting the carriage of dogs on the trams created a new feature of Bradford street life, ie the sight of hounds faithfully pursuing the tramcars on which their owners were riding. The hardship was more apparent than real, as local canines often pursued the cars for pleasure. One of the Thornton drivers observed that an Airedale terrier sometimes accompanied his tram for four consecutive round trips – a total of over 34 miles – and then repeated the feat next day! When faced with the dilemma of a Dog Show in Lister Park the Department supplied special trams for dogs only, although how the animals paid their fares is not known.

The permanent depots at Thornbury and Duckworth Lane were now complete. Well built in local stone with a glass roof and spacious forecourt, they housed 61 cars on 13 roads and 27 cars on 8 roads respectively, and when in 1903 the old steam-tram depot at Thornbury (jocularly known as 'The Far West') received new trackwork, it was able to accommodate 55 trams as well as joiners' and blacksmiths' shops.

On 3rd November 1902 the Leeds Road and Great Horton Road services were experimentally linked, with Stanningley cars running through to Queensbury and Thornbury trams to Southfield Lane. The Horton Bank Top Young Women's Class had already blazed a trail by hiring special Bradford and Leeds tramcars to travel all the way to Roundhay Park, Leeds, a distance of 16½ miles with only one change of car at Stanningley, although the safari lasted two hours in each direction. However, the cross-city facilities were discontinued after 18th January 1903, probably because of timekeeping difficulties.

The momentous year drew to a successful conclusion with the opening of the Heaton tramway. Although a tram service was ardently desired by Heaton folk, fears for the disturbance of their age-old 'peace and quiet' were strongly expressed. Wilmer Road residents wished the rails to be laid in Heaton Road or North Park Road; their neighbours in Heaton Road took the opposite view, while Victor Road and Emm Lane dwellers were equally vociferous.

Having digested petition and counter-petition the Committee ruled that the route should be an extension of the existing North Park Road tramway by way of Victor Road, Buxton Street, Wilmer Road and Emm Lane to the 'King's Arms', Highgate. A connecting line from the Duckworth Lane tramway via Church Street, Heaton Road and upper Victor Road was agreed but not built.

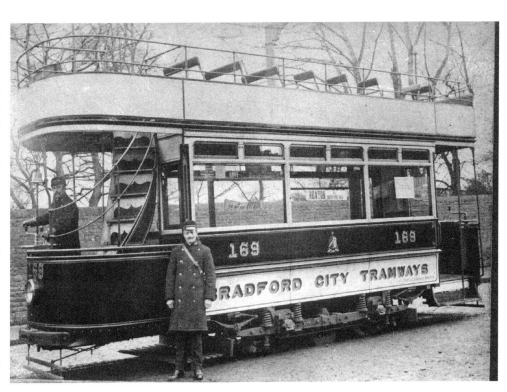

A wintry day at Heaton terminus ('King's Arms'). The photograph was probably taken soon after the route opened in 1902, as the destination display consists only of paper stickers labelled 'Heaton and North Park Road'. The driver bore the splendid name of Cornelius Augustine Horgan. *Courtesy: Mr F. Hartley*

Authorised on 4th August, the tortuous and steeply-graded extension was inspected on 23rd December 1902, by Major Pringle, when after a brief struggle around the sharp, steep curve into Emm Lane, the tramcar reached its picturesque destination below tree-shrouded Heaton Hall. Free travel was allowed for the rest of the day, and a through service to Undercliffe commenced next morning. The high 2d fare led to a virtual boycott, and in February 1903, the cross-city link was severed, the Heaton service being diverted to Rawson Square (then a high-class shopping area frequented by Heaton ladies). As this was equally unsuccessful, the workings to Undercliffe resumed and continued until February 1904. Heaton folk were reputedly the only tramcar users who occasionally tipped the drivers.

During 1903 the white painted bands on the tram poles which denoted stopping-places were replaced by enamelled plaques clamped around the poles. Request stops, in blue, white and black, announced that 'Cars STOP here by request', whereas the red, white and black 'Board of Trade' compulsory stop signs warned that 'All cars STOP here'.

Up to that period all trams had carried a foot-gong to warn of their approach, but from September 1902 they were fitted with a handbell hung on a bracket in front of the driver. Although trams later built by BCT reverted to foot-gongs, most of the original fleet retained the handbells. Steel tyres began to replace the chilled-iron variety in 1903, and Milnes-bodied tramcar 173 received a trolley which dropped automatically if it left the wire instead of springing heavenward; prudently the safety of top-deck passengers was ensured by protective iron hoops.

Following the electrification of the Allerton section in June, the Shelf steam-trams were the last to operate. Mr Harold Smith, who knew them well, wrote years later that,

'Those of us who recollect the closing stages can never feel too thankful for the change to electricity, comfort and cheapness. A voyage up Manchester Road used to be quite an exciting event, with steampipes blowing out at intervals and the engine coming to a standstill.'

After 17th November 1902 the old 'puffing billies' were seen no more in the city centre, being confined to a Bankfoot-Shelf shuttle service worked by one tram per hour. Their lifespan was prolonged by the little Shelf Tramway Company, owners of the 1,286 yard line in Shelf UD, who placed a value of £3,400 on their permanent way, whereas Bradford who wished to buy, relay and electrify it, offered not more than £1,500.

When the lease expired on 31st January 1903, the Corporation promptly cut back the service to the city boundary (Furnace Inn), alleging damage to tramcar springs on the Shelf track, to which the directors retorted that they had recently overhauled their metals and that derailments occurred more frequently on Bradford's own track. At Shelf there was a 'palpable sense of loss', but worse was to come.

On 1st April 'it was rumoured that the cars would stop running in the direction of Shelf', and next morning 'newspapers were not available until much after the usual time.' In other words, the steam-trams had finally retired, Mr Spencer being authorised to sell the last three engines at Bankfoot depot and dispose of the trams for £5 apiece.

The tracks between Odsal and the boundary were quickly lifted, and new foundations, rails and electrical equipment installed, progress being watched by the 'huddled, wet and unhappy batch of passengers 'aboard a solitary Shelf-bound horse-drawn waggonette as they peered 'disconsolately through the wide apertures left by the brown tarpaulin cover. 'They had not long to wait. The first electric car reached the 'Kings Head' on 29th May and the 'Furnace Inn' a week later.

Finally, in June, after arbitration, Bradford agreed to pay the Shelf shareholders £1,950, and track renewal began at once, although heavy rain and urgent commitments elsewhere delayed completion until 1st September, when a quarter-hourly electric service began at last. A week later, having 'settled down', it was linked with Stanningley as a long cross-city service. Horizons were expanding rapidly now, as Halifax trams had also reached Shelf – indeed, the two sets of overhead wires were joined end-to-end at the terminus – and local guidebooks were advertising a variety of inter-town journeys, scenic rambles and circular safaris.

Prior to the disposal of the BST rolling stock, the Tramways Department had decided, on 23rd February 1903, to retain one of the 40-seat single-deck trailers 'to deal with the rush of passengers at certain hours'. Towed to Thornbury and given the number 229, the car was re-mounted on Brush equal-wheel two-motor bogies, with a trolley-mast erected on the clerestory roof. As the platforms were underslung, the car had to be mounted high to ensure proper clearance for the bogies, which in turn were placed closer together than was usual, and two entrance-steps were needed.

The single-decker entered service about September on the Thornbury and Wakefield Road routes, where its unusual length inspired local railway users to name it 'The Low Moor Tunnel'.

In a misguided attempt to relieve congestion at the foot of Sunbridge Road where the Allerton, Duckworth Lane and Thornton tramcars jostled for a place at the crossovers and queue-barriers, the Department banished the Duckworth Lane cars to the Westgate crossover, only two cars per hour being allowed to descend Godwin Street. A weekly loss of 2,000 disgruntled passengers soon prompted a change of mind, but the basic problem of too many trams and too few tracks remained.

The rapidly-improving fortunes of the tramways made possible the introduction of a maximum 2d fare within the City boundary, and some fortunate areas such as Eccleshill found their fares reduced to 1d. Tramcar speeds were then reviewed at the request of Mr Spencer, and Major Pringle duly persuaded the Board of Trade that they could safely raise most speed-limits, ie from 8mph to 12, 6mph to 8 and (on the level) 4mph to 6, but the 4mph restriction for steep descents, facing points and sharp curves remained. Paid meal-breaks were permitted for the first time, with mess rooms at the Forster Square and Bridge Street offices,

although solicitous wives continued to provide drivers and conductors with hampers and tea-jugs nevertheless.

The spectre of company-owned trams on municipal tracks continued to haunt the Corporation, who had been obliged to acquire Parliamentary powers for tramway extensions to fend off threatened incursions from the direction of Wakefield and the Heavy Woollen District.

A Morley and District Light Railways Order 1901 had authorised the acquisitive British Electric Traction Company (BET) to provide tramway facilities from Tingley via Morley, Bruntcliffe and Drighlington to Tong Cemetery unless Bradford extended its operations to Drighlington not later than 1903.

The same deadline applied to nearby Birkenshaw, as the BET's Spen Valley Light Railways Extension Order, 1901 empowered the company to extend to Tong Cemetery unless Bradford exercised their own powers first. In October 1899, the UDCs of Birkenshaw, Hunsworth and Gomersal had invited Bradford to link them with the Corporation tramways, but BET, already negotiating with Dewsbury and Cleckheaton, persuaded Gomersal to accept their company trams instead.

Hard-pressed by the electrification programme, Bradford rose to the challenge. The Drighlington line, mostly single-track with nine passing-loops, was ceremonially opened on 30th June 1903, when the Mayor and the Committee were conveyed by special car (possibly driven by Driver Hornsby) to Tong Lane End, where a horse-brake was waiting to transport them to the 'Greyhound' at Tong for a dinner provided by Councillor Lister. Public service began next morning at frequencies varying between 20 and 30 minutes and at fares of 2d to the boundary and 3d beyond.

The tracklaying gang had already moved to Birkenshaw, where they laid a single track with six loops; for the first time the

Tong Cemetery terminus, 1903, where Milnes car No. 163 (left) is heading for Birkenshaw and No. 164 is returning from Drighlington. The white band on the tram standard has been superseded by the new enamel tram stop sign, and the cast-iron ornamental pole base was a typical piece of Bradford 'street furniture'. *Courtesy Bradford Libraries*

rail-joints were Thermit-welded to provide smoother travel. The trial run on 30th September was performed by Brush car No. 122 experimentally fitted with a Brush 'A' truck and air brakes, and the public service opened immediately. At the insistence of the Great Northern Railway, the Corporation had to pay for the strengthening of the bridge at Bierley Bar, and understandably the company was in no hurry to execute the work, so that for the rest of the year the tram service had to operate in two halves. As the city boundary was only a few yards past Tong Cemetery, the 2d stage was fixed at that point with a 3d fare beyond.

Within a few days of the opening, the BET-owned Yorkshire Woollen District trams from Heckmondwike (and later Dewsbury) also reached Birkenshaw, the two systems being separated by the width of Whitehall Road. Had Bradford been amenable to company tramcars, Yorkshire Woollen would have laid their lines to the 4ft gauge, but on 2nd September 1901, the Corporation had declined to entertain the idea, even though their cars would have been allowed to run to Dewsbury. The company therefore used the 'standard' gauge in the hope of links with its other neighbours, but these never materialised either. Through fares to and from Bradford were agreed, however.

The Tong Street schedules were reorganised so that trams worked to Drighlington and Birkenshaw alternately, with extras to Tong Cemetery as required. A more frequent service was run to Dudley Hill, where a terminal siding was laid into Sticker Lane to avoid delays on the 'main line'. With the exception of the one-way working in the City centre (inwards via Croft Street, Nelson Street and Norfolk Street and outwards via Bridge Street) and a single line where Wakefield Road was narrow, the entire route from Hall Lane to Tong Cemetery was double track.

A proposed link between Wakefield Road and Laisterdyke via Bowling Back Lane was surveyed but not built, as the low bridge spanning the narrow road might have debarred every tramcar except No. 229!

Simultaneously the tracks around the Town Hall were augmented to allow maximum permutations of services or car movements. From 21st January 1904 the Manchester Road

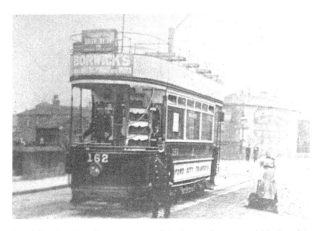

Drighlington terminus was a quiet place where an old lady with her dog could stand in the centre of the road with the conductor of Milnes car No. 162 in 1903. *Courtesy Mr F. Hartley*

tramcars began to load at new queue-barriers in Town Hall Street and depart via Nelson Street and Croft Street, thus allowing their previous reversal-point in Town Hall Square and the outward-bound tracks in lower Manchester Road to be relegated to emergency use.

The cumbersome fare-boxes inherited from the steam era had been rendered obsolete by the expansion of the network, as the conductor was still expected to collect 1d from each passenger every time the tram passed a fare stage. Its replacement was the Barker Bell Punch manufactured by Williamsons of Ashton-under-Lyne, with 'geographical' tickets in two groups based on Forster Square and Town Hall Square respectively. Colours were used to identify the different values, eg child's ½d pink; ordinary 1d white, 2d blue and 3d buff. Messrs J. R. Williams of Liverpool

The 'Halfway House', Birkenshaw, was the meeting-place of Yorkshire Woollen tram No. 24 (left) and BCT Milnes car No. 163 in 1903. Differing track gauges prevented through running.

A plaything of the winds. The canvas blinds attached to the primitive Milnes top cover were no match for the capricious Pennine breezes. Standing at Queensbury terminus in 1903 Milnes car No. 184 is receiving attention to its slipper brakes; the poles on the left belong to the Halifax tramway. *Courtesy Mr F. Hartley*

(later known as 'Autotickets') were the usual suppliers in early and later years, with Oller Ltd of London in the intervening period.

The provision of enclosed top decks on the old steam trams had owed more to a need to protect passengers from the grit, ash and steam emitted by the engine than to climatic considerations, and it was therefore taken for granted that clean electric trams did not need top covers. As early as September 1898, however, passengers were seen to boycott the rainswept upper-decks and dripping seats, and various forms of 'patent dry seats' were tested without success.

On 8th October 1902 Corporation representatives inspected a Liverpool 'Bellamy' top cover – a glass and timber saloon enclosing the central part of the upper deck and leaving the balconies completely open, and six similar covers were ordered from G. F. Milnes for trams under construction at their works. Unsightly and impractical, the covers comprised glazed bulkheads with sliding doors, a canvas roof surmounted by a flat-base trolley on a trolley-plank supported by the bulkheads, and canvas side blinds to pull down on wet days.

Boisterous breezes on the Queensbury route made playthings of the blinds which flew outwards like flapping wings; encountering one of these disturbing apparitions on the road to Stanningley, an indignant carthorse fled and upset a whole cartload of mineral water on the highway. The tramcars concerned, thought to have included Nos. 183/4/6/7/8, soon received glazed windows and tongued-and-grooved timber roofs.

An improved type of cover was therefore designed by the Thornbury depot foreman, Mr Albert Bailey, and unofficially bore his name. Theoretically removable, it comprised a tongued-and-grooved roof mounted on five channel-iron frames to which the glazed sides and bulkheads were bolted, and on the trial car, No. 206, the normal Munro and Rogers trolley mast was replaced by a taller Estler mast which protruded through the roof.

Approving the design on 7th September 1903, the Committee sanctioned the construction of 93 additional 'Bailey' tops and the conversion of the Milnes tops. All were in place by October 1904, being fitted to every type of car except the ex-trailers and 'White Board' cars, at a cost of £35 per car. Most matched the design of the trams to which they were fitted,. ie oblong windows

with radiused top corners for Milnes cars and arched window for the 'cantilever arch' Westinghouse/Brush cars, and a few boasted sash-windows. Except for a few trams equipped with new Hargreaves flat (roof-mounted) trolley bases, most used Munro and Wood masts, which, in the case of the Westinghouse/Brush cars had to be taken from uncovered Milnes cars in exchange for the unsuitable outside-spring Blackwell masts.

Construction of a short branch from Manchester Road to Gaythorne Road began on 21st December 1903, as a means of relieving seasonal unemployment, and was opened for public service on 1st April 1904 in time for the Easter Weekend. Serving a densely-peopled area, the 'Bowling Old Lane' tramway replaced the last of the horse-buses and proved very profitable.

The year 1904 was long remembered for its 'Exhibition weather' – a prolonged spell of fair weather which coincided with the magnificent Bradford Exhibition opened on 4th May by T.R.H. the Prince and Princess of Wales (later King George V and Queen Mary) who also unveiled a statue of Queen Victoria in Morley Street as well as the new Cartwright Hall in Lister

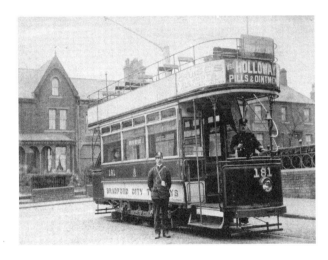

The Bowling Old Lane tramway, where Milnes car No. 181 is seen at the Gaythorne Road terminus about 1904, was one of the Tramways Department's 'money-spinners'. *Courtesy Mr F. Hartley*

Much more practical than the Milnes top covers were the 'Bailey Tops' designed and built at Thornbury, where Brush car No. 57, newly overhauled and repainted, is ready to re-enter service.
Courtesy the late R. B. Parr

Park. In preparation for these hugely-popular events short-working crossovers were laid in Morley Street (Claremont) and Manchester Road, and the derelict horse-tram track in North Park Road (Oak Lane – St. Mary's Road) was relaid and electrified for a special Exhibition tram service from Rawson Square to Lister Park.

Predictably the public declined to toil up the hill to Rawson Square in the blazing sun; instead, they thronged the Saltaire trams in Forster Square and alighted near 'The Spotted House' hostelry in Keighley Road, where a short-working crossover had to be hastily inserted. The track in North Park Road was therefore used for storing trams during the day, and 'football specials' for Bradford City matches were also 'shunted' there for many seasons.

The Tramways Department's most spectacular contribution to the exhibition was the transformation of Milnes car No. 130 into an 'illuminated drawing-room'. The saloon was re-finished

The Bradford Exhibition of 1904 created a tremendous demand for transport to and from Lister Park. Tram car No. 148, labelled 'Special Car No. 4', queues in North Park Road with other Milnes cars which, despite their newness, are already showing signs of structural drooping. *Courtesy Mr F. Hartley*

The 'Bailey Tops' provided better accommodation in bad weather. This view of Milnes car No. 206 shows the staggered '2 and 1' seating arrangement with the trolley mast mounted on a box in the centre of the car. *Photo: Bradford City Tramways*

in walnut with luxurious fittings – mirrors, curtains, a walnut cabinet, four single and two double easy chairs and painted glass panels depicting local scenes. Externally, cream lincrusta concealed the panels; the dashplates were in simulated mahogany, and 988 16-candlepower lamps provided a blaze of colour after dark. The cost was £114.6s. 11d, but the exhibition produced a net profit of £6,000 for the tramways and when it closed on 29th October the car re-entered normal service. Mysteriously, the painted glass panels vanished for eight decades before being presented to Bradford Museums. One enduring legacy of the eventful season was the establishment of two cross-city services – Heaton to Bradford Moor and (as in steam days) Saltaire to Undercliffe.

During the year the carriageway and track beneath Bowling Bridge were lowered by six inches to allow the use of Bailey-top Brush cars, though their slightly-higher Milnes counterparts were still debarred by the 16ft 4ins minimum clearance.

As the developing suburb of Bradford Moor was insistently demanding tramway facilities, the Corporation had to seek a replacement for the only available approach to the area – the inconvenient single-track Harris Street and East Parade lines which could not carry increased traffic. The one practical alternative was the 'appallingly precipitous' direct approach via Church Bank, a narrow, curving and uneven ascent reaching a gradient of 1 in 7. However, if the brow of the hill could be dug out and tipped into the hollow at the bottom, a constant 1 in 9.8 gradient could be created.

The press considered it 'one of the most daring engineering enterprises ever undertaken in Bradford .... almost sufficient to stimulate visions of tramcars recklessly trundling down the Bank in somersault fashion'. Nevertheless the 'Bank' was widened and regraded in the Autumn of 1903, and large crowds assembled on 30th November to watch the ascent of car 122, laden with sandbags to represent a full load and piloted by Mr Spencer who, never a faint-hearted man, also drove the tram downhill 'at a fair speed' and halted it within half its own length with its patent air-brake. A Board of Trade downhill speed limit of 4mph was imposed.

The least-satisfactory 'Bailey Top' cars were the 1898 Brush cars with precipitous stairs and no balcony. Car No. 1, with driver standing to attention, is at Eccleshill terminus. *Courtesy Mr F. Hartley*

Nothing if not intrepid: Milnes car No. 146 returning from Undercliffe in 1903 confidently descends the 1 in 9.8 gradient of Church Bank. The ancient Parish Church (later the Cathedral) stands on the left. *Photo: Bradford City Tramways*

Undercliffe cars were re-routed via Church Bank on 19th December, being joined on 30th January 1904 by the Bradford Moor trams on their two-mile double-track route. At first the new service terminated at Rushton Road where housing development ended, but from April 1906 was extended to Woodhall Road near the junction with the Stanningley tracks. In the interests of safety and the peace of mind of Church Bank users, the whole fleet was fitted with automatic run-back brakes.

Meanwhile, history was attempting to repeat itself in Shipley, where the UDC had obtained parliamentary powers for additional tramways to their boundaries at Nab Wood, Windhill, Baildon Bridge and Frizinghall (Valley Road) and to Saltaire station (Victoria Road).

Bradford were willing to work most of the proposed routes as extensions of their existing network, but were not interested in the Victoria Road, Valley Road or Shipley-Baildon Bridge sections, whereupon Shipley accepted a bid from Mr Quinn (their resident engineer), Mr A.S.J. Musgrave of Settle and Messrs J.G. White of London, contractors, who duly formed a Mid-Yorkshire Tramway Company with the aim of constructing a 19-mile system radiating to Ilkley, Otley, Keighley (via Bingley) and Baildon ('Bay Horse'), with a generating station at Menston.

Most councils supported the scheme, provided that Mid-Yorkshire reimbursed Ilkley for widening 'Crescent Corner', Bingley for making a new road past Bingley Church, and West Riding County Council for improving Cottingley Bridge over the River Aire. Also, Mid-Yorkshire trams would be allowed to run into Keighley but not provide a local service. Significantly, however, the viability of the Valley Road and Windhill routes was dependent on the construction by Bradford of connecting tramways within their own boundaries ie along Canal Road and from Thackley to Windhill respectively. Bradford saw no reason to construct either, partly because neither would be profitable, and equally because of its attitude towards company trams.

Nevertheless the first line, from Windhill to Nab Wood, was built by Mid-Yorkshire. Unexpectedly, Shipley permitted the erection of a corrugated-iron depot in Saltaire Road (Exhibition Road) on the onerous proviso that it would be removed within two years, and the ensuing dispute delayed the work so long that the depot was incomplete when the tramcars were delivered.

As Major Pringle insisted on inspecting the Saltaire-Windhill line at the same time as Bradford's Drighlington route, Bradford had to lend both tramcars and staff, as the Company's own fleet was still under construction. The first inspection, on 2nd July 1903, was a disappointment, as the Inspector disliked the condition of the road surface, and even though the first of the Company's own trams arrived on the morning of Major Pringle's second and successful visit on 23rd July, the only glimpse he obtained of it was when he rode past Windhill station yard (where it was briefly on display) on one of the borrowed Bradford trams, in the company of Shipley, Baildon and Bradford representatives. The Mid-Yorkshire tram was then hauled to the depot site by a team of horses, and was fitted out as an illuminated vehicle for its trial run five days later.

The borrowed trams did a good trade at the start of Shipley Tide, the local holiday week, carrying 9,070 passengers on 25th July with takings of £29.0s.4d. During the period of hire, which ended on 11th August and cost the Company £299.10s.0d, they had to be stabled in the Corporation's tiny 10-car depot in Moorhead Lane, displacing several cars needed for the Saltaire-Undercliffe service and condemning the staff to a long walk home if no staff car was available to and from Thornbury depot.

Painted in cheerful vermilion and cream, the ten Mid-Yorkshire tramcars were powerful and steady-riding though dated in design, resembling Bradford's earliest 1898 purchases. Solidly-built by Hurst Nelson in best oak, they incorporated three 'Tudor Arch' windows per side surmounted by half-lights in amber 'Cathedral' glass, as well as luxuries which included curtains, electric heaters and strap-operated conductor's bells (the bells were later adopted by BCT as a standard fitting).

An animated scene in 1904, with strollers, a handcart, butchers in immaculate aprons and Milnes car No. 135 climbing Church Bank past the ancient Parish Church (now the Cathedral) on its way to Bradford Moor.
Courtesy Mrs D. Burrows

A painting by Mr F. Hartley of Mid-Yorkshire tram No. 3 heading for Nab Wood in 1903, with Baildon Moor in the distance.

The street installations were impressively constructed, with heavy poles, elliptical pole bases and ponderous pear-shaped finials which matched the High Victorian architecture of Saltaire village. The permanent way was laid with 91lb-per yard rail bought from Walter Scott of Leeds.

The short line from Branch to Baildon Bridge was tested on 24th August, but before it could be opened for service, disaster overtook the Company. ' Lord Loch', a valuable chestnut stallion, took fright at the approach of car No. 2 as it descended Saltaire Road and was struck by the tram; it fell, broke a leg and had to be shot. The ensuing damages cost the Company £1,750 plus costs. Financially overstretched, Messrs Quin and Musgrave transferred operations to the contractor, but Shipley refused to relieve them of their obligations, and shortly afterwards Mr Quin was mysteriously drowned at Morecambe.

The Branch-Baildon Bridge route was eventually opened by the new lessees on 14th November. Where the two routes crossed in Shipley town centre ('Fox and Hounds' corner) a complicated series of connecting curves, crossovers and overhead wires earned the crossroads the new title of 'Cobweb Corner', although in

Company days the only curve in daily use was the one which allowed cars from Baildon Bridge to turn into Commercial Street and head for the depot.

Already it was clear that Mid-Yorkshire could not survive. Its existing two routes were too short even to cover their cost: the Windhill-Nab Wood route was described as "startin' wheer nubb'dy lived an' finishin' wheer iv'ribody wer' deead", ie at the local cemetery! Large-scale expansion was now unthinkable, and the strategic track junction at the 'Branch' was denied to the Company by Bradford's refusal to allow private trams on public tramways. As a Shipley councillor ruefully explained,

"If we could nobbut a' getten 'em on t' top road, they'd a' been alreight!"

From 16th November the Windhill trams ceased to run beyond Wrose Brow Road except at peak-hours and weekends, and in December the business was offered to Bradford. Official reaction was mixed, as receipts were only 5d per car mile, and a few days previously Councillor Fred Foster had counted nine passengers on thirteen cars! Nevertheless the purchase was agreed on the basis that Shipley would pay £32,751 for track and overhead fittings which Bradford would lease in addition to purchasing the trams and stores for £7,500.

Thus the latest of Shipley's unlucky tramway ventures passed under Bradford's control on 30th April 1904, when the Nab Wood-Windhill and Branch-Baildon Bridge services were replaced by three new services from Forster Square via Branch and Shipley town centre to Nab Wood, Baildon Bridge and Windhill. The appearance of 'red' cars mingling with the familiar blue cars on Manningham Lane aroused much friendly banter, especially when a 'red' tram shed a wheel near Eldon Place. The ex-Company stock was renumbered 230-239 (not necessarily consecutively) in the BCT fleet.

'Cobweb Corner', Shipley, where the Windhill-Nab Wood line (foreground) crossed the Branch-Baildon Bridge tracks (left to right). Mid-Yorkshire No. 1 is standing in Commercial Street. The 'Sun Hotel' (extreme left) is still a popular Shipley hostelry.

Courtesy: the late R. B. Parr

A gloomy view in old Windhill, where BCT car No. 65 is descending Leeds Road on its way to Nab Wood. *Courtesy: Mr F. Hartley*

The Mid-Yorkshire trams inherited by Bradford proved to be a useful asset when conventional BCT cars were banned from the Greengates route. Car No. 235 is experiencing no difficulty in passing beneath the bridge at Eccleshill Railway Station.
Copyright: Bradford City Tramways, courtesy Mr F. Hartley

The unique four-track layout at Saltaire, where the company tracks had by-passed the BCT terminus, was linked up at the same time as the rails were removed from the vacated Saltaire Road depot, and when the 'missing link' from Windhill Boundary to Thackley (Victoria Street) was completed on 1st July (with unusual staggered railjoints which, when well worn in later years imparted a rolling, drunken gait to the trams), the services were reorganised again, with a new Circular Route operating from and to Forster Square via Shipley. Moorhead Lane depot worked the anti-clockwise service via Bolton, Thackley, Shipley, Otley Road and Branch, returning via Manningham Lane, whilst Bolton depot operated the clockwise service – a much more leisurely affair, since Bolton's low-powered 1898 fleet made 'heavy weather' of the interminable climb from Low Well to Thackley. In Forster Square the track layout had to be augmented to cater for the additional workings.

An unusual visitor to the Circular Route was single-decker No. 229 whose bogies developed the endearing habit of taking different tracks when entering loops, thus causing the car to travel almost broadside down Leeds Road, Thackley.

The little Moorhead Lane depot, now inadequate and outmoded, was superseded in August 1904 by a stylish stone and glass structure at Saltaire, housing 30 cars on six roads that converged at the gate into one track which crossed the Saltaire Road lines to join the 'top road' tramway to Bradford. The Milnes and ex-Mid-Yorkshire cars which inhabited the depot served Baildon Bridge, the Saltaire-Undercliffe route (jointly with Thornbury depot) and (jointly with Bolton) the Circular workings.

In order to serve the isolated village of Sandy Lane the Committee extended the Allerton tramway to the top of Stony Lane. Major Pringle approved the extension on 12th October 1904 and the public service commenced immediately. On several occasions extra cars had to be run on Sundays when popular preachers visited Sandy Lane Baptist Chapel.

The second tramway inspected by Major Pringle on 12th October was a 1 mile 1434 yards extension from Undercliffe to Greengates ('Roebuck') on a continuously-falling gradient. At Eccleshill Station a low overbridge carried the G.N. Laisterdyke-Windhill railway across the road, and as its owners had refused to allow the carriageway to be lowered, a short length of single tram track had to be laid so that the overhead wires could be slewed to one side out of the reach of passengers.

Wyke terminus about 1904, with the new Board School on the left. Milnes 'Bailey Top' car No. 192 is standing on the former steam tram permanent way, with the disused reversing curve extending around the corner to join the third leg of the triangle in Huddersfield Road. When the Wyke tracks were renewed in 1905, the terminus was re-sited in Huddersfield Road, alongside the gas lamp.

Courtesy: Mr R. Brook

When Major Pringle found that at its lowest point the bridge was only 15ft 5½ins above rail level, he refused to allow the use of double-deck cars, as there was less than the newly-introduced 6ft minimum clearance above the top deck floor of Milnes car No. 137 on which he was riding. Consternation reigned until the existence of single-decker No. 229 was recalled. Hurriedly summoned from Thornbury it surmounted Church Bank with ease but was defeated by the sharp 'Cock and Bottle' curve and was obliged to execute a 'three point turn' at the top of Harris Street before commencing a shuttle service between Undercliffe and Greengates from 14th October while comparative measurements of other tramcar types were being taken.

The ex-Mid-Yorkshire cars were found to provide sufficient clearance, and on 31st October their use was sanctioned provided that they were running on half-worn tyres and that passengers were regularly warned to remain seated when passing beneath the bridge. Supplemented by a few suitable 'White Board' cars at rush hours, the 'Mid-Yorkshires' took over the Greengates service, and to forestall complaints from Shipley against the loss of 'their' cars, the Department instituted a cross-city Greengates-Baildon Bridge service via Forster Square and Shipley town centre, cars being housed at Saltaire depot.

A bold decision to provide plush cushions by Lister and Company for the unyielding wooden seats of 120 trams prompted a health warning from the Medical Officer. Sad to relate, his forebodings were well-founded, and within three years the cushions, thoroughly "wick" (alive with fleas) had to be destroyed.

Much more successful was the Tramways Parcels Service instituted on 1st January 1905, following inspection of a similar venture in Dublin. From rented premises at 7/9 Piccadilly, and assisted by three De Dion van chassis with home-built bodies, 60 canvas-lined skeps made by the Blind Institute and a fleet of two-wheeled handcarts, a horde of parcel-boys collected and delivered parcels within half a mile of any tramway and would, on request, collect railway travellers' luggage in advance. Parcels could be handed in at the tramways offices, depots and a network of suburban sub-offices; also they could be given to conductors of city-bound tramcars, and most were delivered the same day, even if received in the early evening. Arrangements were made with Halifax and Yorkshire Woollen for collections and deliveries from and to their areas, and 478,214 parcels were distributed in the first year.

Tramcar operation in Church Bank proved successful and uneventful until the Committee unwisely yielded to pressure to allow a stopping place at Upper Park Gate on a 1 in 14 gradient. On 8th February 1905 – a damp, drizzly day – Driver Stilgoe halted his Undercliffe-bound Bailey-top car (No. 171) at the new stop, only to find, to his alarm, that the brakes would not hold. Slowly the tram began to move backwards, as did the following car, No. 136, on the Bradford Moor service, its driver being anxious to avoid a collision, although the descent of both vehicles was safely regulated by the automatic run-back brake. The situation was saved by ex-steam tram driver Sam Coultas in charge of Greengates-bound 'Mid-Yorkshire' car No. 230 whose stout fender halted the two Milnes cars and enabled all three to resume their journeys. The stop was promptly abolished, and as a means of ensuring that not more than one car would ascend the Bank at any time, a 'skate' (contact) was fitted to the overhead wire at the foot of the hill and at Stott Hill to light and extinguish a red warning lamp.

The diversion of the ex-Mid-Yorkshire fleet to the Greengates route had an unexpected sequel when the clockwise Circular Route cars commenced on Good Friday, 1905, to work through to Nab Wood from Forster Square via Manningham Lane without

37

passing through Shipley town centre. Whereas the 'Mid-Yorkshires' with their centrally-mounted trolley-masts had encountered no difficulties with the short Shipley bracket arms, the first Brush/Westinghouse tram to pass beyond Saltaire became stranded out of reach of the wires, as its trolley was offset to leave the gangway clear. Until the Saltaire-Nab Wood overhead wires could be converted to span-wire suspension, every 'Circular' car which was travelling with its trolley-mast on the 'wrong' side had to travel via Shipley and reverse at 'Cobweb Corner'.

In order to cater for Whitsuntide holidaymakers a few weeks later, the Department organised some unusual workings, such as Stanningley to Saltaire via Barkerend Road; Heaton to Eccleshill and Baildon Bridge to Town Gate (Idle) via Shipley and Thackley.

A year earlier the Corporation had bought from the Bowling Iron Company four acres of land and spoil-heaps for use as extra depot accommodation and a permanent way yard. Opened in 1905, the typically-BCT stone-fronted, glass-roofed depot housed 36 trams on six roads which continued down a long approach to converge into a single line compressed between cottage dwellings in Foundry Lane, where a junction with the Wakefield Road tramway was laid.

The remainder of the site, known variously as Bolling Hill or Bowling Yard, formed the permanent -way depot where a network of tram-tracks, railway sidings and a dual-gauge weighbridge allowed goods to be delivered direct. Three tramcar goods-waggons, two stores trucks and nine salt-trucks, all built at Thornbury, were based in the yard. When the dross (ironworks waste-product) proved to have a commercial value, crushed clinker, shingle and rough ballast were advertised for sale, and the clinker, together with sand dried at the yard, was used in tramcar sandboxes. Unevenly sloping and overshadowed by the brooding dross-hill, the yard became a hive of activity, while the depot provided all the trams needed for the Wakefield Road routes.

The patent air-brake on car No. 122 was replaced by a Westinghouse unit driven from the car axle, with two wooden slipper-brake blocks actuated by the driver's operating valve, but as the Committee deemed it too expensive, it gave way to normal manual braking.

In the summer of 1905 Wyke was tramless for fourteen long weeks while the former steam-tram track was renewed; a service to Low Moor (Common End) was operated as soon as the relaying reached that point, but Wyke residents were displeased, as were Leeds Road folk when the removal of the sub-standard Demerbe rails caused the temporary diversion of their trams via Bradford Moor. More fortunate were the Thornton passengers when their Demerbe track was replaced in manageable stages between School Green and Green Lane after a life of only five years. The Corporation accepted compensation from the rail suppliers for all existing and future claims for defective materials.

Friendly rivalry between the depots was aroused in 1905 when the Department allowed each one to decorate a tramcar for the annual Sports and Cricket Match. Keen competition for the most original entry ensued. Lace curtains and evergreen plants imparted a domestic touch to Bowling car No. 169, while a 'Horton Beef' – a currant teacake – was proudly displayed by the Horton Bank Top staff as the emblem for their tramcar. From 1906 swelling harmony and tuneful melody was offered by the new Tramways Band.

The completion of the new John Street alongside Rawson Market enabled the Department to extend the Rawson Square tracks to a two-way junction with the Duckworth Lane tramway in Westgate, thus providing a useful inter-route connection. Commencing on 13th December 1905 it was used for a new permutation of the Heaton service, whereby on weekdays a 15-minute service was worked from Sunbridge Road bottom via John Street, North Parade and St. Mary's Road – in addition to the already adequate Bradford Moor to Heaton service. Complaints soon arose that whereas the Allerton, Thornton and Heaton trams which now shared an adjacent departure point were fitted with Bailey tops, the Duckworth Lane cars were all 'open-toppers'. However, as the Allerton, Duckworth Lane and Thornton trams all shared the same depot, the complaint was probably exaggerated, and within a few years the depot allocation consisted entirely of top-covered cars.

Ever since the opening of the electric tramways eight years previously, the starting-point for the Bolton Road trams had been in the centre of the carriageway in Forster Square, outside the Post Office, but in order to eliminate the inconvenience of 'swinging' the trolley boom and reversing the seats each time a tram arrived in the Square, from September 1906 the cars were allowed to circumnavigate the Square and load at a point between Canal Road and Commercial Street. Unfortunately, in wet weather passengers sought shelter in office doorways, and the experiment had to be abandoned.

The vacated track on the North side of the Square was then assigned to the Pay Car, which for the next two decades became a feature of city life. Ex-trailer car No. 27 was adapted for this purpose with a hatch in one of the side-windows. Stabled at Bowling depot, it made its unobtrusive way to the Square every Friday morning for the convenience of staff. Never altered or repainted, its Prussian blue deepened to near-black and its ivory to deep yellow, but the gold leaf retained its glitter. By 1926 the increase of traffic and requests for a more dignified method of wage payment led the Department to withdraw the old car.

Meanwhile its fellows, Nos. 25/26/28, had been rebuilt with balconies which increased the top deck seating from 20 to 33, although as most of the seats were doubles, the accommodation was cramped. In their revised form the three trams may have made an impression on J.B. Priestley, who in *Good Companions*, described Mrs Buttershaw's girth as being 'of a breadth far beyond the dreams of the Tramways Committee'! Simultaneously, together with car No. 100, they received new Brush AA trucks (a stronger version of the A and a precursor of the 21E), and car No. 26 was fitted with the first four-shoe slipper brake.

Stabled alongside the dreary drosshills of Bowling Yard, tippler waggon No. 5 was used to transport ballast and crushed clinker for the Permanent Way Department. *Courtesy Mr J. Copland*

The imposing appearance of the fleet was, however, slightly diminished when the proud, shaded-gilt legend 'BRADFORD CITY TRAMWAYS' on the rocker panels was discarded in favour of small, chocolate-brown lettering, with a saving of 10 shillings per car! Other savings were tried also. Between 1907 and 1909 cars Nos. 104 and 120 used Raworth regenerative braking which was reputed to reduce current consumption by 23%, but as no reduction could be detected, manual braking remained as a standard fitting.

Most of the early trams were rebuilt with extended balconies for extra seating capacity. The 1898-vintage No. 18, labelled 'Idle', displays its new shape in Thornbury depot yard, 1908. *Courtesy Mr F. Hartley*

5 - THE CHURCH BANK SMASH

'It streams from the hills, it descends to the plain ...'
(Hymns Ancient and Modern)

Man-made disasters have always caused sensations. Even though the sinking of the *Titanic* and the destruction of the airship *Hindenburg* were insignificant events compared with the overwhelming might of volcanic eruptions, floods and famines inflicted by Nature, nevertheless because they were potentially preventible they made a lasting impression.

So it was with the Church Bank Smash, which caused injuries but no deaths. Pessimists had warned that the Bank was too steep for tramcars, and the one sensational happening which apparently justified their forebodings has often obscured the undeniable fact that for the next four decades thousands of laden trams safely negotiated the hill as a routine part of their daily duties.

On its departure from Undercliffe at 5.56am on 31st July 1907 Milnes car No. 210 made normal progress as far as the 'Cock and Bottle' where Driver Dover halted it with the handbrake. Then, rounding the sharp curve towards the city centre, it gathered speed before the slipper brake could take effect.

Observing that Church Bank was approaching with alarming rapidity, the sole top-deck passenger ran downstairs, leaped off, landed heavily on the pavement and recovered his senses to find a kindly soul proffering whisky. Meanwhile the tram had rushed down the Bank at a speed of which Major Druitt would have strongly disapproved, ignoring the compulsory stop which he had insisted upon, and after leaving the rails at the Well Street junction, had slewed round towards the nearest warehouse and overturned in Forster Square. Its Bailey top was wrenched off and slithered in fragments across the pavement while the passengers and crew lay stunned and shaken in the lower deck.

'The injured ones were travelling on to earn their daily bread,

But were prevented, for they met with accident instead.

Then some were taken to their homes which they so late had left,

And some to the Infirmary, of happiness bereft' –

Fortunately, two fractures, three sprains, two cases of cuts, one of bruises, four of shock and (as revealed by the local poet), temporary loss of happiness were the only injuries sustained by the unwilling participants in the drama.

The noise and crash created a huge sensation in the busy Square; indeed, the reverberations have still not died away, 90 years later. Fascinated crowds watched the lower deck being righted and hauled back on to the tracks. As the leading axle was broken, a small emergency trolley was inserted underneath so that the car could be towed along Well Street and back to Thornbury.

With a new wheelset and a borrowed Bailey top and trolley mast, car No. 210 returned the same night to the scene of its dramatic descent. This time the journey was accomplished without incident, although the tram then quietly retired from public service.

At the ensuing inquiry a week later, Major Druitt attributed the accident to the breaking of the axle as the car rounded the 'Cock and Bottle' corner. All the brakes – hand, slipper and rheostatic – had been fully applied, although an earlier and firmer use of the slipper-brake might have prevented the runaway. Alternatively, the axle might have fractured when the wheels struck the pavement edge. The axle load was about 3 tons per journal with a breaking-strain of 21 tons, but contrary to railway and recent tramway practice the 4ins thick axle was reduced to 3¾ins at the wheel-seat. With a recommendation that no old-type axle should be used for longer than four years, the Inspector closed the inquiry.

For a long while afterwards some passengers alighted at the 'Cock and Bottle' and walked downhill. The 'Church Bank Smash' lived on as an exciting folk memory, and until the last day of the Forster Square trams the more imaginative passengers held their breath as their tramcar forsook the safe levels of the Square for the abrupt ascent of the Bank. The majority of their fellow-travellers scorned such forebodings and never hesitated to stand upstairs or downstairs if all seats were taken. Even a trolley dewirement halfway up the hill held no fears for them – willing hands reached over the balcony rail to assist the conductor in retrieving the errant boom, and a forest of heads craned to watch the clouds of dropped sand scatter as the tramcar wheels began to grind their way up the steep gradient again. The Bradford Tram always got through. Well, almost always!

The shattered top deck of car No. 210 became separated from the lower deck in the 'Tramway Disaster', 31st July 1907.
Courtesy the late R. B. Parr

6 - THROUGH SERVICE

In the early years of the tramways the absence of through services to neighbouring towns presented no problems, as demand was modest, and few objected to changing trams at Queensbury, Shelf or elsewhere.

On the Tong Street tramway where each car worked alternately to Drighlington and Birkenshaw, the need for Corporation and Yorkshire Woollen District drivers to enable passengers to make a proper connection was well ingrained. One day a Drighlington-bound driver who had been waiting patiently at the last passing-loop for the preceding car to return to City, drove cautiously on to the sleepy terminus where he found the car oddly deserted. Tracing its crew to the nearby hostelry he enquired the reason for the delay. "Nay, we're waitin' for t'Woollen District tram", came the slurred reply. Good excuse, but wrong terminus!

At Stanningley, however, the situation was startlingly different, as contrary to anyone's expectations Town Street was daily thronged with passengers changing between Bradford and Leeds tramcars. The reason was that although the Great Northern Railway trains between the two cities, a distance of nine miles, were three times swifter than the trams, the railway fare was 9d but the tram fare only 6d.

On 5th January 1906 Mr Spencer's Leeds colleague, Mr J.B. Hamilton, suggested that a third rail should be laid between the two city centres to enable both Corporations to run a through service. As the proposal would have entailed eighteen miles of extra rail and countless points and crossings, Mr Spencer conferred with his shrewd engineering foreman 'John Willie' Dawson, with the result that at the next Committee meeting only 42 days later he was able to present an ingenious alternative plan whereby the wheels of the tramcars would be able to slide along the axles to adjust themselves to the gauge of either track. He was authorised to conduct a practical experiment and to apply for patent rights, reserving two-thirds of the royalties to Bradford Corporation.

Brush Bailey-top car No. 124, happening to be in the Works, was selected for the trial. Its Peckham truck was dismantled and rebuilt about 6ins wider; the axle boxes were removed and stationary axles fitted. The wheels were shrunk on to sleeves capable of sliding along the axles and revolving around them; each sleeve incorporated a gearwheel constantly meshing with a pinion at each end of the motor armature to provide 4-wheel drive on either gauge.

The wheels were locked into position by individual guides mounted on a transverse shaft which was controlled from a hand-lever near the mid-point of one side of the truck. The guides ran outside the wheels on the Bradford gauge and inside them on the Leeds gauge, being raised or lowered by a platform-mounted lever between the controller and the handbrake.

The handbrake equipment was adjusted so that the shoes moved laterally with the wheels, while the incompatible mechanical slipper brake was replaced by a Westinghouse magnetic track brake hung from the axles and able to conform to the change of gauge.

Although the structure of the top saloon was retained, the Bailey roof was replaced by a full-length canopy cover with a flat trolley base mounted on a trolley plank, and, uniquely, a Leeds-type trolley head was fitted, presumably in case the Leeds overhead fittings were incompatible with Bradford's. For the last time, the full shaded-gilt legend, 'BRADFORD CITY TRAMWAYS', filled the rocker panels, and thick double lining-out was applied below the upper saloon windows, an unhandsome practice which fortunately was discontinued soon afterwards.

Within the Works a portable tapering track had been laid out, and on 26th November the fascinated Committee watched as the reconstructed truck was run along it, changing gauge as it did so. Afterwards the car body was reunited with the truck, and presumably the tram was tested up and down Leeds Road.

At Stanningley the Bradford and Leeds tracks had been linked by a 30ft length of single-line tapering track, and the overhead wires had also been joined up, though with a section insulator separating the Bradford and Leeds supplies. So the stage was set, but would the ingenious experiment work?

On the evening of 22nd January 1907 Mr Hamilton joined Mr Spencer at Thornbury, together with members of their staff. There they boarded No. 124 for a journey to the bottom of Leeds Road and thence to Stanningley, where the locking-gear was raised and the car driven forward. With a low, grinding noise the wheels adjusted themselves to a new gauge; the guides dropped back into place, and the deed was done. With great anticipation the party embarked on their historic journey, travelling on Leeds tracks as far as Branch Road, Armley, where the car reversed for a homeward run to Thornbury. Ingenuity had triumphed, and doubtless Messrs Spencer and Dawson slept soundly that night.

Board of Trade approval having been given, Major Pringle rode to Leeds with the Committee on 16th April when a month's trial was agreed. The following Monday, 22nd April, was the first day on which passengers were able to travel through. With great approval the *Yorkshire Observer* recorded the momentous event.

'The new car ... left Bradford at 8.25am, and arrived in Leeds at 9.30. At Stanningley where passengers have previously had to alight and change cars, they kept their seats, and by the simple movement of a lever the conductor altered the gearing so that the wheels readily accommodated themselves to the broader gauge of the Leeds tramways. On the Leeds section there are several sharp curves, but these were successfully negotiated, and the whole journey was accomplished with perfect smoothness.

Experimental dual-gauge car No. 124, photographed at Thornbury in 1907, had a composite top deck comprising a full-length canopy roof superimposed on a Bailey top, with a trolley base mounted on the roof.

Photo: Bradford City Tramways

Residents of Stanningley watch in awe as a Leeds inspector learns how to negotiate the taper track in Town Street on Bradford car No. 124.
Photo: Bradford City Tramways courtesy the late R. B. Parr

In Bradford the new car is by this time a tolerably familiar object in the streets, but in City Square and at the Corn Exchange, Leeds, it was sufficient of a novelty to arouse considerable curiosity, and although little of the gearing is in view, many persons stopped to make a close examination. On the first journey a driver and conductor selected by Mr Hamilton acted as pilots.'

Despite severe snowstorms No. 124 successfully completed its trials on 25th May, and with the blessing of the Board of Trade commenced a regular though solitary service on 23rd September.

Domestic issues were being dealt with in an equally decisive way. When a drunken passenger on an open-top tram pulled the trolley off the wire on an ascent of Cheapside, and a more obnoxious youth assaulted a conductor, both received a well-earned sentence of one month's hard labour.

The Board of Trade was being pressed to raise the maximum speed limit from 12 to 17mph to legitimise what tram drivers were already doing. The dogs of Bradford were not being forgotten either; as they had never been allowed to board the

cars and had to 'gallop after them' while their owners rode in comfort, the new prospect of 17mph 'gallops' prompted requests for a change of heart. But the possibility of passengers accidentally 'stepping on the tail of a ferocious bulldog and finding its teeth in the back of their leg', encouraged the Committee to maintain its stance until 1910, when accompanied canines were permitted on the upper deck at the conductor's discretion.

The new, steeply-inclined highway from Little Horton to Wibsey, laid partly on viaduct and partly on embankment, was now ready to receive the tramway promised when North Bierley joined Bradford. Surprisingly, the Corporation had to be shamed into honouring its promise by Alderman Enoch Priestley of Wibsey, in whose honour the new thoroughfare was jocularly named 'St. Enoch's Road'. When Major Pringle rode on car No. 26 to inspect the tramway on 9th October, the Black Dyke Mills Band played triumphal music on the open deck of car No. 25, 400 old folk sat down to a good tea, and Wibseyites rejoiced.

Laid with 105lb welded rail and firmly anchored to its foundations, the track was completed in only two months, and with quiet satisfaction Alderman Priestley drove the first car on the day of completion, 4th October. Fearful lest the route might be unprofitable, the Manager had originally proposed a trial service using a converted motor tower-waggon with charabanc seats, and he now recommended a 2d fare. Overruled on both counts, he soon found that the trams paid handsome profits and that the development of Wibsey was greatly enhanced. Cars for the service were provided jointly by Bowling and Horton Bank Top depots.

Within the lively, bustling city, Sunday evening travel was surprisingly heavy. At Frizinghall crowds of over 200 frustrated residents probably intent on visits to church, chapel or relatives sometimes waited 40 minutes before they could board a tram, while at a later hour the throngs at the Forster Square loading points 'beggared description'.

By this time the Bailey top covers were leaking badly, a succession of wet and dry summers having destroyed their waterproof qualities, and passengers often resorted to umbrellas. The Committee visited Leeds, Glasgow and

Flags, bunting and potted plants adorned the upper deck of ex-trailer car No. 25 on its triumphal arrival at the Wibsey terminus (entrance to High Street) when the route opened in 1907.
Courtesy Mr F. Hartley

Manchester to inspect more modern types in use there; the Manchester type with a canopy roof extending the full length of the upper saloon and balconies found favour, and in March 1907 the Works were asked to produce an initial batch of 25.

With a headroom of 6ft 0½ins the new 'Oak Top Covers' had four full-drop windows per side (later reduced to two full-drop and two fixed), surmounted by quarter-lights in Muranese 'cockleshell' glass (originally clear, later yellow). The ash roof-sticks stiffened by L-shaped angle-irons supported a double-thickness pine planked roof interleaved and covered with well-painted duck canvas. The saloon doors slid within the bulkhead, and the birds-eye maple-panelled ceilings were illuminated by four lamps in ground-glass bowls, with a single lamp lighting each balcony. The seating comprised seven double seats per side with five places on each balcony, an overall total of 22 + 28 + 10 = 60.

Brush cars Nos. 111 and 113 were the first to receive 'oak tops' in late 1907 or January/February 1908; for several years only Brush cars were so equipped, and in 1910 75 further tops were commissioned. Unfortunately their height precluded them from passing beneath the 16ft 0½ins Windhill railway bridge and its even lower Greengates counterpart.

Dual-gauge car No. 124 ran over the Town Street taper track for the last time on 10th May 1908, thus allowing Leeds Corporation to begin an extension of their Stanningley tramway to Pudsey. By mutual agreement Bradford surrendered the 88 yards of track and overhead in Town Street while Leeds paid for a new double taper track straddling the Pudsey/Farsley boundary, with a 4ft gauge facing crossover for the Bradford-Stanningley trams. The LCT Pudsey route diverged from the main line and disappeared uphill under the railway viaduct.

A formal through-running agreement covered the division of receipts and ordained that trams would be subject to the byelaws of the Corporation on whose track they were running. Each undertaking was to provide ten tramcars. Accordingly BCT Brush cars Nos. 72, 76, 78, 93, 110, 116,118 and 127 received 'oak tops', and together with No. 111 had their Peckham trucks rebuilt and strengthened; the additional height thus created necessitated a three-bar lifeguard, and a stout wooden sill had to be fitted to the sole bars to accommodate the extra width of the truck.

In order to match the horsepower of the LCT contingent – LCT 87 and 104-112 also with Peckham trucks but GE 37½hp motors – the BCT cars received 35hp 'Witting' motors and B18 controllers taken from Milnes cars. Unlike No. 124, several of them retained their mechanical slipper brakes (for use on Bradford

track only), and the makeshift top deck of No. 124 was superseded by a new 'oak top'. The BCT cars bore prominent white side-destination boards advertising in black letters the legend, THROUGH CAR BRADFORD AND LEEDS' whilst LCT reversed the colours and name sequence.

The through service was ceremonially inaugurated on 7th June 1909, when decorated cars left Bradford and Leeds at 11.15am. LCT Car No. 104 collected its cargo of councillors in City Square before proceeding to Corn Exchange and embarking on its long journey, cheered on its way by Armley schoolchildren. Their Lord Mayor, Alderman Kitson, was content to motor to Stanningley and board the tram in Town Street. Meanwhile BCT No. 118 had taken its civic party on board outside the main entrance to the Town Hall and then travelled 'wrong line ' around the curve into Bridge Street, regaining the correct track at the new Leeds (and Stanningley) departure-point in Leeds Road.

At Stanningley the Lord Mayor (Councillor James Hill) drove No. 118 over the new taper track. The Mayor of Pudsey boarded the LCT car, and the two cars were driven by their respective Lord Mayors to the Bradford side of the junction. The Leeds tramcar then led the way to Bradford where the little procession halted outside the main entrance to the Town Hall before, presumably, 'shunting' in Town Hall Street while the dignitaries devoured a celebratory lunch. Few instances are known of dual-gauge trams straying from their scheduled paths, although Driver Field later recalled having driven BCT No. 124 to Kirkstall Works, Leeds, for bags of sand.

The regular passenger service began on 8th June when cars departed at 15-minute intervals from 5am (Leeds) and 5.2am (Bradford) with a 10-minute service from midday. Saturday and Sunday trams also ran at 10-minute intervals, though no service was provided on Sunday mornings. Both undertakings provided a maximum of six cars for daily service; these ran in batches, taking 55 minutes for the 9½-mile journey – a creditable performance, as the cars carried local as well as long-distance passengers, and there were more than twenty stops between Bradford and Thornbury alone.

At the intensively-used Corn Exchange turning circle there was a mere 2-minute layover and boarding time with a compensatory 7-minute layover in Bradford where cars rested on the southbound track in Norfolk Street to avoid delays to the cross-city Thornbury-Wyke service which had replaced the Stanningley-Shelf workings. The only BCT cars scheduled to reverse at Stanningley were Saturday 'extras' and the last few late-evening dual-gauge trams.

Seen from the forecourt of Thornbury depot on a frosty morning in 1908, Brush car No. 117 exhibits its new oak-framed canopy top, a superior product to the 'Bailey top' glimpsed on the left.

Photo; Bradford City Tramways.

Both undertakings co-operated in ways of maintaining regularity. If a mechanical problem arose in Bradford, the defective car ran into Thornbury depot while a conventional tram, deceptively labelled 'Leeds', conveyed passengers to and from the city centre. In Leeds, Bramley depot performed a similar function, and LCT inspectors sometimes reversed cars at Wellington Bridge to prevent disruption, though the service was usually very punctual. Snow which fell heavily in Leeds in 1912 was brushed aside by snow-brooms, but their efforts were nullified when a BCT car derailed at the Boar Lane/Briggate junction – the heart of the Leeds network – virtually paralysing the system for 25 minutes.

The two-year trials with tramcar No. 124 had led to improvements in the locking-gear, which now embodied a phosphor-bronze lock in a dustproof case between the wheel-centre and the truck frame. Curiously, the Bradford cars were noisier than their Leeds counterparts; on a still day the loud, geary ring of their four pinions could be heard as far away as Eccleshill, whereas the LCT cars rumbled as though they were running on sand, the sound fluctuating as they 'tailwagged' along. Approaching Corn Exchange they could all be heard before they were visible. At Stanningley a lock-up shop was leased for 5s 0d a week as a parcels office, store room and shelter for the fitter who, armed with a grease-gun, lubricated the gears of the trams as they traversed the taper tracks.

Back in Bradford improvements abounded. At Dudley Hill the terminal stub was extended 41 yards to the corner of Cutler Heights Lane to accommodate special cars for Greenfield greyhound stadium; at Idle terminus the rails were carried forward 63 yards into Albion Road where the gradient was easier, and at Greengates a 10-yards extension enabled an extra car to 'shunt' at the terminus. In Town Hall Square (junction with Town Hall Street) and at the 'Cock and Bottle' automatic point equipment was installed; if a tramcar passed under a 'skate' on the overhead line with power 'on', the action of a solenoid caused the point-blades to switch, while a reset-mechanism restored the status quo when the car had passed by. Later equipment installed by Clay and Atkinson at all regularly-used junctions omitted the reset facility.

In a drive to improve the riding-quality of the trams, twelve Mountain and Gibson 6ft 6ins wheelbase 21E trucks were fitted to Milnes cars in 1910/11 in place of their 6ft Brush trucks. A Barber 6-wheel radial truck was tested for two months beneath car No. 224; the middle pair were 'pony' wheels which steered the driven wheels around curves, and a similar 11ft wheelbase truck was tried under car No. 133. The 'radials' were steady-riding but troublesome, and as track brakes could not be fitted, they were confined to the gently-graded Thornbury route during their brief but unfruitful trials.

Automatic signal lights for single-line sections had been installed during 1906 in Wakefield Road and Bolton Road, and in 1909 their use was extended throughout the network to prevent collisions in fog and bad visibility (see page 58). Collapsible platform gates were fitted to all trams for use when they were full, although brass chains superseded them after 1912.

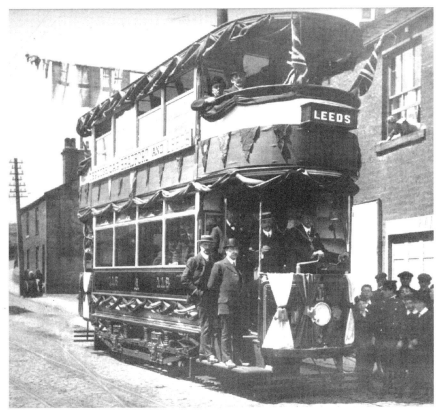

Before the regular through service to Leeds opened, the Stanningley terminus was removed to the Bradford side of Richardshaw Lane bottom, with a 4ft gauge facing crossover visible on this photograph. On board car No. 118 Mr Spencer (in a straw boater) is instructing the Lord Mayor (Councillor James Hill) how to drive the tram over the new taper track for the formal opening ceremony in 1909. On the step are Mr Tom Stirk (traffic superintendent) and Mr J. W. Dawson, engineer.

Following tremendous public controversy the Corporation widened Keighley Road at the expense of Lister Park, but as the tram track had unfortunately been immaculately relaid not long before, it was never resited, and always remained well to the eastern side of the carriageway, an inconvenience repeated some years later after road-widening in Horton Bank, lower Thornton Road, lower Oak Lane, upper Church Bank, Idle Road and at Crossflatts terminus.

However, no amount of smooth, new welded track could eliminate the racket now being created by the Milnes cars (Nos. 129-209, 211-228) which critics condemned as 'cheap' and 'rickety' compared with the 'noiseless' Westinghouse/Brush (Nos. 1-128) and Hurst Nelson trams (Nos. 230-239). Obviously the fault lay in the Brush trucks, as Milnes cars Nos. 219/220 which had acquired Peckham trucks, now ran as quietly as their elder brethren. Despite their elegant appearance, the hundred Milnes products had proved unequal to the demands of unremitting toil and the Pennine climate; moisture had penetrated the joints and the frames had sagged, and drastic reconstruction was becoming unavoidable.

Ever since the introduction of tickets in place of fare-boxes, the conductors had had to carry in their hands all the denominations of tickets required for the various fare values. Hand-held ticket racks were therefore introduced, consisting of metal frames with spring clips to hold separate blocks of 50 tickets each, including 'through' tickets for Birstall (8d), Batley or Heckmondwike (10d) and Dewsbury (1s 0d) on the Birkenshaw trams and genuine through tickets on the Leeds service.

The expense of maintaining a multiplicity of minor depots encouraged the Committee to inspect Manchester's large central depots at Hyde Road and Princes Road as well as Sheffield's Shoreham Street, following which they advocated the replacement of all 'running sheds' except Bankfoot, Bowling and Saltaire (and of course Thornbury Works) by a large establishment between Westgate and Sunbridge Road with access via Grattan Road and Providence Street. However, as the scheme would have entailed the loss of late-night cars as well as causing congestion at peak-hours, it was not pursued.

The black-and-white destination indicator slides in use since 1904 were superseded in 1911 by coloured slides denoting the various services (see Appendix 3a) with black letters on red, yellow, green or white backgrounds. For the convenience of passengers, shelters were provided at the exposed Five Lane Ends, Queensbury, Shelf, Thornton, Tong Cemetery and Undercliffe termini.

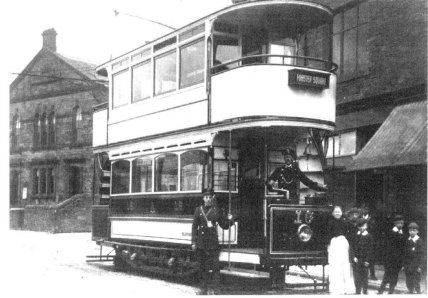

Admired by Eton-collared boys and a lady in an apron at Eccleshill terminus, Brush car No. 16 proudly displays the canopy top which it acquired in May 1908.

7 - TWELVE NEW TRAMS – AND A MYSTERY

Tenders for large quantities of timber were accepted in January 1910. They included American ash and white wood, mahogany, Californian redwood, teak, birch, English oak, Indiana and Austrian wainscot pine, Petersburgh redwood and Archangel redwood and first quality yellow pine, all of which were to be thoroughly seasoned and free from knots or imperfections.

Purchased from local firms such as J. Rushworth, they were needed not only for canopy tops but also for the reconstruction of the Milnes cars, of which No. 152 re-entered service in February as the first of its type to bear a canopy top deck. Car No. 161 which passed through the Works immediately afterwards was found to be so decayed that extra window-posts had to be inserted to ensure that the body was capable of supporting its new upper deck; it thus became the first of the 'six-window' cars which were to be a familiar Bradford feature for almost three decades.

Not all the Milnes cars were rebuilt; some remained in their open-top or Bailey-top state, though even some of the latter had to be strengthened with extra window-posts a few years later. All the canopied cars received new reversed stairs like their Brush counterparts.

The few Brush Bailey-top cars available to negotiate Windhill Bridge were supplemented by Brush cars equipped with special medium-height canopy ('oak') tops, commencing with No. 50 in November 1912 and cars Nos. 52, 55, 67, 49 and 55 thereafter; these wee collectively known as 'Windhill Bridge' cars.

In May 1910, the manager was authorised to construct two completely new car bodies to replace the Church Bank runaway (No. 210) and the long-disused single-decker (No. 229), which were then officially struck off the stock list. No immediate move was made, however, as the Thornbury draughtsmen needed to produce a new, sturdy design which would withstand the rigours of climate, hard work, steep gradients and full loads.

The exhaustive process of finding a form of braking which would fulfil Bradford's arduous operating requirements reached a satisfactory conclusion on 10th April 1911 when the Committee inspected a Milnes car newly equipped with an air-and-oil brake invented and patented by Mr Spencer and Mr Dawson. Descending steep Godwin Street and Church Bank on the trial run Mr Spencer halted the car with the new brake and then applied full power, which normally would have incurred disastrous consequences, but the tram remained firmly rooted to the track.

When the brake was applied, compressed air forced oil into a cylinder, actuating a four-shoe iron track brake first and the wheel brake second; it was available for normal braking or 'emergency' use, and any failure in the system resulted in an automatic brake application. Mr Spencer was authorised to equip twelve cars, and when Board of Trade approval was received, the conversion of the entire fleet was envisaged. The trial car was probably No. 132, which was certainly carrying the equipment by 4th August 1911, and entered regular service on 20th October, being joined by the authorised dozen cars between August 1912 and July 1913. Further units were manufactured by the local firm of Cole, Marchent and Morley, who subsequently supplied equipment to Birmingham, Nottingham, Sheffield, Walsall, West Ham and Johannesburg.

Failure to reach agreement in a dispute concerning through fares in May 1911 promoted Bradford to suggest the Chairman of the Municipal Tramways Association as arbiter, but as he was a close colleague of Mr Spencer the suggestion was rejected by Leeds, who preferred to invite the Glasgow tramways manager. However, as he and the Leeds manager were fellow Scots, Bradford objected too!

Good relations were restored on 20th June when the two cities launched their new 'railless' (trolleybus) systems simultaneously. Bradford's first route, from Laisterdyke to Dudley Hill, connected the Leeds Road and Wakefield Road tramways. The Tramways Committee rode from City to Laisterdyke on a special dual-gauge car, and while the brief inauguration ceremony was taking place, the car presumably travelled on to Thornbury and back, reversing over the Laisterdyke crossover, or, more interestingly, stood on the track curve leading into Sticker Lane which had been laid in 1902 for the proposed Bowling Back Lane line.

The Committee then rejoined the tramcar to meet their Leeds colleagues for a celebratory lunch at Leeds Town Hall, No record of the route taken by the tram in Leeds has survived, but it can be conjectured that it travelled to Corn Exchange and then returned to run via City Square, Infirmary Street and East Parade.

Bradford's first two trolleybuses, alias 'trackless trams', were numbered 240/241 at the end of the tramcar fleet number series. They were soon joined, mysteriously, by an unexplained tramcar numbered 242, whose 'oak top' was built in December, although the complete car was not ready for service until shortly after 1st April, 1912, when it was mounted on a new 6ft 6ins wheelbase Brush 21E truck, one of six purchased shortly before.

Identical in appearance and construction to the rebuilt Milnes six-window cars, No. 242 was clearly not a new tram – indeed, BCT records classified it as a rebuilt Milnes car – but why had

Most Milnes cars had to be rebuilt as 'six-window' cars before they could carry the additional weight of a Thornbury-built oak canopy top deck. Tram No. 162 was photographed in June 1911, on the G. N. railway bridge near Gain Lane, Thornbury.

Photo: Bradford City Tramways

it been given a new, out-of-series number? Despite mysteries surrounding (probably at a later date) the fate of Milnes car 183 and the origins of six-window cars Nos. 116 and 124, the logical though unproved solution is that the lower deck was in fact the resurrected and reconstructed remains of No. 210, victim of the 'Church Bank Smash', which possibly had been retained as a Works store place. Its original number had already been allocated to one of the two new trams authorised in May 1910, and in any case, to reintroduce it under its old number would have ensured instant notoriety and outcry!

Some nine years earlier two local clergymen, concerned at the plight of tram drivers exposed to the elements on their open platforms, had requested the provision of canvas screens or Dublin-style glazed vestibules, but enquiries to other operators had convinced the Committee that 'covered fronts' were not desirable, as tram-driving was 'one of the healthiest occupations'. The drivers, in their storm capes, gloves, hats and warm Melton woollen overcoats, might have been expected to disagree, but instead they distrusted the idea of being surrounded by large sheets of fragile glass. However, when drivers on the through service began to notice vestibuled cars in service in Leeds, their union requested a trial in Bradford. A Birmingham-type canvas screen failed to please, and the Thornbury draughtsmen devised a more elegant solution.

In June 1912, the fleet was augmented by the new cars sanctioned two years earlier. The first complete bodies built at Thornbury Works and the first to incorporate glazed vestibuled

platforms, they took the two vacant numbers 210 and 229. On 1st July the Committee rode to Thornbury on No. 210 and were impressed by its neat, trim and handsomely-painted appearance.

Sturdily braced by concealed lateral and longitudinal rods, the teak-framed lower deck with its four side-windows and opening half-lights had mahogany exterior panels, oak furnishing, maplewood ceilings and longitudinal seating for 22. Seven pairs of double seats occupied the upper saloon; each balcony had a curved seat for four with a single seat over the stairwell, giving a total of 38 seats upstairs and 60 overall (and later 62 when trapdoors with seats were fitted over the head of the stairs).

The angular timber-framed vestibules comprised solid dadoes surrounding mahogany panels, and above the end window a narrow grille admitted fresh air to the saloon. As a protection against snow and rain (there being no windscreen wipers) a screen normally housed in a recess above the grille could be pulled out to partially shield the windscreen. A used-ticket box was neatly incorporated into the bulkhead panelling, and the vestibule was enclosed by glazed folding doors which gave drivers complete protection from the weather.

As 'power' (ie air/oil) braking was fitted, a space-saving vertical handwheel replaced the conventional hand and slipper brake fittings, serving chiefly as a parking-brake. Relieved of the need to wrestle with heavy manual controls, the driver was provided with a pedestal seat which fitted into a slot in the floor. Like No. 242, No. 210 was mounted on a Brush 21E truck with Witting 35hp motors and BTH B.18 controllers, and its twin,

The first tramcar built by the Corporation at Thornbury Works was No. 210, which entered service on 14th June 1912. Its design incorporated glazed platform vestibules, folding platform doors, a pedestal seat for the driver, and a 6ft 6ins Brush 21E truck which gave steadier riding qualities.

Photo: Bradford City Tramways

This interior view of No. 210 shows the handsome, polished woodwork, maplewood ceilings and hanging straps for use by standing passengers. On the platform can be seen (left to right) the BTH controller (replaced later by a Dick Kerr unit), the pedestal seat, the air/oil brake column and handle, and the folding platform doors, now closed. *Photo: Bradford City Tramways*

No. 229, differed only in having Phillipson's side-guards initially. The Committee happily voted £8,400 for twelve similar cars. The characteristic native BCT tramcar was born.

Perversely the drivers disliked both their seats and the platform doors, and eventually the unwanted luxuries were removed.

The outstanding success of the Leeds through service attracted interest from other quarters. Halifax and Bradford representatives met in October 1912 to discuss a dual-gauge service via Shelf, but the scheme foundered when Halifax's Parliamentary Bill, 1915, had to be withdrawn (see Chapter 8). Obviously, in view of the formidable gradients to be encountered between Northowram and Halifax, the track brakes would have had to operate equally efficiently on either gauge, a requirement not achieved with the existing dual-gauge cars.

Discussions were held also with Yorkshire Woollen for a dual-gauge service to Dewsbury, but with a similar lack of success.

The Coronation of T.M. King George V and Queen Mary on 22nd June 1911 inspired the Corporation to construct upon the truck and underframe of car No. 10 a replica of the royal crown. Brilliantly illuminated by 1,100 coloured bulbs, it visited each route in turn; after dusk its mighty glow was visible for miles as it made its welcome progress through the gaslit streets and dark country roads.

A few weeks later Bingley UDC sought discussions about an extension of the Nab Wood tramway into their area, and (later) an extension from Allerton to Ling Bob, Wilsden. Similar moves by Baildon UD councillors for trams to Baildon were defeated by their own colleagues who, fearing absorption by Bradford, unkindly asserted that people 'moved to Baildon to get away from trams!'

Much of the original tramcar equipment, bought at a time when 60 or 70 miles per day were considered a fair day's work for a tram, was now becoming inadequate for heavier cars, faster schedules and a daily workload of over 200 route miles. Tenders for up-to-date units were therefore sought, resulting in the purchase in 1913/14 of no fewer than 98 Hurst Nelson 21E 7ft-wheelbase trucks at £81 each, with Siemens 40hp motors, resistances and circuit-breakers, Dick Kerr DB1 K4 controllers and Cole, Marchent and Morley 'power' brakes.

The dual-gauge trams were in need of modernisation too. Their 35hp 'Witting' motors, originally designed for open-top cars and leisurely schedules, were wilting under the strain of weightier bodies, heavy passenger loadings and high average speeds of 10mph including stops, and the heat generated by an 18-hour day affected them so severely that they had to be rewound twice yearly instead of once every four years. At the end of 1913 they were replaced by new Dick Kerr DK19A double-drive 40hp motors (ie with a pinion at each end of the armature) for whose larger diameter the Peckham trucks had to be built higher with a bracing bar at the bottom.

Their Brush bodies were similarly becoming overstrained by the through-running, and one by one most were replaced by solidly-rebuilt 6-window Milnes bodies. Between 1912 and 1916 Nos. 76, 78, 110, 116 and 124 exchanged trucks and fleet numbers with Milnes Nos. 142, 161, 136, ?183 and ?149, though Milnes Nos. 143, 172, 177 and 242 retained their numbers when they superseded Nos. 93, 111, 118 and 127 (not necessarily respectively).

On the evening of 7th February 1913, while Driver Willie Gill and Conductor Barker were examining the sandboxes under the lower saloon seats of car No. 88 as it reposed at Allerton terminus, the tram was struck broadside by a violent wind which blew it over. Many windows were broken, and the car was laboriously righted next day. The ensuing Board of Trade report advocated the installation of a wind-gauge at Thornbury depot and a rule that conductors should lower the upper-deck side windows on exposed routes in gale conditions. They did so, but windblown passengers promptly raised them again!

In common with most operators Bradford possessed powers to transport goods over its tramways, but wisely forbore to use them, as corteges of coal, cauliflowers or codfish would not have been conducive to the punctuality of passenger services. Household goods – parcels, prams, pushchairs, bicycles, rolls of linoleum and bundles of newspapers were however regularly deposited on the front platform of service cars under the nominal control of the driver. Entertaining mishaps occurred occasionally.

As his tramcar swung into the steep curve of Church Bank. Driver Hornsby observed that the pram recently positioned behind him was now rapidly making its way back to Forster Square, and a similar dilemma occurred at the same place as Driver Alf Bromyard on car No. 132 was just reaching the first parallel power notch. An old but determined man leaped aboard with two piles of books in his arms; one of the piles toppled into the road, followed by its owner and the other pile, and the tram halted as quickly as the air-and-oil brake would allow, ie with a typical brief runback which always alarmed the passengers.

The delayed action caused by the length of time taken by the oil to enter or leave the valve also created wheel-spin when cars started from rest on a steep ascent, so that drivers often used the manual brake in such places. Although safe and easy to operate, the air-and-oil brake was not faultless; a drop in pressure could lock the tram so firmly to the rails that a fitter with a long spanner had to be summoned to release it.

Nevertheless the staff had complete confidence in it, as on the day when tram

High winds and not Alexanders' Glenlivet Whisky caused Brush car No. 88 to fall over at Allerton terminus on 7th February 1913. It is being laboriously raised by the traditional expedient of block and tackle.

No. 184 was late in leaving Undercliffe. Turning out of Otley Road towards Church Bank the driver daringly applied power, waiting until the very summit of the Bank before making a firm brake application which almost ejected the passengers from their seats.

Duckworth Lane schedules were speeded up when the single line in Toller Lane was replaced by a handsome 'boulevard' with a centrally-placed row of trees separating the inward and outward tracks. New ways of making the permanent way more permanent were foreshadowed by experiments in Bowling Yard with ferroconcrete track foundations; the new method was used in Toller Lane, on lengths of the Stanningley and Thornton routes due for renewal, and for an extension to Bailiff Bridge authorised in 1910.

The Tramways Parcels Service was popular and well used from its inception in 1905 to its enforced abolition in 1949. Seen here in Norfolk Street about 1913, the conductor of through-service car No. 78 (ex No. 161) is helping the smartly-uniformed 'parcels-boy' to transfer a cartload of packages to the tramcar platform.

Photo: Bradford City Tramways

8 - BAILIFF BRIDGE, BINGLEY AND BAILDON

Tramways to Bailiff Bridge and beyond were first discussed in 1903 as part of a proposal for a long extension of the newly-electrified Wyke route as far as Brighouse. Unfortunately, tramway operating rights in Brighouse had already been acquired by Halifax Corporation whose 3ft 6ins gauge cars reached the town on 26th February 1904, and Bailiff Bridge on 13th October.

In 1911 residents of Wyke Lane besought the Corporation to resume negotiations, and a year later Bradford opened discussions with Brighouse, Halifax and Huddersfield with a view to purchasing the Bailiff Bridge-Brighouse line and establishing a link with the Huddersfield tramways. While declining to sell, Halifax offered to lay a third rail from Bailiff Bridge to Brighouse and a 4ft gauge extension via Rastrick and Fixby. This imaginative scheme was defeated by local tradesmen at a town's meeting in Halifax, and a second attempt to include it in the Halifax Corporation Bill, 1915, was equally frustrated.

Huddersfield Corporation were interested nevertheless. Their 1913 Parliamentary Bill embodied a proposed line to Brighouse via Bradford Road from their existing tramway at Smithy, and in December 1914, they reached agreement with Brighouse Corporation that the latter would apply for an Order for a Light Railway which Huddersfield would construct to the 4ft gauge between Brighouse and Smithy, where a taper-track would connect with their own 4ft 7¾ins gauge lines. Also, on or before 1st August 1921, Huddersfield could request Brighouse to exercise their powers to acquire Halifax's 3ft 6ins Bailiff Bridge tramway and convert it to 4ft, thereby facilitating an 11.63 mile Bradford-Huddersfield dual-gauge service.

In preparation for the service the Huddersfield manager, Mr R. H. Wilkinson, experimented in 1916 with a new type of handbrake suitable for use on dual-gauge cars; it acted upon a brake-drum fixed to the extended armature shaft and was thus independent of gauge-changes. Sadly, these progressive preparations were to be directly affected by the later vicissitudes of the existing Bradford-Leeds dual-gauge service.

Nevertheless, Bradford persevered in linking the systems as far as possible. Work on the extension from Wyke down the wide, quiet road to Bailiff Bridge crossroads began on 9th August 1912 and ended on 11th March 1913, when a successful trial run was followed two days later by Major Pringle's formal inspection.

Soundly constructed with thermit-welded high-silicon rails laid on ferroconcrete, the line was double track throughout except for the terminal stub adjacent to the end of the Halifax Corporation tramway. A precautionary crossover was laid at Shirley Manor within the city boundary, as the outermost part of the route lay in Hipperholme UD (and the stub terminus in Clifton parish). Equally well-designed was the overhead equipment, with the usual James Russell poles, finials and scrollwork, span-wire construction and wires suspended directly above the tracks.

Tastefully decorated vestibule car No. 210 carrying the Lord Mayor, tramways officials and members of Hipperholme and Brighouse Councils inaugurated the route on 17th March, after which the public service opened as an extension of the Thornbury-Wyke workings.

Formal Parliamentary approval for the construction of tramcar bodies by the Corporation was included in its 1913 Act, although

Possibly on a trial run to Bailiff Bridge prior to the opening of the route, Brush car No. 161 reveals slight collision damage to its platform dashplate. Previously No. 78, a through-service car, it has retained underneath its fender the stout wooden block which prevented cars mounted on dual-gauge trucks from overriding normal trams on lower-slung trucks. *Courtesy the late J. A. Pitts*

the first three of the twelve new cars authorised by the Committee a year earlier had already entered service between May and July as Nos. 240/1 and 243, the two tracklesses Nos. 240/1 having been renumbered 502/501 in 1912. Virtually identical to the two prototypes apart from their new Hurst Nelson trucks, each car took seven weeks to build, and no fewer than 225 men were now engaged in the construction of new tram and trackless bodies, routine overhauls and the reconstruction of older bodies. The skeletons of Milnes car No. 198 and ex-Mid-Yorkshire No. 239 were used as the basis of BCT-style four-window bodies with 'oak tops' and open platforms, while No. 213 was similarly treated but with vestibuled platforms. No other pre-1904 trams were so radically reshaped, although Nos. 9 and 54 received modern vestibules while retaining their original body design.

New opportunities were now beckoning a few miles north of the city. In 1910 Keighley Corporation had launched a service of motor-buses via Bingley to link their own tram terminus at Stockbridge with Bradford's Nab Wood outpost, but as the primitive contraptions proved unreliable, Bingley UDC revived their discussions with Bradford.

Amicable agreement was reached whereby Bradford would construct and maintain a tramway through Bingley and Crossflatts to Morton Lane at Bingley's expense and pay the interest on the capital and sinking fund, while Bingley would supply electricity at reasonable charges, refund the rates, grant Bradford a lease which would terminate on the same day as the Shipley lease (17th May 1932) with power to renew it, and when the lease finally ended, pay Bradford the outstanding value of the installations.

The ensuing Bingley Tramways Order 1912, required the UDC to provide a 40ft minimum road width in Main Street, whilst the West Riding County Council were to widen Cottingley Bridge from 22ft 3ins to 39ft and improve Ryshworth Corner between Crossflatts and Morton Lane. On 5th May 1913, Bingley urged Bradford to begin work, but when asked when Cottingley Bridge would be widened, airily replied, "Not this year!"

Bradford proceeded nevertheless, and the track from Nab Wood reached a temporary terminus at Ann Street by the end of the year. The overhead wires continued through the town to the main feeder point at Millgate, but as the high-tension cables from the Coney Lane generating station of Keighley Corporation (from whom Bingley had contracted to buy electricity) were not ready when Bradford completed work on 12th January 1914, Major Pringle could not inspect the line until 29th January.

On 3rd February a stately procession comprising vestibule car No. 229 driven by the Lord Mayor, canopy-top car No. 187 piloted by the chairman of Bingley UDC and open-top car No. 144 were met at Ann Street by a vast, enthusiastic throng of Bingley folk. The public service began as soon as the speeches died away, and despite the 3½d fare (later reduced to 3d after protests) it was hugely patronised.

The highly-scenic nature of the long rural side to 'The Throstle Nest of Old England' was emphasised by the bucolic description of some of the seven passing-places, eg

'88 yards South-east of the watertrough ... 32 yards east of the hedge between the fields opposite Bankfield'.

Upper: There was hardly a bare head in sight when tramcar No. 210 arrived at Bailiff Bridge for the official opening on 17th March 1913. Two smartly-dressed reporters are busily noting the speech being made from the balcony by Alderman Priestley.
Photo: Bradford City Tramways

Lower: Smart new Bradford-built No. 240 advertises the varying delights of Bottomley's Mint Rock, Nubolic Soap and Jacob's Cream Crackers before reversing at Four Lane Ends in 1913.
Courtesy Mr F. Hartley

Bingley folk turned out in force to greet tramcars Nos. 229 and 187 at the ceremonial opening of the route as far as Ann Street on 3rd February 1914. *Photo: Bradford City Tramways*

Newly-built five-window car No. 247 entered service on 30th May 1914, and was photographed near 'Bankfield', between Nab Wood and Cottingley Bar.

With a double line through the town, the installations were all of high quality, British Mannesmann weldless stepped poles being used for the first time, while the overhead wires were suspended close together for ease of maintenance.

By this time more than 40 of the new Hurst Nelson trucks were in use, several with Witting motors pending deliveries from Siemens. In an attempt to maximise the benefit of their longer wheelbase, the next tramcars built at Thornbury, Nos. 244/5, were built to an increased overall length of 30ft 4ins with a seating capacity of 68 (71 when trapdoor seating was fitted). Distinguishable by their five side-windows, they were completed by the end of 1913 but not put into service until April 1914, when they were mounted on the new trucks complete with Siemens motors, Dick Kerr controllers and air-and-oil brakes. Identical cars Nos. 246-8 appeared later in the year, when No. 247 paraded its impressive lines on the Bingley tramway where its high capacity would have been welcome, but as Bingley cars participated in the cross-city run to Undercliffe with its sharp 'Cock and Bottle' curve, the 'five window' cars took up residence at Duckworth Lane depot, proving useful on the Duckworth Lane service as well as the Thornton route where their stately roll on entering loops was reminiscent of ocean liners.

Car No. 249 introduced two design improvements: longer and more spacious platforms and 'three-quarters direct' stairs instead of the previously-preferred reversed stairs which limited the driver's view. With 70 seats (73 with trapdoor seats) it proved to be the highest-capacity car ever operated in Bradford, as Nos. 250-252, last of the dozen trams authorised in 1912, reverted to the previous, shorter four-window design albeit with the new stairs, platform length and 62 (later 65) seats, entering service in December 1914.

Tests with the new trams indicated the value of modern braking systems. Car No. 244 weighing 12 tons 6cwt 1qr 14lb underwent seven tests in Leeds Road near Dick Lane, using every possible permutation of brake types and an application of the sand-pedal. Relying solely on the handbrake the car had a stopping-distance of 87ft at a speed of 17.83mph, but with all

brakes applied (rheostatic/air-oil/mechanical) it halted within its own length. Mr Spencer commented proudly that,

"From the passengers' point of view a tramcar (rail-borne) is more desirable than any public vehicle running on the road surface, but a Railless Car or Motor Omnibus is better than nothing at all".

Bingley folk dissented from the latter statement: they allowed their Keighley bus service to lapse altogether, without replacement, and welcomed the completion of their tramway. On 25th August the route was extended to a new crossover in Main Street (Post Office) in preparation for Bingley Feast Week. The final extension to Crossflatts (Micklethwaite Lane) was delayed by the discovery of a layer of sand near Bingley Church which called for stronger track foundations, but the service to the final terminus 6 miles 1700 yards from Forster Square was opened on 13th October. There was no ceremony, as a 'European War' had broken out unexpectedly, and already 94 staff had enlisted. The last 500 yards of tramway authorised by the 1912 Act were indefinitely deferred until Ryshworth Corner was improved.

When the widening of Cottingley Bridge was completed early in 1915, the half-laid double track on the bridge was transformed into a long loop commencing near a farmhouse which obstructed drivers' vision, resulting in several near-collisions between tramcars entering and leaving the single line.

The cost of the tramway exceeded the borrowing powers by £5,891. It transpired that the ferroconcrete foundation laid as far as Bingley Church had been authorised only as ordinary lias lime concrete, and that there was sufficient rail in stock for another 3¾ miles of single track – perhaps Mr Spencer had become over-confident, but the firm foundations and surplus rail were to prove a great boon in coming years.

With the opening of the Bingley/Crossflatts service the Manningham Lane schedules were reorganised. The Circular Route was extended to Cottingley Bar and the Bingley/Crossflatts cars alternated with the Saltaire cars in the cross-city journeys to Undercliffe. The public response was gratifying: at Whitsuntide, 1914 the Bingley cars were 'bulging with passengers'.

There were drawbacks, of course. Imposing fines on a group of non-resident drunkards, the Bingley magistrates expressed a hope that the novelty of riding from Bradford for drink would wear off. It did not. Ten years later Driver Hornsby discovered a drunk fast asleep in his late-night tramcar after he had 'shedded' it in Saltaire depot.

In March 1914, the Committee had invited tenders for 50 new tramcar bodies, and a few weeks later had voted to inspect new types of tramcar in use elsewhere. Presumably, having done so, they wisely concluded that the home-built product was superior, as no more was heard of tramcar purchases. When the survival of more than 60 open-top trams evoked criticism, complainants were advised that many who rode 'outside' actually preferred to do so, as it was healthier for them if sufficiently clad. Drivers who had taken a liking to vestibuled platforms occasionally took steps to avoid driving open-platform cars: allocated an open ex-Mid-Yorkshire car on a cold day, a Heaton driver 'accidentally' upset his tea-can into the resistances, thus sparking off brief but effective 'fireworks'.

The Great Yorkshire Show held near Bradford Moor terminus from 22nd to 24th July 1914, created a tremendous demand for the Thornbury, Leeds and Bradford Moor cars, and many of the last-mentioned had to be sent via Harris Street. The sun shone; parasols twirled and holidaymakers happily disported themselves in the straw 'boaters', Eton collars, graceful dresses and hats of a people, confident in their future, who believed in 'making the best of themselves'.

Eleven days later Britain was at war. Mobilisation followed swiftly: on 13th August the 2nd West Riding Battery of the Royal Field Artillery marched out from Lister Park, and to help them on their way, open top tramcars towed their 15 lb guns and ammunition carts as close as possible to the Western Front in Flanders, ie to Drighlington tram terminus.

A year previously Baildon UDC had overcome their earlier misgivings and obtained Parliamentary sanction for a 1,749yd extension of the Baildon Bridge tramway to Station Road. The line was to be leased to Bradford on the same terms and for the same duration as the Bingley and Shipley leases, and was to be laid as double track with a stub terminus; the overhead wires (span-wire in Otley Road and bracket-arm in Baildon Road) were to be energised by power bought from Shipley. Borrowing powers were granted on 30th July 1914, when guns were already sounding in Serbia; on 7th September Baildon UDC decided to widen Baildon Road but pressed Bradford to lay the tramway immediately. Bradford sensibly preferred to lay the rails in the centre of the highway after the widening.

National events then intervened. H.M. Treasury vetoed all new projects not already begun, and setts provisionally laid out in Baildon Road were hastily retrieved. The powers lapsed in 1915, although Bradford undertook to build and work the tramway as soon as construction costs and interest rates returned to their pre-war level.

The picturesque nature of the Bingley route is typified by this view of a six-window car crossing Cottingley Bridge about 1915.

Courtesy the late R. B. Parr

9 - GREAT WAR

An influx of Belgian refugees on 15th October 1914 served as a warning that the war was going to last longer than had been expected in the euphoric days of August. The newcomers were awarded free passes for unlimited tramcar travel, as were members of the Armed Forces, Boy Scouts assisting the war effort and the Lord Mayor's Relief Fund workers.

Outstanding track repairs were completed with some urgency. The Branch to Saltaire section was relaid with new foundations and welded joints, though the Bingley cars had to be briefly diverted via Otley Road and Saltaire Road when a car ran off the temporary track laid alongside the roadworks. Along parts of the Thornbury and Stanningley route new foundations were laid, but the existing rails were retained and welded.

A growing shortage of staff caused by enlistments to the Armed Forces enabled the Department to prune unnecessary services. In January 1915 the Circular Route was replaced by a Forster Square-Bolton-Thackley-Shipley-Nab Wood service operated wholly from Bolton depot, with 'extras' to Thackley and Briggate (Shipley) as required. In February the Baildon Bridge-Greengates cross-city service was split so that Forster Square to Baildon Bridge passengers could enjoy their first taste of top-covered cars, operated from Saltaire depot, whilst the luckless Greengates residents continued to enjoy the exclusively open-top facilities furnished by the ex-Mid Yorkshire cars and Brush-built Nos. 30-34 and 36-40. Then in May the Rawson Square to Heaton service was eliminated, this being the last of a series of permutations (Sunbridge Road to North Park Road via Rawson Square, Rawson Square to Heaton via North Park Road etc) forced on the reluctant Committee by adamant councillors to augment the perfectly adequate Bradford Moor-Forster Square-St. Mary's Road-Heaton service. In October some tramcar stopping-places were abolished to reduce wear and tear and current consumption; the loss was scarcely felt, as some stops were barely 200ft apart.

In March 1915 the illuminated car made several evening forays for Armed Forces recruitment purposes; ironically it had to return to depot by 8pm to avoid contravention of new Defence of the Realm regulations by its brilliant lamps. For the first time in history a partial blackout had been imposed as a precaution against aerial attacks. Tramcar headlamps were discreetly masked, and interior lamps were painted a lurid orange and shielded with cardboard shades, while the Leeds Corporation trams running into Bradford were distinguishable by their awesome green interior lighting.

The gas street-lamps were heavily shaded too, making it difficult for conductors to locate the overhead wire when changing the trolley at the termini at night. Automatic trolley reversers were therefore erected at all termini in regular use; at Duckworth Lane, Heaton, Thornton, Shelf, Drighlington, Birkenshaw, Greengates and Eccleshill the reversers were suspended beneath long bracket-arms, but elsewhere span-wire suspension was used, and the Shelf, Drighlington and Birkenshaw apparatus was later converted to span-wire.

At Thornbury and Dudley Hill the existence of trackless overhead equipment with wires of opposite polarity called for more complex reversing equipment, and at Stanningley no reverser was provided until about 1933, partly because so few cars reversed there during the dual-gauge era and also because the carriageway and pavements were too narrow.

The automatic equipment, with reverser frogs situated 13ft 6ins from the centre of the track, quickly exposed a lack of trolley standardisation. Whilst vestibule car No. 251 standing 15ft 11ins high with a 15ft 10ins trolley cleared the frog by a margin of 1ft 10ins, open-top No. 37, 14ft 1ins high with an offset trolley mast and a 15ft 5ins trolley boom cleared it by only ½ins, and Bailey top No. 215 with an offset 14ft 10ins boom did not even attempt it. Yet, on 22nd May 1918, there were still twelve different lengths currently in use, ranging from 15ft on 'Bailey tops' 141 and 208 and 15ft 9ins on through service car No. 116 to 17ft 4ins on the five-window cars.

By March 1915, 339 out of a total BCT staff of 1,363 had either enlisted or been directed to munitions factories, and 'lady conductors' had to be employed, not without misgivings on the part of the management who feared that they would possess insufficient strength to apply the mechanical brakes, change the points or swing the trolley.

From the special training-school which was set up for them, apocryphal tales soon spread. Asked what she would do if a tram ascending Church Bank halted and began to roll backwards, one of the trainees is reported to have replied, "I would run upstairs and change the indicator!" Perhaps for that reason a pilotman rode on the rear platform of every Church Bank car throughout the war, but in fact the ladies learned quickly and gave devoted service. Some were drafted in from country areas, like Gertie from Gargrave who accompanied Driver Hornsby until his regular conductor, Lionel, returned from the wars.

The fitting of air-oil brakes had been halted with a maximum of 75 cars thus equipped, the allocation between depots being surprisingly mixed. Horton Bank Top had one car; Bolton had Milnes six-window No. 157 on a Brush truck; Saltaire had Milnes Bailey-top No. 199 on a Siemens-motored Hurst Nelson truck; Bankfoot had Milnes six-window cars Nos. 190-4/6; all the Duckworth Lane cars had air-oil brakes; Thornbury had thirty-six but Bowling none. More sensibly-distributed were the 57 open-top cars: Thornbury had fifteen and Bolton with its exposed routes had four out of a depot complement of nineteen whilst Duckworth Lane had none.

Wartime conditions did not diminish Yorkshire humour. When an anonymous complainant requested "less noise" from tramcar No. 221, Frizinghall residents proposed a contest between No. 221 and their own nominee, No. 75, the proceeds to go to charity. They had, they stressed, no desire to be rid of No. 75.

"When we hear it leave Bingley on a morning", they claimed, "We know it is time to sit down to breakfast if we intend to catch it when it reaches Frizinghall. At midday our wives put the potatoes on directly they hear it leave Undercliffe. Some people boil eggs by it – from the Park-side points to the penny stage for a hard-boiled one or from Emm Lane stop for a soft-boiled one!"

Tramcar types could also be distinguished by their characteristic sounds – the old Westinghouse cars emitted a 'contented purr' and the ex-Mid-Yorkshire trams an 'urgent warble'. A different 'warble' resembling a harmonium chord was produced by the axle-driven air compressor of the air-oil brake cars.

In a drive to eliminate most of the original equipment BCT ordered 100 trucks from Mountain and Gibson Engineering Company, with Brown Boveri GTM 11 motors. Unfortunately M. & G. passed into liquidation, and in default 25 trucks (presumably to BCT design) were ordered from Messrs Hartley, Dauston and Richard Ltd. Neither these nor the Brown Boveri order materialised, and the elderly equipment 'soldiered on' patiently.

Patience was exercised by passengers too. The 'canopy switches', ie circuit-overload boxes fitted to the underside of the platform canopies, relied on a fuse which had to be replaced by the driver when it 'blew'. One day a tram beginning the long climb to Horton Bank Top had hardly left Tyrrel Street when the

Thoroughly rebuilt and mounted on a Hurst Nelson truck after capsizing at Allerton, No. 88 was used in 1915 to demonstrate the new trolley reverser at Duckworth Lane terminus. Awaiting its turn at the bottom of Little Lane is six-window car No. 155. White stripes were painted on the tram standards to assist pedestrians during the wartime blackout.

switch blew out with its usual blue flash and sharp report. Persistent repetitions soon exhausted the stock of fusewire, and the driver, rolling back the saloon door, tentatively enquired whether any lady passenger might lend him a hairpin. By the time that the capricious circuits had done their worst, the saloon was filled with ladies whose hair was unfashionably hanging down to their shoulders.

Ferocious gales on New Year's Day 1916, blew trees and debris across tram tracks and overturned a 'Windhill Bridge' canopy car, No. 67 at Ivy Place, Idle Road, fortunately without much damage – indeed, the canopy top deck gave three more decades of service. Then on the evening of 5th March warnings of possible air raids by German Zeppelins were circulated, and as part of the agreed 'air raid drill' the power was switched off and the trams unceremoniously halted. Using the departmental telephones provided at each terminus the drivers rang for instructions and had messages conveyed by the police to their anxious families. Fortunately the raid did not materialise, as the Department had problems enough.

The Works staff, depleted by a third, were battling to keep pace with routine maintenance; one elderly man was struggling with a line of worn-out controllers, and consequently only one total reconstruction – a vestibuled six-window body – was possible during the year, although ten top decks were built for bodies remodelled six months earlier. Cars were laid up awaiting major rehabilitation, including a Bolton-based car whose aged body had habitually moved at every joint as it swayed to and fro over the staggered rail-joints at Windhill, until the day when the creaking ceased and the alarmed driver realised that the body had ominously settled into a permanent sideways lean. Trams were hard-pressed, particularly the through-service cars whose patronage had increased by 22%. The recruitment of 52 part-time auxiliary drivers relieved matters slightly.

Lifting up his eyes to a visionary future, the Burnley tramways manager declared his belief that 'in time' the North-East Lancashire and adjacent Yorkshire 4ft gauge networks "would have physical connections from Bradford down to Darwen and the Rossendale Valley." However, despite the desire of Keighley and Bingley to bridge the two-mile gap between their systems, no prospect ever existed of the necessary fifteen-mile connection 'over the Moss' from Keighley to Colne, and through trams from Bradford Moor to Bacup or Wyke to Whitehall were never anything more than a whimsical pipe-dream.

Far more important in Mr Spencer's eyes was the impossibility of repairs to the 59 miles of permanent way, the increasingly damaging consequences of which he correctly assessed as one of the 'unascertained liabilities of the future' for which the Corporation needed to accumulate sizeable financial reserves.

From October 1916, evening travel was officially discouraged; service frequencies were reduced, and last trams on the Allerton, Thornton and Wakefield Road services ran half an hour earlier. Then in December Mr Spencer was co-opted by the Admiralty to set up a Shipyard Labour Department, leaving Mr Dawson and Mr Tom Stirk in full charge of the tramways engineering and traffic departments respectively, reporting regularly to Alderman Priestley.

Mr Dawson was kept busy. Twenty-one trams had been 'totally dismantled' because moisture had penetrated their body frame, and to protect the remaining cars he adopted a wartime livery of plain, unadorned 'Navy grey' and white with white hand-painted numerals, thereby enabling the paintshop to double its output.

Then, acting on a request from the Ministry of Munitions and the Phoenix Dynamo Company, he organised the construction of a 4ft gauge munitions tramway from the company's forge in Dick Lane to Phoenix Works in Leeds Old Road, with 1 mile 87 yards of line and sidings laid on sleepers except where it crossed and joined the Leeds Road tramway and intersected the Leeds Old Road line near Bradford Moor terminus. Thornbury Works built a 'steeple cab' tractor (electric locomotive), two flat trucks and a truck for the transporting of aeroplane parts, while two tipper waggons and two additional flat trucks were loaned by the Permanent Way Department.

A trial run was made with the 'tractor' over the Dick Lane sidings on 7th February 1917 when, despite ice and mud on the rails a total of 50 tons was hauled at 4mph with motors in series and 10mph in parallel. Next day seven trucks and a total load of 70 tons were successfully hauled from Dick Lane to the forge. Less successful was an exploratory run with a ballast truck to the Leeds Old Road premises, as the truck 'rocked violently' on the street tramway crossings, but following alterations the line went into partial use in March and into full operation in July, a driver being loaned by Thornbury depot whenever Phoenix Works required his services.

The munition tramway's moment of glory arrived in May 1918, with a visit by King George V and Queen Mary who travelled on truck No. 11 which had been specially fitted with seats.

In his journal Mr Dawson recorded that on 13th February 1917 he had:

'...visited Mr Watmough at Leeds Tramway depot, Kirkstall, and discussed with him the question of discontinuing the repairs to the through cars and concentrating the labour on the repair of ordinary service cars. He stated that he had had considerable difficulty in maintaining the dual-gauge cars in service, mainly on account of damage caused to the locking gear due to change of drivers; also failures of armatures had become of serious moment, also wreckage of cars by collision. He had the same number of men working for him as before the War, but so many were inexperienced, he had difficulty in keeping cars available for service.

I pointed out that our maintenance of the dual-gauge cars seemed to be somewhat less than his, but agreed that considerably more labour was required to maintain these cars in service than the ordinary cars; our own shortages were caused by a refusal to work overtime and a recent snowstorm. We were however steadily recovering, and hoped in a short time to be able to supply a sufficient number of cars for service requirements.'

The rudimentary nature of the locking gear sometimes led to derailments when it became worn. In 1917 Milnes car No. 78 strayed from its tracks and caused mortal damage to No. 9, Town Street, Stanningley, and one of the BCT drivers claimed to have driven the full length of Wellington Street, Leeds, with his wheels locked to the Bradford gauge, though the damage to the paving would surely have constituted a major 'diplomatic incident'. Schedules were interrupted in 1916 when an LCT car returning from Pudsey derailed on turning into Town Street and blocked the tracks.

Human error caused chaos at the height of the Leeds rush hour when a BCT driver failed to operate the automatic points at Corn Exchange, allowing his tramcar to enter Call Lane instead of New Market Street. Prevented from reversing by the solid mass of Leeds cars following behind, to the fury of the LCT inspector his tram had to proceed to the single line in Call Lane where it reversed and loaded its passengers while Leeds trams for Wortley, Rothwell and York Road as well as West Riding company cars for Wakefield queued endlessly. And of all the routine reports of damage to overhead equipment, the most distant incident ever recorded was dated 3rd September 1917, when the trolley of a BCT tram dewired on a frog at the top of Bishopgate Street, Leeds and caught on a span-wire; the trolley head was wrenched off and fell on the hapless head of a passing cart driver.

These entertaining mishaps did not detract from the popularity of the through service. Sales of tickets in the first full year – 136,504 on LCT and 146,210 on BCT cars – had risen to 197,741 and 205,138 respectively in 1916/7, and a 50% increase in rail fares was to boost them to 317,600 and 308,637 a year later. But car 72, last of the original BCT contingent, retired worn out in 1916 and could not be replaced. Some months previously both Corporations had approved charges to be paid if either Department hired a car from the other in case of need.

However, plans for a new generation of Bradford through-service trams were apparently afoot. The first of these, No. 205, was completed in June 1917 and observed some time later resting on a temporary works truck, displaying the distinctive sill at the base of the rocker panels which would accommodate the extra-wide dual-gauge truck. Similar in dimensions to the vestibuled six-window cars, with 6ft vestibuled platforms and ¾ direct stairs, No. 205 had four side-windows on both decks and a particularly elegant and symmetrical appearance. But in the final desperate months of the War the needs of the other tram services took precedence, and No. 205, first of the 'high four window' cars, entered general service on a conventional Hurst Nelson truck, being joined by four 'new' vestibuled six-window cars, Nos. 185, 191, 193 and 197, the first built for over a year, though 41 cars had been thoroughly overhauled and 98 repainted grey and white.

By this time the valiant tram drivers were working thirteen days out of fourteen with the assistance of 300 lady conductors,

and special Sunday morning services were being run for munitions workers.

On 8th January 1917 – a dark, windy sleety day – six-window vestibuled car No. 193 arrived at Wyke at 6.30am. Driver Hudson alighted to hand a parcel to a city-bound driver and then found to his horror that during his brief absence No. 193 had moved off down the gradient, already beyond recall. After an ineffectual attempt to re-apply the air-oil brake, lady conductor Eva Hewitt abandoned ship, leaving the empty car to gather speed into the gloom.

Almost a mile further downhill BCT-built car No. 250 had halted at the 'Red Lion' to set down passengers, and was pulling away across Whitehall Road when No. 193 caught up with it and smashed into it so violently that it demolished the rear platform, sliced half the roof away, ripped out the seats, flung the twenty passengers into a heap and propelled No. 250 100 yards before thunderstruck Driver Newboult could halt the cortege. All were injured: a collier and lady conductor Jenny Regan died in hospital. The coroner ruled that the brakes had been insufficiently applied, and both cars were repaired at a cost of £190.

On an equally dreary morning a year later (1st February 1918), newly-overhauled Brush car No. 88 descending through Allerton

Bradfordians in their best Whitsuntide clothes stroll through Forster Square while tram No. 216 and other cars admit passengers for Saltaire, Heaton and elsewhere. In the distance can be seen the Post Office, partly masking the Parish Church, now Bradford Cathedral *Photo: Bradford City Tramways*

For the Phoenix Munitions Tramway the Corporation built several vehicles including (left to right) waggon No. 11 on an ex-Mid-Yorkshire truck, a waggon on a Peckham truck and a 'steeple cab' tractor capable of hauling 40 tons with ease. *Photo: Bradford City Tramways*

village unexpectedly gained speed as it approached Chapel Lane corner, left the rails, slewed across the road and capsized, killing Driver Gill who, by sad coincidence, had been aboard the same tram when it was blown over on the same route in 1913. The tram had subsequently been rebuilt with new teak frame and Hurst Nelson truck, but this time the damage was terminal, and the car was scrapped. Presumably the driver had been taken ill, as the brakes had not been applied.

At the insistence of the Committee Mr Spencer was released by the Admiralty on 16th March 1918, just in time to deal with a

strike of platform staff in protest against having received a substantial war bonus denied to the ladies. The rates were soon equalised, but the financial effect coupled with an alarming rise in the price of materials brought about a substantial fares increase – penny stages were increased by 50% and workmen's fares doubled. In August the number of tram stops was further reduced, and once again no track renewals were carried out during the year.

Compelled to use his depleted workforce as effectively as possible, Mr Spencer immediately arranged with Mr Hamilton for the labour-intensive through service to be suspended after the last BCT car had departed from Leeds and the last LCT car had left Bradford metals on Easter Sunday, 31st March 1918 (LCT archives however recorded the date as 25th March). No account was taken of the holiday, and the unsuspecting press commented that on 1st April,

'The cars were very busy. The Leeds line ... did a big trade, although for some reason there were no through cars.'

Amazingly, no public announcement was made. At the next Committee meeting on 15th April Mr Spencer merely stated that, "The through service has been discontinued for the present by arrangement with the Leeds Corporation Tramways Department," attributing this shortly afterwards to "the shortage of labour and materials consequent upon the War."

The Stanningley service, thus unexpectedly resumed, was worked principally by the long five-window cars, Nos. 244-9, drafted in from Duckworth Lane and assisted briefly by a few of the redundant dual-gauge trams such as No. 78. Meanwhile another 'high four-window' car, No. 214, had been built and another, No. 218, planned, while the dual-gauge trams they were evidently intended to replace stood in line inside Thornbury depot, their trucks undergoing overhaul one by one.

Mr Spencer's return was regrettably brief: in July 1918, he was appointed Tramways Operating Manager for the London Underground Group, and left Bradford on 31st October, after twenty years of illustrious service. His successor was Mr Richard Henry Wilkinson, M.Inst.T., A.M.I.E.E., General Manager at Huddersfield since 1904 and previously with Liverpool and Oldham.

BRADFORD CORPORATION TRAMWAYS.

NOTICE TO DRIVERS and CONDUCTORS.

Instructions for Working of Single Line during Fog or Snow Storms.

The Signals for working the single line (when unable to see through) are now in operation and must be worked according to the following instructions :—

Signal lights have been placed at each loop and the lights will be operated by the Conductor turning the switch, which will be found inside the box affixed to the pole.

White and Red Lights Burning—Line Open.
White Light only Burning—Car going in same direction.
Red Light only Burning—Car coming in opposite direction.
No Lights Burning—Car in block going in same direction, Second Car waiting to come through from distant loop, or failure of signal apparatus.

The Signal Regulations are the same as those used under the automatic signals excepting that the Conductor will have to switch off the **red light** before entering the single line and **switch on the white light** when leaving the single line.

The arrows marked on the door pointing in the direction in which the car is to travel, indicate which switch to use.

The Driver will be held responsible for the correct carrying out of these regulations.

Should both lights be turned out at the same time, the Conductor of the **outward bound Car** must put his lights in again, thus giving the Car to City preference.

The Conductor of the first Car out must put all signal lights in each day (whether it be foggy or otherwise) without fail.

The Conductor of the last Car must see that all lights are switched off.

R. H. WILKINSON,
General Manager.

TP 9859—9000 (50).

One of Mr Wilkinson's first Traffic Notices.

10 - RECONSTRUCTION AND IRRESOLUTION

"If the trumpet give forth an uncertain sound, who shall prepare himself for battle?" (Corinthians, ch. 14 v 8.)

Mr Wilkinson's analysis of his new responsibilities was not encouraging. Four years of war and enforced neglect had reduced the once-flourishing undertaking to a sorry state, with miles of worn and corrugated track and a fleet of 252 cars of which, at its lowest ebb, only 99 were fit for regular use. Not all services were fully operated; for a while the Allerton cars terminated in the village instead of continuing to the terminus.

Staff released from the Forces did not immediately realise that the old practice of assigning an individual tramcar to each driver had long been abandoned. Catching a passing glimpse of the battered, shabby vehicle which had once been his pride and joy, a returning veteran greeted his employers with eloquent reproach. "Ah've seen it!" he exclaimed. Rehabilitation began without delay, and within a month 117 trams were available.

At the Committee meeting on 9th December 1918, Mr Wilkinson voiced his impression that Bradford's trams were "topheavy" or too tall for their gauge, and obtained permission to build a trial car 6ins lower than usual, in the hope that it would be able to pass under all the low bridges.

Also, he was permitted to introduce illuminated route number indicators of the type which he had devised for the Huddersfield trams earlier in the year, in which metal stencils were superimposed on a square opal glass panel. The route numbers themselves were grouped in relation to the city centre departure points, and the Chairman very properly directed that his own route should take precedence! Hence:–

TYRREL STREET: Wibsey 1, Southfield Lane and Horton Bank Top 2, Queensbury 3, Lidget Green 4;
SUNBRIDGE ROAD: Four Lane Ends 5, Allerton 6, Thornton 7, Duckworth Lane 8;
LEEDS ROAD: Thornbury 9, Stanningley 10;
TOWN HALL STREET: Bowling Old Lane 11, Shelf 12; Bailiff Bridge 13, Wyke 14, Odsal 15;
NORFOLK ST/NELSON ST: Drighlington 16, Birkenshaw 17, Tong Cemetery 18, Dudley Hill 19;
FORSTER SQUARE: City to Undercliffe 20, City to Greengates 21, Saltaire to Undercliffe 22, Bingley and Crossflatts to Undercliffe 23, City to Bingley and Crossflatts 24, City to Saltaire 25, City to Baildon Bridge 26, City to Frizinghall 27, City to Heaton 28, Bradford Moor to Heaton 29, City to Bradford Moor 30; Idle 31 (and later, Five Lane Ends 31A), Nab Wood via Thackley 32, Eccleshill 33.

As the urgent need for rolling-stock greatly exceeded the Works bodyshop capacity, tenders for new trams and equipment were sought, resulting in the following orders placed in 1919/20:–

Car bodies: 46 English Electric (the initial 26 were ordered from the United Electric Car Co. (UEC) which merged with Dick Kerr Ltd to form English Electric (EE) before the cars were delivered)
Trucks: 113 Dick Kerr 21E wide-wing 7ft wheelbase, and 25 Boving Engineering Works (Stoke-on-Trent) – built to BCT specifications as a more solid version of the Hurst Nelson 21E 7ft truck

Motors:
26 pairs Dick Kerr DK31B 50hp
88 pairs Dick Kerr DK31(A) 45hp

114
all to be manufactured by EE at their Phoenix Works, Thornbury.

Controllers:
32 pairs Dick Kerr DB1 Form K4B
62 Dick Kerr DB1 Form K4

94
(as 123 pairs of K4s had been bought 1912-5, up to 217 cars were thus equipped by 1921)

Timber bought for Thornbury-built cars included Beecroft & Wightman's best English ash and wainscot oak, Petrograd red, pitch-pine floor laths and Columbian pine, redwood and birch, also American Veneer Company 3-ply bird's-eye maple ceiling panels.

Having estimated that traffic requirements would not exceed 258 tramcars, the Tramways Department decided that the fleet numbers should correspond with the size of the fleet. Accordingly the initial batch of 26 English Electric cars was allocated the numbers 233-258, and existing BCT cars numbered up to 252 had to be re-numbered (see fleet list). A second and equally far-reaching wave of renumberings ran through the fleet with the arrival of the second consignment, Nos. 213-232, between 17th February and 9th August 1921 – for instance, the 'mystery car', No. 242, was renumbered 142 in 1919, but in 1921, in an effort to group it with other Milnes rebuilds, it became No. 115, the original holder of that number having been 'reborn' as No. 91! Other groupings were attempted, eg Nos. 140-164 were all four- and five-window cars built to pre-Wilkinson designs, but in many cases a tramcar's age and origin could no longer be deduced from its fleet number.

The first of the English Electric trams delivered from Preston in 1919/20 resembled No. 235 (seen in Bowling depot yard in the later Wilkinson livery) with high balcony 'tins' but eventually all the 'Preston' cars were identical with No. 214 overleaf.
Photograph courtesy BCT

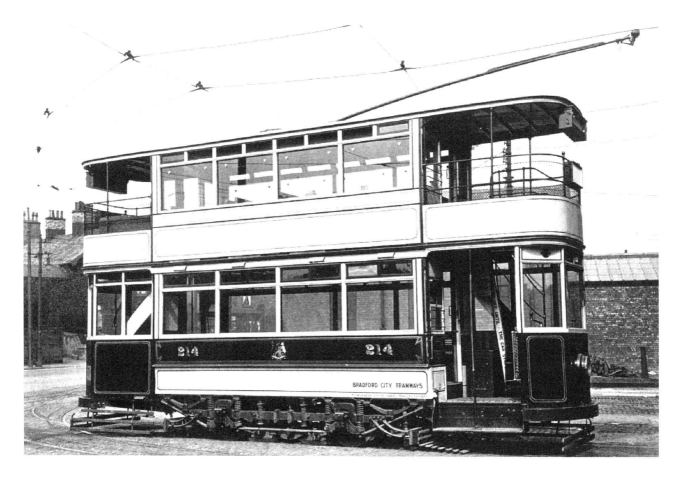

Car 214 of the second English Electric batch, seen here at Thornbury before entering service on 17th February 1921. The wooden 'rubbing-strip' taped to the trolley boom prevented damage from accidental de-wirements. This was a feature which could be seen on all Bradford's trams from around 1908 onwards.

Photo courtesy Mr R Brook

The first of the new English Electric cars, No. 233, left the company's Preston works on 8th September 1919, but as the trucks were delivered without wheels, spares from BCT stock had to be used, delaying the car's entry into service until 20th October. So desperate was the need for rolling-stock that when the top deck of No. 234 suffered damage in transit, the car ran as an 'open topper' for a few days with a second-hand trolley mast and incongruous old, faded top deck side panels which did not match the much higher balcony 'tins'.

Identical in length and seating capacity with the last pre-war cars (Nos. 250-2, now Nos. 150-2), they had medium-height (5ft 8ins) top decks which allowed them to negotiate every bridge except Greengates. Their bodies were teak-framed with galvanised-iron lower-deck side panels and vestibule panels; top deck windows were of frameless plate glass, and the balcony seats were of slatted wood which allowed rainwater to drain through instead of lying in pools as on the BCT plank seats. Dodson and Smith three-bar lifeguards with Phillipsons' side guards were fitted initially but soon replaced by the Tidswell variety.

Proposals to fit air-oil braking having been abandoned, the new cars were equipped with tripod-mounted handbrakes and mechanical four-shoe iron track brakes applied by a horizontal brass (later iron) handwheel, also tripod-mounted. The efficiency of the new track brake was such that it was gradually fitted to the entire fleet, and, with one exception, there were no more 'runaways'. Another welcome innovation was canopy-hung roller-blind destinations which by 1926 had replaced all the coloured indicator slides.

Easily distinguishable by their squat appearance and full-width fenders, the English Electric cars were known variously as 'the Prestons', 'the big cars' or, less politely, 'the Tanks' on account of their massive silhouette and weight, a factor which induced Mr Wilkinson to reduce the height of the balcony 'tins', commencing with No. 247. The trams then resembled their Huddersfield cousins, especially when the manager introduced Huddersfield-style lining-out upstairs in bright blue on the panels, balcony 'tins' and side-window posts. These changes applied to the 'native' cars also, and high 'tins' disappeared by 1925.

When new, most 'Prestons' sported EE 'Arabic' numbers on the vestibules, and also on the side-panels from whence they had been banished on BCT cars in 1917. Numbers 241-3 and 246-250 ran temporarily in grey undercoat with 'Spencer' numerals, but the 1921 arrivals proudly displayed the full post-war livery. By that time all the wartime Navy grey had given way either to full livery or a temporary unlined blue and white.

Happy to spread the benefits of modernity around the network, the Department allocated Nos. 233/239 to Saltaire depot, Nos. 235/240 to Bowling, Nos. 236/8 to Duckworth Lane and Nos. 234/7 to Thornbury; later Nos. 241-256 went to Bowling, Nos. 213-219 settled at Horton Bank Top and the rest at Thornbury and Saltaire. It was several years before a 'Preston' car ventured up Manchester Road, and only occasionally was one loaned to Bolton depot, although on Friday evenings a Saltaire-based 'Preston' tram was used for the Briggate-Town Gate (Idle) working in connection with late-night shopping at Shipley Market. Uniquely, in 1926 Nos. 223/225 ventured to (but not under!) Greengates Bridge to assist the normal service cars at a period of exceptional demand.

The new cars suffered 'teething troubles', of course, such as axle failures, and until 'run in', the track brakes had 'an uncanny knack of going out of order'. The handbrake handles had to be lengthened for better leverage; the trucks were considered hard-

By 1920 the tramcar loading arrangements in Forster Square were totally inadequate, especially when motor cars began to force their way through the crowds. In this scene a six-window car (No. 204 or No. 226) approaches Church Bank en route to Bradford Moor while 'Preston' car No. 254 loads at the Undercliffe queue-barrier and six-window tram No. 170 (still in wartime grey and white) waits in the background. *Courtesy Mrs D. Burrows*

full load, No. 63 could not pass beneath Greengates Bridge. While hurried calls were made to Thornbury, the tram returned to the terminus to await sufficient weights and sandbags to depress the springs and allow it to escape, never to return.

A special lowbridge 5ft 6in canopy was therefore built for the next new car, No. 64, which with new Boving truck and the first of the Huddersfield-style route number boxes successfully reached Greengates on 30th September, being joined by Nos. 65-69 in October and November. With No. 64 came also the elegant gilt 'Clarendon' fleet numerals, much more legible than the angular 'Spencer' numerals used since 1898; on No. 64 they were shaded in pale blue, but commencing with No. 65 a pleasing rose-red shading was used. Bradford's tramcars were now among the smartest and most attractive vehicles in Yorkshire, though the competition was fierce and opinions not unanimous!

The need to differentiate between the varying body heights was met by code letters painted on the staircases, ie GB, WB and B, denoting respectively Greengates, Windhill and Bowling Bridges. Cars bearing no code letters were debarred from all three.

The return of peace had not been accompanied by a renewal of the calm tranquillity which subsequent nostalgic generations attributed to the pre-war era. Railway and coal strikes in the Autumn of 1919 imposed pressure on tramcar services, although in Bradford industrial relations were assisted by the establishment of a Tramway Employees' Social Club.

Released at last from the protracted horrors of the War, the Easter crowds gladly set out for the parks, woods, glens and

riding until adjusted, and at first No. 253 delighted in derailing on the Heaton route's Buxton Street curve, but thereafter the roomy 'Prestons' proved to be useful and adaptable vehicles.

The Thornbury coachbuilders had been busy too. Adjusting their programme to accommodate parallel priorities, they constructed two vestibuled six-window cars, Nos. 192 and 163 (later 113) in March/April 1919, a 'high four-window' car (another 163) immediately afterwards, and then four more vestibuled six-window trams, Nos. 194/6/9 and 201 (the last to be built with high balcony 'tins'), by which time the first all-new car since 1914 had been built to Mr Wilkinson's medium-height version of the 1912 design.

Resembling Nos. 250-252 (soon to become 150-152) except for shallower waist-panels, straighter rocker panels, a medium-height (5ft 8ins) canopy top and an absence of air-scoops in the vestibule quarter-lights, the new tram, No. 63, resplendent in

the magnificent Wilkinson version of the pre-war livery, completed its trial run in September 1919, and was confidently despatched to Greengates, where, for the first time, a carload of delighted passengers arrived at the 'Roebuck' dry and warm. But on the return journey watchful eyes detected that, relieved of its

Heralded as 'Bradford's Newest Tramcar' at its debut on 30th September 1919, No. 64 was the first top-covered car to make a successful return journey to Greengates. Above, passengers are boarding in Forster Square, while (below) the tram squeezes beneath the low railway bridge.
Photos: Bradford Daily Telegraph and Bradford City Tramways, courtesy Messrs J. Copland and F. Hartley

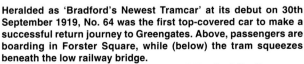

Seen passing in Manchester Road (Broadway Avenue) about 1922 are old No. 9 – an 1898 tram which had received a modern vestibule in 1914 – and open-ended Brush car No. 91, previously No. 115. Both are using trolley-skids in place of the usual wheels.

moors; the queues at the corner of Market Street extended twice around the block, and takings were double anything previously recorded. Fortunately the chaos caused in Forster Square by the demand for tramcars had at last been recognised; in January 1919, the first of several designs for a Tramways Centre had been unveiled.

There was anger in the Town Hall two months later when the Chairman of Finance (Councillor Joseph Stringer from Idle) successfully proposed that the hard-won Tramway Reserves Fund should contribute £30,000 to reduce the city rates at a time when the Tramways Committee were committed to spending £131,000 on new trams and track renewal. Adding insult to injury, he insisted that the tramways should make up the deficiency by borrowing £45,000 for their commitments and repaying it – with interest – from future income. This civic short-sightedness contrasted with the generosity of the tramways and the Bradford Traders' War Fund Committee who freely conveyed 20,000 children of the City's soldiers, sailors and airmen to Peel Park for tea, buns, games, races, prizes and entertainment by the City Police Band.

In January 1920, Mr Wilkinson altered the upper saloon seating of car No. 150 (ex No. 250) from seven pairs of double seats per side (total 28 seats) to three double pairs per side facing a longitudinal bench for six, a reduction of four seats but an increase in leg-room and (unofficially) standing capacity. For the next seven to eight years this arrangement was used in most cars including the 1921 delivery of 'Prestons'.

Then, concerned by the heavy wear on the overhead wires caused by the 6ins brass trolley-wheels, the manager experimented with a soft-iron trolley-skid which he claimed would reduce friction. Following a 3,391 miles trial with car No, 106 on the Bowling Old Lane section between 12th August and 15th December 1919, he was authorised to convert the trams based at Bankfoot, Bowling and Duckworth Lane depots. When predictably the rate of wear increased formidably, he instructed that worn stretches should merely be 'patched', but the overhead line staff had no qualms about renewing half a mile of wire at a time if necessary. When defeat was finally conceded about 1923,

lighter trolley heads with 4ins or 5ins wheels were introduced, and no tram ever again used skids.

In Sunbridge Road where despite the existence of two track crossovers and two separate loading points for the Duckworth Lane (8) and Allerton/Thornton (6/7) routes, intolerable congestion led to the removal of the Duckworth Lane cars to the upper queue barrier and the other cars to a new terminus 200 yards higher up the hill outside the Co-op Emporium (now 'Sunwin House'), an amazingly inconsiderate and naturally unpopular move. Although the Allerton cars later returned to their old haunts, the banishment of the Thornton cars was permanent. Alternative plans for commodious sidings in Tyrrel Street (between Sunbridge Road and Ivegate) were disapproved, probably because the area was used as a taxi rank. The situation was partly eased in December 1920, when rush-hour extras on the Duckworth Lane section which had hitherto reversed on the crossover at the bottom of Westgate were diverted to a new terminus in Rawson Square as service 8A.

The serious backlog of track repairs was now being remedied. Work begun in Manchester Road in May 1919 had been so delayed by the railway strike that despite the best efforts of the newly-invented 'pneumatic pick' it was not completed until August 1920. For much of the time the surviving ex-Mid-Yorkshire trams were drafted in to negotiate the temporary tracks in place of the heavier and more precious six-window cars.

Next, the track gangs moved to Church Bank, causing the usual diversions via Harris Street, where tram traffic was controlled by an employee perched in a strategically-placed armchair hoisted halfway up a tram standard at the Harris Street/ Humboldt Street junction, using green and red flags by day and lanterns by night. Manor Row and Thornton Road (Four Lane Ends to Fairweather Green) were dealt with next, and in main thoroughfares single-line sections were doubled wherever possible.

An early 1920s view of Manningham Lane with six-window car No. 170 and 'high four-window' tram No. 157 returning to City. Between the two trams can be seen the entrance to Lister Park and the statue of its former owner, 'Sam' Lister, Lord Masham.

For the Birkenshaw section where the foundations had deteriorated but the rails were sound, the Manager who from the day of his arrival had taken a keen interest in the eighteen-strong fleet of tracklesses, tentatively suggested in July 1920, that instead of renewing the track, the Committee should replace the trams by a Tong Cemetery-Birkenshaw trackless shuttle service. Quickly recovering from sensations of blank amazement, the Committee instructed him to lay new foundations and re-use the existing rails with Sandberg hardening treatment to prolong their life.

The derelict munitions tramway at Thornbury was removed, releasing the land for Corporation housing.

In October 1920, Bingley revived their earlier request for an obviously unremunerative extension of the Allerton tramway to Wilsden, but Mr Wilkinson offered tracklesses instead. Baildon, still hankering after their tramway, were reminded that costs still greatly exceeded the 1914 estimates, and when a primitive bus service from Baildon Bridge was launched on 16th August 1921, the dream finally died.

The body-building programme continued with six six-window vestibuled cars (Nos. 170/1, 204, 161 later 210, 183 and 226 later 198) in January-June 1920, and three 'high four-window' trams (159, 107 – briefly 118, a replacement for the withdrawn dual-gauge car – and 157) by the end of the year, followed by a thorough rebuilding of one of the original six-window cars (No. 158 later No. 169).

Meanwhile the large square route-number stencils, clumsy and inconvenient, had not spread beyond the Wibsey (1) and Greengates (21) cars, and by December 1920, all the canopy-top cars and 'open-toppers' had been fitted with smaller and more easily-manageable Manchester-style oblong boxes and stencils.

As a current-saving measure the automatic operation of single-line signals was converted to manual methods whereby tram conductors alighted to switch off the red light before the car entered the single-track section, and switch on the white light on leaving it.

Lack of precision in the Shipley lease had caused a long dispute about responsibility for the repainting of the tram standards, and consequently, none had been repainted since 1903. In 1920 Shipley treated the Otley Road installations to a few coats of silver paint, thereby conjuring up a startling vista from the Branch of an apparently solid mass of silver poles, bracket arms and scrollwork. When the Windhill poles were painted a more restful green, the rusting scrollwork was removed, and by 1927 all scrollwork both in Shipley and Bradford had vanished, often revealing hidden corrosion.

The Corporation trackless fleet continued to inspire the Manager with an enthusiasm not shared by its users. Increasingly convinced that one day tracklesses would supersede trams, he pioneered a 51-seat double-decker which commenced service on the peripheral Bolton-Bankfoot route on 3rd November 1920. By an ill-timed coincidence the Bolton Road and Eccleshill permanent way was due for renewal, thus encouraging Mr Wilkinson to recommend that as the adjacent, thinly-populated Idle and Thackley tramways were uneconomic, the trams on all three services should be replaced by double-deck tracklesses. His economics were challengeable, as the lightly-used Idle and Thackley tracks were debt-free and not yet worn out.

However, while the Lord Mayor of Birmingham, on a recent visit, had been deeply impressed by the new trackless car, the residents of Bolton and district, who knew it well, were not.

"The first time I boarded the new trackless in snowy weather it refused to start", said one. "When it did, it careered all over the road before it would take the slight incline ... and eventually we had to get off and walk."

Councillor O'Neill confirmed that the trams were safer in all circumstances including icy weather, a statement which he possibly recalled four years later.

Equally sceptical that tracklesses could adequately replace their trusty trams, the Committee decided to undertake all the necessary track repairs in Bolton Road and Eccleshill, even

'High four-window' car No. 107, seen at Wyke about 1921, was built as No. 118, a potential successor to the dual-gauge trams, but spent its entire working life (1920-1949) on conventional Boving and Dick Kerr trucks. *Courtesy Mr R. Brook*

allowing a touch of modernity in the form of tarmacadam paving to be applied to the Eccleshill section. Also, pleasingly, from November 1921, some of the 'old original' trams at Bolton depot made way for 'a better standard of car' in the form of new 'Windhill Bridge' No. 21, followed by Nos. 56, 77, 50 and 57.

The new No. 56 had replaced its Bailey-top predecessor in circumstances which belied the claims of tramcar superiority. Approaching the Five Lane Ends junction in thick fog on 3rd February 1921, Driver Benson had misjudged his whereabouts and allowed the tram to strike the points at excessive speed. After jumping the rails and hitting the kerb at an angle, it toppled over. Its broken remnants were converted into a snow-plough, and at Five Lane Ends a pane of red warning glass was fitted to one of the gas street lamps. Tramway morale revived a month later when the tiny trackless fleet was found to have incurred a £14,222 loss, compared with a growing tramway profit.

The outbreak of a coal strike soon afterwards affected power supplies so acutely that a 25% reduction of tram services had to be imposed. During June no trams operated before 6am, from 10am to mid-day or between 2.30pm and 4pm, the gap being filled on every route except Thornton, Tong Street, Bolton Road and Bowling Old Lane by a rabble of charabancs, primitive buses and converted lorries provided by members of the Bradford Motor Owners Association. The return of full tramway services was greeted with relief by everyone except the bus owners who for the first time had enjoyed the fruits of public service within the city and were busily establishing bus services from outer tram termini to outlying villages.

The 1921 bodybuilding programme was the last to produce more than one design of lower decks. The 1919 design pioneered by No. 63 having been adopted as a new standard, three bodies were built in the Spring – No. 70 (later No. 11 and probably the last new car to receive an air-oil brake), No. 74 (later No. 39) and No. 86, differing from No. 63 in having larger windscreens surmounted by a wooden strip in place of the traditional quarter-lights. Then came two 'high four-window' trams, Nos. 164 and 158, two

more 1919-style cars, Nos. 24 and 21, in the summer, and finally in October No. 160, last of the ten 'high four-window' trams seemingly intended for the Leeds through service.

Although a parcels service to Leeds had been operated since November 1918 by a trackless converted into a waggon fed from the tramway overhead wires with a trailing 'skate' in the groove of the tram rail, the passenger through-service was still dormant. Throughout 1919 Leeds had been reluctant to resume running until the permanent-way between Bradford Moor and Farsley Old Road recovered from its indifferent state of health, but in February 1921 the technical press reported that 'Leeds were willing to renew the agreement, but Bradford had not expressed an equal readiness'. On 7th April the 'Yorkshire Observer' stressed that those who appreciated the advantages of the through cars were eagerly awaiting their reinstatement.

However, the rehabilitated dual-gauge Peckham trucks were no longer in evidence – obviously newer trucks would be needed – and their DK19A motors were converted to DK13 single-drive for general use. When the points and crossings at Stanningley wore out, they were replaced by plain track with a significant 6ins gap on the Pudsey/Farsley boundary. On 14th July 1924 the Tramways Committee declined to make further payments for the Spencer-Dawson dual-gauge patent, an action not lost on Huddersfield, who had already built their Brighouse route to their

When 'Bailey Top' car No. 56 capsized in fog (through driver negligence) at Five Lane Ends in February 1921, its shattered remains were transformed into snowplough No. 14 (later S.7), and was replaced by a new 'Windhill Bridge' tram seen here about 1928 at the later Eccleshill terminus (Mechanics' Institute).

Photos: BCT and Mr F. Hartley

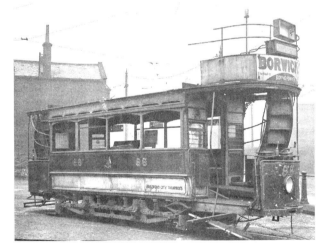

Seen here at Crossflatts terminus on a warm day about 1926, tramcar No. 11 began its life in February 1921, as No. 70 on a Hurst Nelson truck and ended its career in May 1950, as No. 247 on a Dick Kerr truck. The last new car to be equipped with air/oil brakes, it was also the first built with large windscreens.
Courtesy the late Dr H. A. Whitcombe

Street. By this time postwar track rehabilitations were at their height, restricted only by the need to await formal powers to borrow the necessary capital. In Little Horton Lane, however, where drivers had to take special care between Holme Top and Southfield Lane to prevent their trams from being 'shaken to pieces', legal niceties were ignored, and work began forthwith. All curves were planned with a minimum clearance of 15ins between cars.

In lower Thornton Road the old Demerbe rails used by the Lidget Green cars had been due for renewal in 1914, but the War, road-widening and the resiting of Post Office cables had delayed the work until 1922, and not surprisingly the transformation was held to be 'wonderful'. During the relaying seven or eight isolated trams provided a shuttle service between the bottom of Listerhills Road and Lidget Green, where the tiny depot and the adjacent tracks accommodated them overnight.

In the upper reaches of Thornton Road the first instalment of an intended 'super-highway' from Bradford to Colne via Haworth was being laid out as an unemployment relief measure. Between Fairweather Green and School Green the old, winding country lane with its high hedges and single-line-and-loop tramway was dramatically superseded by a sweeping 60ft carriageway flanked by grass verges on which sleeper tracks had been laid. Although the carriageway itself continued to the entrance to Thornton village, the retention of 'Bishop's Buildings' at the corner of Chat Hill obliged the outward-bound trams to veer across the road and join the inward line at the 'Junction Inn', Old Road, thence continuing on the grass verge by means of a single track as far as School Green, where the street track resumed. The road was formally opened by the Prince of Wales (later King Edward VIII) in May 1923.

Ex-trailer car No. 27 served for many years as the Pay Car, and is seen here in Forster Square on 'pay day' in 1925. The building on the left (headquarters of Woolcombers Limited) served as the Corporation Transport headquarters from 1929 to 1974.
Photo: Mr F. Hartley

own gauge. As Huddersfield manager Mr Wilkinson had been interested in dual-gauge working: had professional jealousy intervened, or had he been deterred by the technical problems? The Pudsey press, relying on hearsay, laid the whole blame at Bradford's door, but documentary evidence is lacking. Nevertheless, the unique enterprise was at an end.

Another remnant of the Spencer era, No. 195, last of the quaint Bailey-top cars, was withdrawn either in December 1921, or at the following Whitsuntide. Conversely its Milnes colleague No. 88 (ex No. 144), hitherto an 'open-topper', received a new lease of life with a DK21E truck and a canopy top rescued from scrapped car No. 11; it retained its three large side-windows. Car No. 176 was treated likewise in April 1922.

At Great Horton a new crossover and fare stage at the 'White Horse' had been adopted from January 1921 as a 'shortworking' terminus in preference to Southfield Lane, and lower down the same line the Claremont/Mannville Terrace crossover was used during Armistice Day solemnities at the new Cenotaph in Morley

Old Thornton Road, between Fairweather Green and modern Rhodesway, was a sea of mud when Thornton-bound Brush car No. 12 was photographed there about 1920.
Photo: City Surveyor, courtesy Mrs D. Burrows

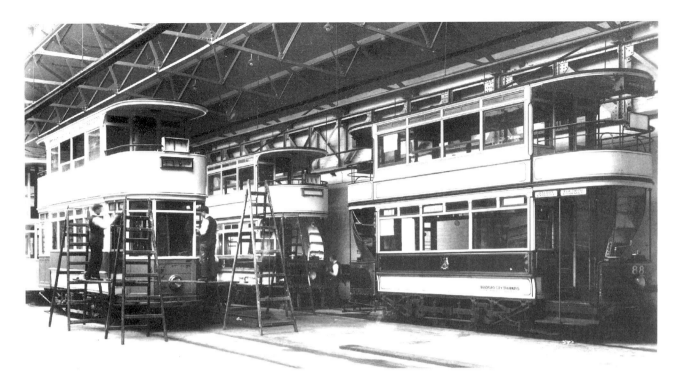

Their infinite variety ... all four trams photographed in the Paintshop in December 1923, had high-type canopy tops but were otherwise different. New Thornbury-built No. 19 (far left) was nearing completion; an unidentified 'modern six-window' car was receiving a blue and white undercoat (left) while Brush car 104 (ex No. 117) was being lined out. Tramcar No. 88 (right), originally Milnes car No. 144, was unusual in retaining three side windows when it received a new DK21E truck and a second-hand top cover from car No. 11 in 1921/2.   *Photo: BCT*

The Forster Square tramway station, laid out between June and October, 1922 used the triangular central island as a loading-point. Around the perimeter tubular-iron gangways resembling cattle- or sheep-pens provided queue-barriers for services to Greengates (route 21), Undercliffe (20/22/23) and Bradford Moor (29/30) on the south side, Bingley/Crossflatts (23/24) and Baildon Bridge (26) on the east, and Heaton (28/29), Saltaire (22/25) and Frizinghall (27) on the north. Cars returning from Manningham Lane to City only (24-28) circumnavigated the island anticlockwise, using the central tracks south of the island to overtake trams loading at the barriers. The Undercliffe (20), Greengates (21) and Bradford Moor (30) to City cars reversed as previously near the end of Ship Alley (later Broadway) whilst the Bolton Road (31-33) tramcars continued to reverse outside the Post Office and load in Bolton Road.

The new facility, well-planned and efficient, was at first resented by Saltaire passengers unwilling to cross the Square to their new departure point – they preferred to loiter at the end of Market Street and 'leg on' as the trams passed, a practice which drivers discouraged by driving past at the best speed they could muster.

Gerald Brailsford was one of those athletic passengers.

'Tramcars were a spirited element in our daily life', he wrote years later. 'We became expert in jumping on and off the moving cars. A favourite leaping-on place was at the sharp curve at the bottom of Cheapside. No need to walk to the sheep-pens where the cars started. Once, however, I was hampered by the chap in front and began to be dragged up Cheapside still clutching the handrail until the conductor hauled me aboard with one hand on the scruff of my neck.'

Others were even less appreciative of the splendid new facilities. The possibility of holding the annual cattle fair in the 'pens' instead of St. James' Market was frivolously raised by appropriately-named Alderman Trotter, who quickly learned, however, that tramcar travellers did not relish being likened to horned beasts. The same dignitary was once refused admittance to an already full tram in Norfolk Street. "But I am Alderman Trotter!" he expostulated. "Ah don't care if tha's Councillor Cowheel!" came the unperturbed reply. "Tha's not gettin' on this tram!"

For the year ended March 1923 the largest-ever profit of £112,109 was achieved. Prudently £52,109 was put into reserves and £47,000 to renewals, but rate relief claimed the rest. Postwar inflation having eased, fares and wages returned to their previous level with a promise that the latter would rise or fall by 1s 0d for every 4-point change in the index. Takings were increased by a new weekly pass sold for 2s 0d (one fare stage), 3s 6d (two stages) and 4s 6d (maximum), as more passengers began to travel home for lunch.

At Thornbury a new 'Car Depot and Repair Works' opened in March 1923, alongside the existing depot, and incorporated engineering, woodworking and paint-shops. A 169-yard track connection from Leeds Road led to a traverser (with a 20ft turntable) which ran the full length of the Works, thus eliminating the need for a track fan.

The tramway between Saltaire and Nab Wood, laid twenty years previously in the leisurely days of the Mid-Yorkshire company but now heavily used by the popular Bingley service, had deteriorated to a point where up to three derailments in a fortnight were being encountered. Shipley UDC asked Bradford to renew the track while they were relaying the Saltaire-Frizinghall section. The work, begun in January 1923, eliminated single-line lengths as well as the quadruple track layout outside Saltaire depot, so that a continuous double track then existed from Forster Square to Nab Wood.

Still hankering after the completion of their tramway as far as Morton Lane, Bingley UDC applied for a further legal extension of time (as they did every year until 1926) and somewhat naively asked Keighley Corporation what prospect there was of the oft-discussed Stockbridge-Morton Lane tramway link. Keighley's tramways, however, were in their last days, and

Above: In 1922 a Tramway Station was laid out on the island in Forster Square, enabling passengers to queue patiently in the 'sheep pens'. Car No. 183 (left) is loading at the Undercliffe barrier while car No. 113 (centre) waits behind a Baildon Bridge tram prior to proceeding to the Heaton barrier (centre left). Unfortunately Bolton Road car No. 13 (right), still in prewar livery, is excluded from the new arrangements. *Photo: Bradford City Tramways*

Left: The 'Tramway Station' was put to the test at holiday periods, when queues encircled the island. On the Milnes open-top car (No. 46?) the Wilkinson-type seating arrangement, part transverse and part longitudinal, can be clearly seen.

Courtesy the late R. B. Parr

Bradford suggested tracklesses instead. Tracklesses were proposed for other long extra-mural routes too, but overwhelming opposition from everywhere except Clayton defeated the Corporation's plans, thus weakening their hopes of forestalling a future incursion of competing private buses.

The creation of a dual-carriageway between Odsal and Low Moor enabled the Corporation to resite the Wyke tramway on a sleeper track in the central reservation. Meanwhile at Park Avenue the 1898-vintage track was kept busy by football and cricket 'specials'; at August Bank Holiday, 1923, a capacity crowd of 25,000 attended a 'Roses' match while a further 20,000 failed to obtain admittance.

Changing patterns of behaviour were noted by newspaper correspondents. 'No one enters a crowded tramcar nowadays without noticing the differences between the manners of today and those of twenty years ago', wrote one. 'It was then rare for a woman to be allowed to stand while a man sat. Now it is frequent!' The age-old puzzle as to where flies go in winter-time was mirrored in the new query, 'Where do tram passengers come from in wet weather?'

Newly-completed car No. 6 was photographed in June 1923, at the entrance to the spacious new Thornbury Works where the traverser with its 20ft turntable and BTH controllers was capable of transporting vehicles to and from the engineering, body and paint shops. *Photo: Bradford City Tramways*

Certain themes, albeit in different guises, reappear in every generation. "It is amazing to see the number of school-children who travel citywards by tram every morning", commented a surprised Bradfordian. "It is even more amazing still when one sees the parents of those same children walking to business and waving to their offspring as the tramcar passes. Is the youth of this city less vigorous than it was formerly?"

An increase in width of tramcar lower decks from 6ft 3⁵/₈ins (over the pillars) to 6ft 6⁵/₈ins was made so that for the first time BCT-built cars could be mounted on the DK21E trucks bought in 1921. The first, No. 52, new in August 1922, inherited its medium-height 'Windhill Bridge' canopy top deck from the old 'white board' car which had borne the number since 1900, and although most post-1919 cars received new medium-height top decks, sixteen of the 'wide' bodies received full-height tops from withdrawn cars; presumably their extra breadth gave them sufficient stability to overcome Mr Wilkinson's fears about 'topheaviness'.

Also overcome once again was Mr Wilkinson's yearning for tramway replacement by tracklesses. In order to relieve growing unemployment in Bradford the Committee voted to borrow £205,968 to renew miles of tramway including Otley Road, Horton Bank Top to Queensbury and Odsal to Shelf. As part of the Shelf section was to be laid on a roadside sleeper track raised slightly above the adjacent road surface, contrary to legislation, special powers had to be obtained before the Minister released all the capital required.

Bolton depot, built as a temporary structure in 1898 and now an unsightly mass of rust, was rebuilt in concrete in May/June 1924, during which time its tram fleet was divided between Thornbury and Saltaire depots.

The unpopular abundance of open-top ('low-deck') trams on the Greengates service – old 'white board' cars assisted by a few Milnes cars on Brush trucks – impelled Thornbury Works to build six more 'Greengates Bridge' cars, (Nos. 70-75) between March and September 1924. Although their overall height of 14ft 2ins matched that of the earlier batch, Nos. 64-69, their bottom saloon was slightly lower, thus allowing a little more headroom in the cramped top saloon and a little less damage to gentlemen's bowler hats!

Never a man to be deterred by opposition, Mr Wilkinson reiterated in 1924 that the tramways should be abandoned one by one when the tracks wore out. Basing his argument on an

At the end of the era of open platforms, high balcony 'tins', coloured destination indicator slides, route number stencils and air/oil brakes, six-window car No. 166 was photographed at Duckworth Lane with Driver Borritt and Conductor Holdsworth.
Photo: Miss A. Holdsworth, courtesy Mr J. Copland

average track life of fifteen years and an average outlay of £70,000 on track renewal, he forecast that complete renewal would cost £1,050,000 compared with only £603,320 for trackless overhead equipment, feeders and road reinstatement.

Austerely the City Treasurer pointed out that highway maintenance costs would increase, and that tracklesses were shortlived and more expensive to maintain; furthermore the trackless licence fees would cost £18,900 per annum. Unable to accept that their 250 trams could be replaced by 270 single-deck tracklesses with only 37 seated passengers and room for 25 'standees', the Committee again overruled him and pressed on with track modernisation including improvements to Duckworth Lane terminus in the interests of traffic flow, and a new track-fan

in the adjacent depot yard. Shipley also indulged in a modest orgy of renewal on the Baildon Bridge section, and a few new sets of points at Windhill.

Two spectacular collisions occurred when a fire-engine smote a Drighlington tram at Westgate Hill and a lorry bearing four tons of stone made a distinct impression on a Shelf car. Less sensational but more frustrating was a cow, en route from Otley to Heaton, which took such a liking to the 'four foot way' that it ambled in front of a Baildon Bridge car from Shipley to the 'Branch', impervious to the angry bell-clanging which accompanied its stately progress.

By the 1920s the delights of fresh air for tram drivers had diminished, and their union requested that the many open-platform cars should be vestibuled. Accordingly in February 1924 Milnes car No. 114 received a prefabricated so-called 'temporary front' clamped to its existing round steel dash and projecting beyond it to accommodate the swing of the handbrake handle. The fender was extended to protect the vestibule from collision damage, but the hand-rung driver's warning bell was retained despite the existence of more convenient footgongs on all BCT-built cars. Visually less pleasing than the conventional angular BCT platform vestibules but quicker and cheaper to instal, 'temporary fronts' were fitted to all the 78 open-platform canopy-top cars but not the 'open-toppers'. As the process was spread over two years, 500 storm caps for drivers were bought for 4s 6d apiece.

Gradually the old wooden-shoe slipper brakes were giving way to the much more efficient iron four-shoe mechanical track brakes, a process not completed until 1928. Commencing with car

Good views of Shipley town centre in the tramway era are rare. Here six-window car No. 183 returning from Baildon Bridge has just crossed 'Cobweb Corner' (alias Fox Corner) and is approaching the railway bridge opposite the Market Square.
Courtesy Mr E. Thornton

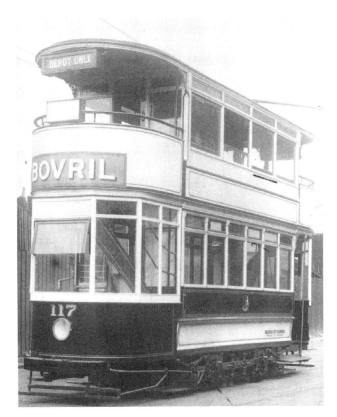

The fitting of 'temporary glass fronts' to open-ended trams between 1924 and 1926 was the beginning of a gradual modernisation programme. Car No. 117 (ex No. 86 ex No. 143) has gained a canopy-hung roller-blind destination while temporarily retaining its route-number stencils and 1912 vintage Brush 21E truck.

Photo: Bradford City Tramways

No. 26 in September 1925 all new bodies incorporated a stout brass rail across the windscreen which drivers could use to gain extra leverage when applying the handbrake.

Among the many provisions included in new byelaws for the conduct of tramway passengers were clauses prohibiting smoking and the carriage of dogs in the lower saloon, spitting or standing on the upper deck, travelling on platforms or staircases, playing musical instruments, swearing, intoxication, damage to seats and the wearing of clothing which might soil the seats or other passengers clothing – workmen's cars excepted. Most passengers were well-behaved, however, and vandalism was almost entirely unknown.

Granville Wilkinson, like all enlightened folk but unlike grumpy J.B. Priestley, appreciated the Corporation trams.

'I was once coming home on the Bowling Old Lane tram', he wrote. 'As it wound its way through the dark canyon of mills, a group of men who were sitting outside at the back of the tram burst into song. They must have been members of a glee union or something like that. To my ears they sang so beautifully; and I shall remember it to my dying day. Then as the tram reached the stop at the start of Gaythorne Road they clattered down the steps with their cheery "Goodnights".'

Less cheery was the Tramways Department's reaction to a City Council edict that the postwar 1½d stages must be replaced by 1d stages of approximately a mile each. Correctly forecasting that income would fall by over £700 a week, Alderman Priestley soberly stated that they had 'reached the parting of the ways'. "While we have been able to pay our way in the past", he stressed, "we are now in a position where the Council has overridden the Committee."

Weekly passes and cross-town overlapping stages had to be discontinued, obliging passengers to re-book in the city centre. Demand remained high, however, prompting a request for 'light toast-rack cars to be run to the penny stages (eg Park Gates) to relieve the long-distance cars', a notion which understandably attracted no support whatever.

In pursuit of a more practical future the Committee resolved to renew part of the Great Horton tramway for £17,043 and Allerton (Four Lane Ends to Chapel Lane) for £31,350, the section between Bullroyd and Yew Tree Lane to be laid on a central reservation in a new dual-carriageway.

However, having been reminded of the Manager's estimate that the well-worn tracks from Bolton Junction to Idle and Thackley needed total renewal at a cost of £107,616 compared with only £50,849 for tracklesses from the City centre to both termini, they felt obliged to vote for tracklesses. A delegation despatched to sample the latest trackless developments at Birmingham and Wolverhampton returned highly impressed, but confusingly a similar deputation to Glasgow was informed that neither they nor their children would see the end of tramways.

Renewed rumblings in Idle led to heated exchanges in the Council Chamber. Recalling how the development of Idle and Thackley had been assisted by the tramways, Councillor Nutton claimed that all the 400 employees at the Jowett car factory in Bradford Road travelled by tram, and proposed that the track be relaid as far as Five Lane Ends. Alderman Stringer queried why his district should be singled out to lose its trams when other tramways elsewhere in the city also operated at a marginal loss.

The Chairman, Alderman Priestley, reminded his colleagues that Bradford's tramways had never been a burden on the ratepayers; they had in fact repaid all their loans and contributed £180,000 to rate reductions. Quoting the phrase, "Let the fat fry the lean" from his native Wibsey, he stressed that if the Corporation began "lopping off" individual sections because they did not pay their way in isolation, the entire system was doomed. Better days were in store, and they would weather the storm. Refuting the notion that trams belonged to a bygone age, he hoped he would not live to see the day when they were abolished. His wish was to be granted.

Controversially on 6th June 1925 the City Council voted 33 to 32 in favour of Idle tracklesses, and in July Mr Wilkinson borrowed a new Garrett demonstration trackless for free trial trips for recalcitrant residents. But although several hundreds of Idle passengers sampled the novelty, they dismissed it as greatly inferior to their trams, especially when the brakes proved inadequate and only a hurriedly-produced coping-stone wedged under a wheel prevented disaster near Springfield.

A further petition and remonstrances from Alderman Stringer finally induced the Council to relent a month later. The trackless threat was deferred pending the construction of the new King's Road (Canal Road-Five Lane Ends), and the Bolton Junction to Five Lane Ends tram track was duly relaid in the Autumn, albeit at minimum cost and without welded railjoints.

In recognition of the greatly-increased use of the highways by motor-vehicles the City Engineer's Department removed lengths of disused track – the long-abandoned horse-tram rails in Oak Lane adjacent to the old depot which had been a cinema since 1914, the remnants of the steam-tram reversing triangles at Four Lane Ends and Chapel Lane, and the unused curves from Leeds Road into Sticker Lane and from the Stanningley route into Farsley Old Road.

Similarly, tram-stops were progressively staggered so that cars travelling in opposite directions did not stop side by side, obstructing other traffic, but the process was not complete until 1938/9, by which time more than one tram driver had mistakenly acted upon a starting-signal from another tram. An obstruction of a different kind incurred a £3 fine with 28s 0d costs when a lorry driver impeded a tram from Nab Lane to Bingley (two miles), causing it to be eight minutes late.

Maximum-capacity tram services were needed for another Great Yorkshire Show near Thornbury in July 1925. Leeds City Tramways issued through tickets available on Bradford cars as far as the main entrance near Pudsey Lane End, thereby provoking most justly a last, wistful protest that,

'We recall the days when cars ran through. It is surprising that through cars have not been reintroduced.'

It was even more surprising that the Corporations and the passengers never compelled the managers to reintroduce them.

Bradford, with its myriad mill chimneys and domestic coal fires, was a smoky, grimy place, and only at Bank Holidays was it possible to see clearly from one side of the valley to the other. In Leeds Road and Manchester Road the cityward side of the tram standards was visibly blacker than the other, and tram cleaners at Bankfoot and Bowling always had a harder task than their more fortunate colleagues elsewhere.

The overhead wires were similarly affected. Lack of use coated the copper with verdigris and soot which, when disturbed by a trolley wheel, caused noisy crackling and blue sparks. When track repairs in Nelson Street or Croft Street caused Bankfoot-bound trams to revert to the old pre-1904 line across Town Hall Square and into lower Manchester Road, the continuous arc which flowed around the trolley head sometimes set fire to the grease which lubricated the trolley wheel. Frost produced similar fireworks, and serrated 'ice-cutter' trolley wheels were fitted to the snowplough cars to keep the wires clear. For the most part, however, the wheels rotated with a smooth, sparkless hiss beneath bright, burnished wires.

At street level the presence of 'greasy' and icy rails required vigilance, although a combination of sensible 'notching up' and

judicious use of the sand-pedal prevented wheel spin when cars were starting up from rest. On one occasion, however, the driver of a city-bound car ascending Harrogate Road towards Undercliffe realised that oil leaked on to the rails from a lorry was causing the tram wheels to lose adhesion. The momentum gradually ceased, and imperceptibly the car began to creep back downhill. Coolly sauntering through the saloon before the passengers had time to notice, the driver depressed the sand pedal on the rear platform, bringing the car to a grinding standstill, and with the help of the front sanders completed the interrupted ascent. Full sand-hoppers and one or two spare sandbags stowed under the stairs were a guarantee of safety at most times.

During winter months if there was any likelihood of frost, ice or snow, each depot sent out a 'night car' to keep the tracks and wires clear. Up to 11pm on 6th December 1925 there had been no significant chill and therefore (in those pre-weather forecast days) no reason for precautions. However, during the dark hours a dense fog gathered, and a thick white frost coated the ground.

Punctually at 5.33am Brush 'temporary front' car No. 8 trundled out of Bolton depot and climbed towards Five Lane Ends in order to provide the first departure from Idle at 5.48am. Soon after beginning the long, steepening descent of Bradford Road, Driver Knowles sensed that he was no longer in full control of the car. He wound down the track brake a little more firmly and applied sand. Still the tram continued to drift downwards, and a full application of the handbrake failed to hold it.

Now dropping sand continuously he called to his conductor, Charles Caudwell, that he could not halt the car, and as it slid with locked wheels screeching on the ice-filled rails down the 1

A busy scene in Tyrrel Street, 1924. 'Modern six-window' car No. 203 is setting out for White Horse while Brush car No. 14 and a 'Preston' car load for Lidget Green and Wibsey respectively.

in 13.7 gradient of Thorp Garth both men peered anxiously ahead from the front platform into the gloom. Like 'a flash of lightning' No. 8 hurtled past a workman repairing a gas leak, tobogganing off the track and flattening a street lamp before crashing thunderously into the Alexandra Hotel, whose entire front wall collapsed on the car. Conductor Caudwell was killed instantly, and Driver Knowles died before he could be extricated from the wreckage.

When tidings of the disaster reached Thornbury depot, Inspector Munt and Bolton shed foreman Edgar Oughtibridge set forth in the towing-car, old No. 189, descending Bradford Road at a cautious 6mph but nevertheless experiencing loss of adhesion at the top of Thorp Garth and three car-lengths further down, but by dint of continuous sanding they reached the terminus safely. There they found No. 8 buried under rubble and reduced to waist level. Its wheels had barely penetrated the ice, and the brakes were wound on so tightly that a long spanner was needed to release them. A closer examination revealed a vital shred of evidence – a piece of paper in one of the hoppers, which clearly had impeded the flow of sand.

In a happier vein, the Halifax Road reserved track from Crawford Avenue to Bowman Road, begun in September 1924, was now in use, although the temporary survival of a few cottages near Netherlands Avenue obstructed the outward track and necessitated a short section of single line. The renewal of the remainder of the Shelf track, in the carriageway, was deferred and in consequence of later events was not carried out. Many tracks in the city centre were relaid, and in upper Harris Street the 1888 steam tram rails were at last replaced by good, part-worn rail on the original foundations.

Thornbury Works was enjoying its most productive year, with thirteen new tram bodies, 53 overhauls, 61 repaints and eight partial rebuilds. For reasons never explained, new car No. 40 received reversed staircases in contravention of Ministry regulations; they were ultimately replaced by normal 'three-quarters direct' stairs probably salvaged from car No. 67 nine years later.

Meanwhile, increasingly disturbed by developments elsewhere, the Corporation had, in August 1925, reluctantly obtained powers to operate petrol buses in isolated parts of the city where trams and tracklesses had never penetrated.

Old Bingley, about 1925. 'Preston' tram No. 225, still in maker's paint and advertising Hardy's, the well-known Bradford jewellers, is passing Myrtle Place on its way to Crossflatts. In Bingley the tram poles always retained their ornamental scrollwork around the bracket arms, above which was a fitting carrying (left) the tramways telephone lines and (right) a single low-voltage wire used for testing the electrical efficiency of the permanent-way rail bonds. *Copyright:* Keighley News

11 - A NEW BEGINNING?

'Behold, I make all things new' (Revelations 21 v 5)

Despite all that was to happen later, the year 1926 began promisingly with a decision by the Tramways Committee to invest £50,717 in new permanent way for Manningham Lane, Leeds Old Road and lower Barkerend Road. In a move to relieve congestion in Tyrrel Street a kerbside loading siding in Thornton Road was being designed for the Lidget Green cars, and track repairs and renewals were being speeded up by the purchase of motor tipper-lorries in place of two of the old, leisurely tram-hauled ballast trucks.

The modest process of tramcar evolution continued placidly. More mechanical four-shoe track brakes were fitted to older cars still equipped with wooden shoe brakes, and roller-blind destinations and route numbers began to replace the inconvenient slides and stencils on all cars except the 'open-toppers' and those due for early replacement. The programme for the fitting of 'temporary glass fronts' to the open-platform trams reached completion with Brush car No. 101 in April, and all trams incorporating Mr Wilkinson's upper-deck seating arrangement received ceiling-mounted handrails to help passengers making their way along the gangway. A visit by Major Hall of the Ministry of Transport resulted in a welcome if unspectacular raising of speed limits – itself an acknowledgement of increased brake efficiency.

Simultaneously an attempt was made to solve the old problem of long-distance passengers being crowded off their tramcars by short-distance travellers for whom short-working cars were provided. From March 1926 a 2½d peak-hour minimum fare was imposed on the Shelf, Bailiff Bridge and Wyke (12-14) services to deter passengers who wished to alight before Odsal, but embarrassingly the scheme was too successful, because if the cars filled up at the City loading-point (Town Hall Street) with the people for whom they were intended, naturally no one alighted before Odsal, and consequently passengers waiting at intermediate stops could not board. The scheme was shortlived.

Much more popular was the City Electrical Engineer's proposal for lighting all the tram and trackless routes by electricity, following a trial in Halifax Road earlier in the year. Within eighteen months the installations were complete, and the Shipley, Clayton and Queensbury UDCs were so impressed that they did likewise. In the other areas outside the city the dim glimmers of gas lighting were retained, except at the Drighlington and Bailiff Bridge termini where the local councils paid BCT 3s 2d per week for maintaining a large overhead lantern fed from the tram wires.

Thoughts were turning at last to the possibility of radically modernising the design of the tramcars, which, despite the continuing modifications, were still being built to an updated version of the 1912 pattern. The obvious need was for a fully-enclosed top deck which would allow all seats to be occupied in all weathers. Neighbouring Huddersfield, Mr Wilkinson's previous undertaking, were about to order their first all-enclosed cars for their new Brighouse route, and on 25th May 1923 the Thornbury draughtsmen produced a drawing of a 'Vestibule Car Body, Enclosed Type'. An adaptation of the current 'wide' body with medium-height roof, it was to provide 37 seats upstairs and 22 down.

But would such a car be stable in high winds? Calculations indicated that it would withstand a 70mph side-wind, compared with 78mph for the equivalent balcony car, but Mr Wilkinson was not convinced. Obsessed ever since his appointment with the fear of top-heaviness, he had in addition to introducing lower (medium-height) canopy tops in 1919 also begun to reduce the depth (and hence weight and wind resistance) of the high balcony 'tins'. Ironically, the only tram overturned during his managership had been 'Bailey-top' medium-height 'Windhill Bridge' car No. 56.

The issue was decided by BCT's braking systems, as the Ministry disapproved of all-enclosed double-deckers reliant solely on mechanical braking on hilly 'narrow gauge' networks. Modern air brakes would have overcome Ministerial objections as in Colne, but would have increased operating costs. The alternative Spencer-Dawson air/oil brake, despite its undoubted usefulness, had caused formidable rail wear as well as pools of sticky oil at stopping-places; decreasingly used since 1919, it was discarded altogether in 1926. The drawing was therefore filed and forgotten, and a different approach was tried.

Mr Wilkinson's experiences with tracklesses had led him to reject double-deckers in favour of single-deckers with a high standing-passenger capacity. Applying similar principles to tramways he concluded that no double-deck tram could operate as safely or efficiently as a single-decker, especially on the 'narrower' gauge. A drawing of single-deck bogie brake mechanisms was therefore studied on 21st June 1924.

Then, alerted by the rapidly developing threat of private bus competition, in February 1926 the Works produced a design for a revolutionary single-decker on the basis of Mr Wilkinson's new-found belief that 'to maintain the supremacy and popularity of the tramcar its average speed must be raised to the highest level consistent with safety'.

Forster Square in 1926. Car 170 at the 'sheep pens' prepares to depart for Church Bank and Bradford Moor.

Courtesy Mrs D Burrows

A central entrance was to ensure quicker loading and unloading, and only one motor per bogie would be used, with silent worm-drive and railway-style side-coupling rods to ensure good rail adhesion.

Intrigued, the Tramways Committee gave consent on 8th February 1926 for the construction of one experimental car at an estimated cost of £2,000, and within a few weeks the project had begun under the chairmanship of Councillor Irvine Smith, who had replaced Alderman Priestley in tragic circumstances.

Enoch Priestley, JP, was born in 1854 and, on the death of his father only ten years later, took command of the family's egg and butter business. At the age of 27 he was elected to North Bierley Local Board, serving as chairman of its successor, North Bierley UDC, so regularly that he was dubbed 'Mayor of Wibsey'. On incorporation with Bradford in 1899 he rose through the ranks to succeed Councillor (later Sir) James Hill as tramways chairman in 1905. On 3rd February 1926 he was knocked down and killed by a locomotive when crossing a goods yard in fog. In 1986 his aldermanic hat and mementoes were presented to the City Museums in the presence of the Lord Mayor, Councillor W. A. Nunn, himself a former BCPT employee. Alderman Priestley's death undoubtedly marked the passing of an age; hard times now lay ahead.

Since 1925 the Corporation had been locked in battle with the West Riding Automobile Company who for some time had operated a bus service from Wakefield to Drighlington tram terminus and now wished to extend it into Bradford city centre. Aware that the battle was becoming a test case for other private operators to the potential detriment of its tramways, the Corporation withheld the requisite licences long after the Ministry of Transport had threatened legal action.

The fateful events of May 1926 changed the course of transport history beyond recall. When the General Strike was declared, the tramwaymen's union instructed its members to cease work in sympathy, contrary to their agreement which stipulated one week's notice on either side. In consequence no Corporation tram or trackless left the depots from 6th-10th May. A volunteer tram service to Thornbury (9), Southfield Lane (2) and the city boundary at Frizinghall (27) was provided on 11th May; next day 34 cars were in use, and on the 13th normal services were resumed, to everyone's relief.

It was soon obvious, however, that the status quo had not returned. The private buses had flocked into the city during the Strike and could not be dislodged; indeed, the Ministry compelled the Corporation to issue licences for private bus services to all the surrounding towns – and every one of them ran along a Corporation tram or trackless route. In theory they could not 'poach' the Corporation's passengers, but in practice they did, and were actively aided and abetted by the many people who had been angered and alienated by the tramways strike. Motor buses, previously unknown in Bradford, had overnight become fashionable and popular, and the shortcomings of the tramways were suddenly viewed in a new and critical light.

Although the penny fares imposed a year previously against the Manager's advice had substantially increased patronage, the revenue had decreased and the net surplus at 31st March 1926 had been halved. The Manager had therefore warned that if the cheap fares policy were to be retained, the Committee would have to cease raising loans to pay for track renewals, as the loans made no provision for depreciation and (in his view) effectively shackled the Corporation to tramcars in perpetuity. As predicted by Mr Spencer in 1917 the bill for the backlog of repairs caused by the War had already doubled the annual charges for interest and sinking fund.

The Manager therefore advised the Committee to pay for all future track renewals out of the reserve fund, to abandon any tramway which did not warrant a 10-minute frequency, and to judge each route on its merits when renewals were needed. For the first time, the committee paid heed to the Manager's long-term advice, and were never again as ready to renew track as previously.

The issue came to a head only four days after the end of the Strike, when the Committee announced that Manningham Lane would be closed to all traffic except trams from 27th May to 8th July to facilitate the track relaying programme agreed in January, and (although they did not say so) to divert the private buses away from Bradford's premier tram route.

Resentment fomented by the Strike boiled over immediately. Tradesmen and residents angrily petitioned the Corporation, and the Property Owners Association asserted that if the track relaying were necessary (which they doubted), buses could be used temporarily as far as Park Gates and trams beyond.

At a specially-summoned Council meeting the leader of the anti-tram faction, Alderman Anthony Gadie, proposed that the Manningham Lane track be merely 'patched up' until the leases of the adjacent Shipley and Bingley lines expired in 1932, when a Corporation bus service to the city boundary (only) should be instituted, thus abandoning Shipley and Bingley to the private buses.

A lively scene in Forster Sqaure, 1927. Car 100 (foreground) is returning from Frizinghall; queueing on the left are numbers 2, (route 30), 64 (route 21), and 156 (route 29); car 151 (route 26) is turning round the island, with cars 176 and 32 on the right.
Photo Walter Scott, Bradford

The inadequacies of his reasoning were quickly exposed by Councillors Pullan, Palin and Walter Hodgson, who pointed out that,

(i) Manningham Lane carried the heaviest tram traffic in Bradford and had earned no less than £175,000 out of a grand total of £660,000 in 1925/6;

(ii) the tramways contributed £100,000 each year to the Corporation Electricity Department, paid rates on the tracks and tram standards and maintained the road surface between the rails and for eighteen inches outside them;

(iii) as trams were by far the most efficient carriers of passengers, many more buses would be needed as replacements, thus intensifying congestion;

(iv) arguments that the private buses had been an adequate substitute for the trams during the Strike were misleading, as thousands had received lifts from motorists, and thousands more had walked.

By a majority vote the Council agreed to the relaying but not to complete road closure, and with round-the-clock working the task was finished by 17th July. Making use of temporary track and the intermediate crossovers at Drewton Street, Grosvenor Road and Park Gates, the Department renewed each track in turn on a ferroconcrete foundation with thermit-welded railjoints, except at the Oak Lane junction where rails lined with manganese steel were laid on quick-setting cement. Between the rails the concrete was covered with a 2ins layer of smooth mastic asphalt, and motorists as well as tram passengers voted it a magnificent job.

Nevertheless the trams did not escape unscathed. Troubled by the recent events and mindful of the Manager's advice that tramways which did not merit a minimum ten-minute headway should be discarded, the Committee revoked its 1924 decision to construct a new reserved-track tramway in Allerton Road, and voted to replace the Allerton (6) trams by motor buses. Rejected by the Council, the decision was reaffirmed by the Committee who, however, consented on 28th June to substitute trackless cars as soon as Parliamentary powers could be obtained.

Shortly afterwards, on 4th September 1926, a new trackless service to Clayton commenced to share overhead wires with the Lidget Green trams along the whole of their route; indeed, the Manager would have been happy to withdraw the trams altogether, but since much of the permanent way was quite new he was overruled, although the number of trams serving the route was reduced by a maximum of four. When the new tramway kerbside loading siding in Thornton Road came into use on 16th March 1927, the trams and tracklesses began to share a common departure point.

Similar kerbside loading arrangements were contemplated for the Thornbury and Stanningley services at the bottom of Leeds Road, but as the highway at that point was narrow and congested, the Committee agreed to lay a new, long siding in nearby Hall Ings, with a passenger waiting room. The new terminus came into use in July 1927, but delays in the construction of the waiting room prompted suggestions that the Tramways Band should boost the spirits of the disappointed public by playing selections from 'Patience' and 'There's a long, long trail a-winding!' Finally completed in April 1928, as a roomy but draughty facility built in concrete, glass and tile with internal queue barriers, it was promptly dubbed 'Tut's Tomb' in honour of Lord Carnarvon's recent Egyptian discoveries.

The driver-training school based at Thornbury depot had the regular use of old open-top car No. 26 – the 'school car' – which set out each weekday morning in search of a quiet line such as Park Avenue on which trainees could learn how to start, stop, de-rail and re-rail a tramcar. The 'school' instructors must have been unusually concerned about their pupils' welfare on 26th

November 1926 as they took with them an electric radiator to heat the saloon. Absent-mindedly they failed to disconnect the radiator on their return to depot, and during the night the tram caught fire and caused a blaze which destroyed not only itself but also Brush car No. 93, five-window car No. 144, six-window car No. 196 and the top deck of six-window car No. 136, and damaged Brush cars Nos. 17 and 38, vestibuled Brush car No. 54, BCT car No. 97 and snowploughs Nos. 13 and 20 as well as No. 8, a partially-completed replacement for the Idle 'runaway'. The damage, excluding the depot roof which also suffered, was estimated at the large sum of £7,703. New BCT 'wide' bodies were subsequently built for Nos. 93 and 196, whilst tall No. 136 received a new medium-height top deck which enabled it to pass beneath Bowling Bridge once more.

The tumultuous year ended on a prudent note when for the first time for a decade Christmas Day services were operated, and from the following Whitsuntide, Sunday morning services were instituted, although the frequencies were low, eg the Heaton route was served by one car to and from Forster Square only (service 28).

Bradford's wool textile industry – the city's major employer – was inherently subject to fluctuations in demand, and during the winter of 1926-7 no fewer than 14,190 employees were 'laid off', with a consequential effect on the tramways. For a while the only profitable routes were the Thornton, Greengates, Wibsey and Bolton Road sections where housing development was taking place; ominously the longer-distance passenger figures plummeted by 480,250. However, a decision to standardise all fares over 1d at 2d any distance within the City boundary not only reversed the loss of trade to the private buses but substantially increased the income. Unexpectedly, therefore, the financial year ended happily with a £13,569 tramway profit which was reduced to £7,935 by the loss-making tracklesses and motor buses. The all-powerful Finance Committee promptly seized £10,000 for rate relief, leaving the Tramways Department to fall back on reserves!

Bus competition was fiercest on the Baildon Bridge (26), Saltaire (22/25), and Bingley and Crossflatts (23/24) routes where the Keighley-based Premier Transport Company had succeeded in 'legitimising' its Keighley-Bradford service by claiming that Bradford's trams were unable to cope with the demand for travel to and from Bingley, especially at rush hours and holidays. The claim was based upon shaky foundations, as Premier's small single-deck buses could not compare with the much larger trams, most of which provided 65 seats and room for at least fifteen standing passengers. At the 1927 Easter weekend, for example, the trams earned £8,666 on Bingley and Crossflatts journeys by providing maximum services and carrying such phenomenal loads direct from and to Bradford that Shipley UDC had to request a few Saltaire-Crossflatts 'extras' at holiday times. Through tickets to Keighley were first issued on 2nd July 1926; passengers changed to or from a Keighley Corporation bus at Bingley or Crossflatts.

Competition was by no means one-sided. When two of the private bus drivers were fined for exceeding their legal 12mph speed limit, complaints were voiced that even at 20mph motorists could not keep pace with the trams. The various long, level sections of track in Keighley Road and Shipley invited fast tramcar travel, and with a skilled driver the usual gentle, swaying motion of the trams changed to a more vigorous movement as they sped past Nab Wood Cemetery, sometimes causing unwary passengers to slide off the well-polished wooden seats!

A ten-day visit by the Manager to Buda-Pesth resulted in a recommendation in May 1927 that on the Duckworth Lane (8) section the overhead equipment and cars should be adapted for bow-collectors in place of the traditional trolleys. The

Committee's decision to await the result of experiments elsewhere was a wise one in view of the presence of trackless overhead wires and complex junctions in the city centre. The retention of the trolleys thus ensured both compatibility and flexibility.

A considerable sensation was aroused by the unveiling of the single-deck saloon bogie car commissioned in February 1926, completed a year later and proudly exhibited to the Committee and invited guests on 8th March 1927. The break with tradition could not have been more dramatic, and the onlookers could have imagined that a railway carriage had strayed on to the streets, for what they beheld in the forecourt of Thornbury depot was a neat, symmetrical and very long vehicle with clean, simple lines and straight, flush panels not painted but varnished in their natural mahogany grain.

For ease and speed of loading and unloading the entrance was in the centre, and it was dropped to within a few inches of the road surface. The body was crowned by a deeply-domed ivory-painted roof into which the indicators and route numbers had been neatly incorporated. Significantly the brass-rimmed headlamp was surmounted by the imposing fleet number 1, symbolic of the new beginning which the gleaming car and its intended companions were to inaugurate.

Equally inviting was the interior. Folding doors opened with a hiss of compressed air to admit the guests to the two saloons – one for smokers and the other for those who preferred purer air. The floors were carpeted with thick green linoleum; four 'diffusing lamps' or ground-glass bowls graced the maplewood ceiling of each saloon, and the driver in his enclosed compartment with its conveniently-placed controls was comfortably seated.

Luxurious, deeply-upholstered red leather seats awaited the passengers too, and at a stroke of the electric bell the magnificently-appointed car glided imperceptibly over the points and crossings into Leeds Road where the guests quickly found themselves travelling smoothly, steadily and silently at 35mph, faster than any tram (except runaways) had ever travelled in Bradford.

A few minutes later at Stanningley terminus they watched admiringly (and no doubt the Leeds Corporation crews enviously!) as the conductor 'walked' the long trolley to the opposite end in readiness for the return journey. When the car reached Thornbury Mr Wilkinson, at the controls, was overcome with a rare moment of exhilaration; he encouraged No. 1 to speed down the Works siding and did not halt until the driver's compartment overhung the Works traverser pit. His shaken passengers were never sure whether the incident was intentional or accidental.

'No car has so radically departed from previous practice', the technical press pronounced. 'Mr Wilkinson has shown much enterprise in devising measures for coping with bus competition, and has deserved success in the fullest measure.' At last Britain's tramways were beginning to fight back. Glasgow's single-decker 1089 and London's 'Bluebell' were both unveiled in the same month and aroused equal interest and anticipation.

Officially designated 'the Pullman Car', No. 1 commenced trials over the whole network, though not without mishaps. Rounding the never-used curve in Forster Square from the Undercliffe barrier to the Bingley barrier it reputedly carried the 'sheep-pen' railings with it, and when sent on the Heaton route it declined altogether to turn into St Mary's Road. However, descending the Thornton sleeper track it attained an astounding 55mph, thus earning itself the topical title of 'the Sixty Mile an Hour Tram'.

Normally housed at Thornbury depot with a precautionary 1ft gap (instead of the normal 6ins gap for lesser cars) between adjoining fenders, No. 1 entered daily service on the Thornbury and Stanningley (9/10) run where it received yet another title – 'the Leeds Road Flyer'. There it was scheduled to remain until joined by other speedy cars, the Committee having accepted on 13th June the manager's proposal that fifteen pairs of existing DK31 motors should be rewound by their makers to produce increased horsepower.

In fact, the first 'high-speed cars', newly-built double-deckers Nos. 79 and 94, had already shown their paces in June, to the astonishment of passers-by and the delight of small boys. Presumably they were making use of four of the six DK31/1C 60hp motors previously tried in Warsaw and Birmingham and currently on hire from English Electric; in Bradford they achieved speeds 20% higher than average.

Enthusiasm for modernisation abounded. From that date all new cars were 'high speed', and whenever finances permitted

'Pullman' car No. 1 prepares for its spectacular trial run in March 1927.

Photo: BCT

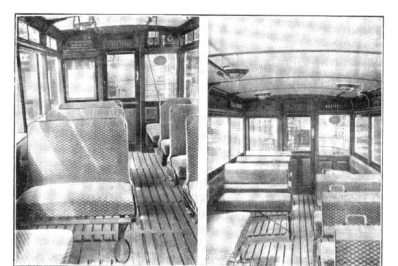

(the cost was £200 per car) batches of existing trams had their DK31A or B 45/50hp motors rewound to DK31D 60hp.

How fast could they travel if the Board of Trade maximum speed limit of 20mph was ignored? In the absence of speedometers no one could be sure, but when an inquisitive Wyke driver gave his steed its head on the reserved track from Odsal to Low Moor a few years later, he was 'flagged down' by a startled Huddersfield bus driver who informed him that he had attained 43mph at the very moment when his trolley had left the wire and begun systematically to smash each overhead street lamp it passed!

By December 1927 six of the new 'first class' trams, Nos. 1, 79,94, 103, 105 and 16 had been despatched to Horton Bank Top depot for exclusive use on the Lidget Green (4) route, where they had no difficulty in keeping up with the Clayton tracklesses. Nos. 103, 105 and 16 incorporated yet another well-received innovation: Listers' fawn moquette-upholstered seating in both saloons. The lower saloon seating was arranged as three single and three double transverse seats, two corner seats for two and another two for three (total nineteen, a reduction of 3 compared with the longitudinal wooden seating used since 1898), whilst the upper saloon retained the Wilkinson design of two five-seater longitudinal benches with six double transverse seats (total 37 including balconies). A modest improvement to the interior lighting was achieved by the removal of the ground-glass lamp covers.

On the whole, tramcar accessories were usually kept to a practical minimum. No Bradford tram ever sported traffic indicators, brake lights, speedometers or driver's mirrors, though the last-mentioned were briefly contemplated in 1925. Windscreen wipers (hand-operated) were unknown until the advent of modernisation, and only car No. 1 had electric bells, although Nos. 3 and 4 had 'Numa' pneumatic bells on both decks.

It was tacitly acknowledged that the trams, armed with the full majesty of Parliamentary powers, were still the monarchs of the highway, moving wherever the tracks directed and halting whenever passengers wished to board or alight in the carriageway. Rash or incautious motorists soon learned, to the sound of tinkling glass and rending metal, that the contest was not an equal one. Confronted by rubber-tyred vehicles darting or skidding into their path, tram drivers always knew that their stout fender would deflect the intruders with impunity; only buses, lorries, traction engines and other trams could inflict serious damage.

The down-to-earth usefulness of the trams was a feature of city life. Although a brief banishment of the Forster Square cars to temporary termini elsewhere in July 1924, had in the eyes of the press demonstrated 'how much pleasanter and safer it would

be if the city centre could be cleared of trams altogether', this uncharitable view was not shared by the thousands who converged there daily. A more practical observer in June 1927 described how a 'sudden rush of holiday folk to Forster Square intent on taking advantage of the generous 2d tram journeys to the country proved once again the superiority of the trams over the present buses in moving large crowds in quick time.'

As if to emphasise this, the trams managed to convey 55,442,660 passengers in six months with a handsome profit, although the price was packed cars at rush hours with long waits at intermediate stops. Most mornings Wakefield Road residents waited, not always patiently, as car after car passed without stopping, while Queensbury passengers claimed that at lunchtimes they were prevented from boarding by short distance riders who could have caught the White Horse trams.

Sometimes tramcars proved useful for recruitment purposes, including a cricket team hastily selected from passengers on the 12.10 to White Horse who played an 'eleven' from Great Horton Parish Church the same evening. Tramcar design also lent itself to cultural activities. In October 1927,

'... two Bradford Grammar School students whose ages would be thirteen and fifteen respectively were seen engrossed in a scientific and learned game of chess upon the upper deck balcony of a City-bound tramcar which sped along Manningham Lane shortly before 9 o'clock this morning. They were using a pocket chess equipment to good advantage, and were completely dead to their environment. The wind tousled their hair. The sun twinkled. Fellow passengers came and went. The car swam and thundered past busy streets and yellowing gardens. A 'two-seater' down below violently grazed its mudguard against a dray, with a resultant flow of hot words from the dray driver. There were other street incidents, but the two players remained riveted to the little chess board.'

Small wonder then that 270 residents of Bolton Woods, rattled and jolted by their primitive tracklesses, petitioned for 'a car service', though sadly their prayers went unanswered.

Minor service adjustments were made from time to time. On the eve of the Strike the Corporation had acquired its first motor buses, and on 27th April 1927 a few of these commenced a service via the new King's Road which not only served the new Swain House Estate but also continued over the Idle tramway from Five Lane Ends to reach the Greengates (21) tram terminus. On the same day the Nab Wood (32) via Thackley tram service was cut back to Saltaire (depot); a relic of the old Mid-Yorkshire company Nab Wood-Thackley Boundary service, its journeys beyond Saltaire had long been superfluous.

Across the city the Odsal-Oakenshaw trackless wires were extended into the city centre in order to frustrate private bus competition. As on the Lidget Green route the trams and tracklesses shared the overhead wires in Croft Street, Nelson Street and Manchester Road, commencing 24th October 1927.

At Duckworth Lane terminus the track had been cut back by 79 yards, from Washington Street to Little Lane, when the permanent way was renewed in 1924, but when this was found

to obstruct Little Lane traffic the track was re-extended by 40 feet. Similarly at Dudley Hill the Sticker Lane siding was lengthened to 180 yards for the Greenfield Stadium 'specials'; both extensions were carried out in March 1928. A few days later a profit of £30,495 on the tram services was announced, and this time not a penny was confiscated for the Rate Fund.

The redoubtable 'John Willie' Dawson, colleague of C. J. Spencer in many innovative ventures, retired in November 1927. Originally Engineering Foreman at Thornbury Works, his talents had ensured his promotion to Assistant Electrical Engineer in 1906 and subsequently to Works Superintendent. Mr C. E. Barton, chief draughtsman, succeeded him.

Meanwhile the question of the extension of the Bailiff Bridge (13) route to Brighouse had re-surfaced. In November 1921 Brighouse Corporation and Hipperholme UDC had offered to exercise their option to acquire Halifax's short 3ft 6ins gauge Bailiff Bridge-Brighouse line and either sell or lease it to Bradford. However, Halifax cunningly invoked the 1870 Tramways Act to insist that if the two councils took over the Bailiff Bridge branch, they would also have to acquire the portion of the Brighouse-Halifax route which lay within their boundaries, whereupon the negotiations foundered.

Nevertheless, when the end of their extended tenure approached, Halifax authorised their Chairman to reopen discussions, and by September 1927, there was agreement that Bradford would pay Halifax a total of £7,500 ie, £5,000 for the regauging of the Bailiff Bridge-Brighouse tracks to 4ft and the laying of 1.7 chains of rails to connect the two sets of metals at Bailiff Bridge, £500 for renovation of the overhead line and £2,000 for the goodwill.

In Brighouse there was to be mixed-gauge track from Bonegate to Commercial Street to accommodate the Halifax-Brighouse trams which were to use a 3ft 6ins gauge terminal stub alongside a 4ft gauge stub for the Bradford-Brighouse cars, while at the opposite side of the crossroads was the 4ft 7¾ins gauge terminus of the Huddersfield-Brighouse tramcars. So, despite fundamental doubts as to the future of Bradford's tramways a significant expansion as well as a unique tramcar meeting-place were being planned.

But first, notwithstanding the Bradford Tramways Committee's enthusiasm, the hurdle of the City Council had still to be tackled, and predictably there was opposition. Councillor

Pearson believed that they should not spend money on 'a derelict track', and Alderman Blythe declared that the days of the 'lumbering juggernauts' were numbered. Alderman Gadie condemned the very notion of extending outside the city – an ironic comment from the man who as Waterworks Chairman was to win lasting acclaim for vast reservoirs served by a full-scale Corporation-owned passenger-carrying steam railway, 30 miles outside the city! And in true Bradford fashion Councillor Robinson enquired why anyone should want to go to Brighouse at all.

The answer was, of course, that Brighouse, not Bailiff Bridge, was the natural terminus; many people worked there, and the extended service would be popular and profitable. Other cities such as Leeds and Sheffield were also extending their tramways. The Council duly voted on 14th November 1927 to promote a Bill enabling them to purchase, regauge and link up the tracks, operate motor buses outside the City (though not into Brighouse unless Halifax consented) and (less pleasantly) to replace trams and trolleybuses by motor buses if desired.

In December a detailed examination of the Bailiff Bridge-Brighouse route showed that after regauging, the distance between tracks would be only four feet, and that if the largest BCT cars (the 30ft 4ins-31ft 8ins long five-window type) were used, on one of the curves the minimum clearance between passing trams at roof level would be only 9ins, but no objection was raised. Curiously, no one informed the Committee of an earlier examination of the rail profiles which had revealed that the track was in fact so well worn that the wheel flanges would soon commence riding on the bottom of the rail groove; accusations of 'dereliction' were dangerously near the truth.

The imminence of through bus services from Huddersfield to Bradford via Brighouse was not considered important, as the bus fares would be high enough to protect the trams. However, conflict between the two modes of transport did not arise, as in late February 1928 Halifax broke off the negotiations, possibly over the issue of tramcar kerbside loading at Brighouse terminus. Duly amended, the Bill received the Royal Assent on 28th August, and Bradford purchased the Bailiff Bridge-Brighouse track as part of an intricate deal whereby on 30th March 1929, Halifax withdrew the trams which used it and agreed to their replacement next day by a Huddersfield-Bradford bus service jointly worked by Huddersfield, Bradford and the Hebble Bus Service. The abandoned track was removed by West Riding County Council at Bradford's expense about three years later, and the Bradford-Bailiff Bridge (13) tram service, deprived of many of its passengers, was reduced to a part-time provision from 9th November 1932.

Elsewhere in the city the 'high speed' upholstered trams had proved so popular that £10,000 was voted for additional rewound

A change of driver for the 'Leeds Road Flyer', alias Pullman car No. 1, outside Thornbury Depot on a return journey from Stanningley about 1928. The 'modern six-window' car behind it is No. 210.

motors, more upholstery and the purchase of an 'Electrolux' vacuum cleaner for the moquette. The latest seats, leather-covered by Laycock Engineering, were extra-comfortable, long and wide, and, when used in the upper saloon, were arranged in transverse 2-and-1 fashion, further reducing the top-deck seating to 33. Ultimately leather was used upstairs and moquette downstairs.

The 'Leeds Road Flyer' meanwhile had most unfortunately not maintained its early promise, and thoughts of further single-deckers had been quietly forgotten. The fault lay in the bogie coupling-rods whose bearings could not withstand the powerful torque of the motors; no matter how often they were renewed they wore unevenly, causing the couplings to clank like an old goods locomotive. Also the small diameter of the wheels tended to cause loss of rail-adhesion when the car was being braked at speed, and the resultant 'flats' which developed on the tyre surfaces had to be wastefully ground off in the Works every three weeks, thus allowing critics the opportunity to enquire where 'the mystery car' was, and how much it had cost.

When it transpired that the final cost was £3,992 1s 6d – double the original estimate – both the 'Flyer' and its creators passed under a cloud, and for the rest of its career the car was to be seen disconsolately tailing older, slower cars between City and Stanningley – a sad fate for such a brave and innovative venture. Perhaps the bold fleet number 1 had been a bad omen; almost-contemporary London County Council and Portsmouth Corporation tramcars numbered 1 similarly failed to usher in a new era.

The 'flats' which afflicted the 'Flyer' were not unknown on the other BCT tramcars, but on these they were avoidable and thus incurred severe reprimands, as the process of carborundum-grinding them out shortened the life of the tyre. Accordingly drivers who detected the tell-tale rhythmical thumping noise as the tram rolled along usually took surreptitious remedial action at the outer terminus: they wound down the slipper brake hard to jack the wheels clear of the rail, then partially applied the wheel

brake as well as a few notches of power. This unusual activity was always a puzzle to waiting passengers, as the tram sounded to be moving even though it was actually static, but by the time they stepped on board the 'flat' had been ground away by the brake shoes.

Approval for roofs for the open-air Forster Square 'sheep pens' led to the erection of a trial 'glazed awning on iron pillars with a narrow glazed facia beneath the eaves' at the Heaton (28/29) barrier in March 1928. Similar 'awnings' without the facias were then approved for the other island barriers in all-day use ie Undercliffe (20, 22/23), Greengates (21) Bradford Moor (29/30), Bingley/Crossflatts (23/24), Baildon Bridge (26) and Saltaire (22/25).

Alderman Mrs Kathleen Chambers enquired acidly why the Heaton passengers had been so specially favoured; they had 'only a short distance to travel and get their clothes dry when they got wet through'. As for fears of visually spoiling the Square, she claimed that 'A Council which had allowed the erection of the Post Office in front of the Cathedral had no right to refuse shelters in the name of beauty.' The worthy lady forbore to mention that the longer-distance (Saltaire) passengers whose cause she was championing were not Bradford ratepayers, and that the ill-sited Post Office had been erected two generations previously!

The additional shelters were erected in October/November 1928, at a time when many of the barriers were out of use while the Cheapside track was being relaid and the Manningham Lane services were using temporary termini – Heaton and Baildon Bridge cars in Rawson Square and the remainder at a specially-laid crossover in Manor Row.

Two elegant ladies board 'temporary glass front' car 138 while the conductor examines the 'awning' erected over the Heaton queue barrier in Forster Square in March 1928. The dome of the LMS goods office rises above the tram, and the Midland Hotel is visible in the background.

Courtesy: Mr F. Hartley

An old, faithful servant: Milnes car No. 120 (ex No. 150) seen below at Undercliffe survived in occasional use until August 1931.

Photo: Mr F. Hartley

No 'awning' was installed at the Greengates (21) barrier, however, and Harrogate Road passengers were fated to derive little benefit from the three new 'Greengates Bridge' cars, Nos 80, 90 and 92, which had just entered service. Six months earlier, on 16th April, the Manager had informed the Committee that the Street Improvement Committee intended to widen Harrogate Road, thus necessitating the re-siting of two sections of track at a cost of £7,893. As the remainder of the track between Undercliffe and Greengates was due for renewal in 1932 at a further cost of £36,528, the Committee had agreed that motor buses should replace the trams, and tenders for Leyland 'Titan' buses had been accepted in June.

Presumably, no one had thought of notifying the Works bodyshop of changed circumstances, so that when cars Nos. 80 and 90 made their debut in August, they were allowed no more than one trial trip to Greengates, and were never seen there again, while unfortunate No. 92 was denied even that privilege – perhaps awkward questions would have been asked. All three had 'wide' bodies incorporating upholstered seats, high-speed motors and newly-introduced frameless plate-glass windows (with Rawlings lifting mechanism) on the upper deck – luxuries never to be sampled by Greengates folk who continued to endure the wooden seating and 'slow' motors of the earlier 'Greengates' cars, not to mention the Spartan comforts of their peak-hour open-top assistants. Reluctantly car No. 70 made the final ascent from Greengates terminus at 10.57pm on 11th November 1928. The long decline of Bradford's tramways had begun.

Apart from the overhead crossing of the Bolton-Bankfoot trolleybus wires at Undercliffe terminus, which was quickly removed, the Greengates wiring remained intact for about two years, being re-attached to new poles wherever road-widening occurred, as the Manager intended to instal trolleybuses when the Undercliffe tramway closed. However, measurements taken in 1930 indicated that double-deck trolleybuses could not squeeze

beneath the railway bridge, and the tram wires were quietly removed. The displaced 'Greengates' cars – Nos. 64-75 and 80, 90 and 92, were shared out between all the depots, enabling their extra-low ceilings and door lintels to make an unfavourable impression on the heads and hats of a wider clientele.

The year of mixed fortunes drew to an end. Some improvements had been achieved – on the Halifax Road reserved track the single-line bottleneck at Hillstones had been eliminated at last, and much of the track leading to Dudley Hill had been renewed, although beyond that point the line to Tong Cemetery was to be merely 'kept in repair' despite its heavy usage. Trolleybuses were once again being proposed for Thackley at a cost of £43,572 compared with £148,000 for complete renewal of the worn-out tramway.

Although the Chairman had declared that there was still a place for all three forms of transport, Bingley UDC had already agreed to 'grant facilities' for future trolleybus replacement of trams, and a Parliamentary Bill was being prepared for trolleybus powers on all tram routes where not already authorised. The mighty winds which buffeted the Queensbury cars on 23rd November 1928, compelling their drivers to halt only at sheltered stopping-places, were merely the forerunners of even mightier tempests which were to shake the Department.

Looking back, there had indeed been a new beginning, though not for the trams. For them it had been a false dawn.

'Beauty and the Beast' was the title given to this photograph by *Commercial Motor* in November 1928, but which was which? Squat, lowbridge Leyland 'Titan' No. 367 collecting passengers at the former Greengates 'sheep pen' or roomy, symmetrical Brush car No. 36 (ex No. 72 ex No 128)? The tramcar gave 29 years of service, but the bus retired, worn out, after only seventeen years. *Photo: the late Mr G. Crowther*

12 - SACKINGS AND SPECTRES

Notwithstanding the likelihood that the tramway network was going to contract considerably within a few years, routes not specifically threatened had to be properly maintained, and during 1929 Croft Street, St. Mary's Road, Leeds Road (Harris Street-Hall Ings) and Whetley Hill (Arthington Street-Ashwell Road) were treated to smooth new permanent way. Conversely, the cost of removing track and reinstating the road surface when routes closed began to cast a shadow over tramway finances, as the Ministry had ruled that it should be paid for out of revenue. So the trams were to pay for their own funeral.

The design of the tramcars was undergoing yet another minor change. The 'wide' lower-deck type in vogue since 1922 had been intended for mounting exclusively on Dick Kerr trucks, but with the withdrawal of older cars, Boving and Hurst Nelson trucks were now more readily available, and the body width was therefore decreased by 2¾ins to accommodate all three truck types. The last 'wide' car, No. 53, which was also the last car to inherit an existing canopy top deck from its predecessor, had entered service in October 1928, and the next pair to leave the Works, cars No. 23 and 55 on Boving trucks, were not only built to the new 'intermediate' width but also sported flush steel-panelled vestibules in place of conventional wooden panelling. On No. 23 the panels comprised two sheets welded together horizontally, whereas on No. 55 (and six-window No. 207 soon afterwards) one-piece sheets were used, but as it proved quicker and cheaper to repair wooden vestibules in the event of collisions, the experiment was not repeated.

By this time all trams built or bought since 1919 were earmarked for 'high-speed' motors, an improvement which was also extended to many of the 'high four-window' and equally tall 'vestibuled six-window' tramcars – to the detriment of their availability, as the increased size of the motors necessitated the insertion of extra leaves into each carriage spring; always unable to pass beneath the Greengates and Windhill bridges, they were now too high for Bowling Bridge also.

By March 1931, 73 'high-speed' cars were in service, and 140 trams, mostly post-war, had been upholstered. Bankfoot depot had received a quota of the speedier cars in order to match the Manchester Road tramcar schedules to those of the Oakenshaw trolleybuses, to the envy of the Stanningley drivers who frequently complained of their slow (or 'scrap', as they called them) 1914-vintage 'five-window' cars. Confidently the Chairman promised high-speed upholstered cars for every route within a few years, though his announcement failed to please the city's Safety First Council, disturbed by a recent 'high-speed' tram journey from Odsal to City which had taken no more than 5¾ minutes, an average of 23.4mph inclusive of stops. No complaints were received from the passengers, however!

Static improvements were in progress too. During the summer of 1929 the Tramways Department removed from the old, gloomy headquarters at 7, Hall Ings (on the eve of their demolition) to No. 11, Forster Square, overlooking the 'tram station', and, more

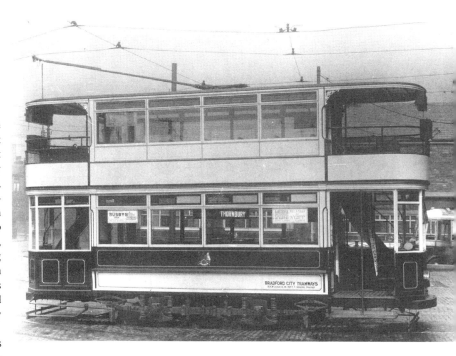

Before entering service in October 1929, tramcar No. 125 was photographed outside Thornbury depot to demonstrate its design improvements – frameless plate-glass upper saloon windows and reduced upper deck lining out, which produced a cleaner, less elaborate effect. The truck is one of the sturdy Boving units purchased in 1919. *Photo: Bradford City Tramways*

humbly, a waiting room was erected at Birkenshaw terminus at the joint expense of BCT and Yorkshire Woollen.

Financial results for 1928-9 provided an ironic contrast: the £9,640 profit accrued by the trams and the parcels department was converted into a £6,221 loss by the tracklesses and buses, in addition to which a deficit of £17,500 on the purchase and resale of a private bus company was charged to the trams. Not surprisingly the fares had to be raised; the maximum fare was now 2½d within the city and 3d outside.

In November the installation of trolleybus equipment on the Allerton (6) tramway reached completion, and following a triumphal excursion on a newly-delivered double-deck trolleybus, the last tramcar ran on the evening of 30th November 1929. Embarrassingly the new, highly-acclaimed vehicles proved unequal to the steep climb through Allerton village which the

Descending Allerton Road between Chapel Lane and the new Rhodesway, tram No. 80 (ex No. 127) halts at Street Gap Farm to pick up a passenger. *Photo: Mr F. Hartley*

old, slow-motored trams had surmounted uncomplainingly. Although the deficiency was rectified by the manufacturers whose fault it was, antagonistic councillors added yet another complaint to their mounting catalogue of grievances against the Manager.

Duckworth Lane tramcar passengers acquired kerbside loading facilities similar to those now enjoyed by the Allerton trolleybus passengers at their queue barrier a few yards away when a new siding was laid in lower Sunbridge Road early in 1930.

Several of the now elderly 'temporary front' cars were withdrawn from service, as was the old illuminated car (once No. 10) whose role was assumed by No. 33, the last of the 'white board' and Brush open-top tramcars. Surprisingly six open-top Milnes cars were retained for special duties – Nos. 10 (ex 145), 46 (ex 146), 120 (ex 150), 137, 168 and the towing-car, once No. 189.

Observing that private buses now outnumbered the trams on the Manningham Lane section, the manager urged the Licensing Committee to impose a 6d minimum fare on all non-Corporation

Last days of the Saltaire and Thackley route, 1930: three-year old car No. 29 under new trolleybus wires enters the short section of single track at Town Gate, Idle. *Courtesy Mr A. D.Packer*

A lively scene at Stanningley about 1930: five-window car No. 146 has delayed crossing over to the 'down' track at the terminus to allow a slow-moving veteran motor-car to chug past. A pedal cyclist keeps pace without difficulty!

Copyright: Woods of Bradford

buses within the city boundary, but when his actions became known, widespread protest and public condemnation followed.

Since the summer of 1929 the long-threatened Thackley and Saltaire (32) trams had been witnessing the relentless onward march of trolleybus poles and wires along their route. Old controversies had died away; the shaken and jolted passengers could no longer summon strength to sign petitions, and the most vociferous opponent of change (Alderman Stringer) could not deny that partly through his actions as Chairman of Finance the Tramways Department no longer possessed the means to afford complete track renewal. Even Shipley UDC had consented to the conversion, driving a shrewd bargain as they did so.

In their last days the Thackley trams had to undergo severe trials, not least a fearsome rail-joint at Windhill which, if approached incautiously, would jar the entire car and cause the lifeguard tray to drop with a clatter on to the setts. Wisely the Department never despatched a 'high-speed' car to those perilous seas, and only one tram (21) ever offered upholstered comfort to its passengers.

The last car, No. 57, quietly left Saltaire on the evening of 29th March 1930, clattering across 'Cobweb Corner' and inching under Windhill Bridge before beginning the patient climb to Thackley, at which point the electricity supplies, long accustomed to the leisurely ways of the trams and fearful of what the morrow might bring in the form of power-hungry, fast-accelerating trolleybuses, nervously blew a fuse and left No. 57 and its passengers temporarily marooned in the night.

The closure relieved the Bolton depot staff of the need to segregate their trams; previously they had had to arrange schedules so that the low 'Windhill Bridge' cars worked alternate journeys to Eccleshill (33) as did the more miscellaneous Idle (31) cars. However, the Idle tramway was next for closure, though not before a trial of strength had been staged in Idle Road, where a new Saltaire via Thackley trolleybus swerved to avoid a wagon and wrecked the vestibule of an Idle tram.

A more serious collision occurred in Cheapside on 27th July 1930, when a chronically impatient West Yorkshire Road Car bus tired of following a tram downhill, pulled out into the path of approaching car No. 164 and violently derailed it, splintering the vestibule. Although the tram conductor and passengers were thrown to the floor, they fared better than the occupants of the bus, whose heads smashed through the windows. Breakdown gangs took an hour to separate the vehicles, and the bus driver was deservedly fined for dangerous driving.

The slow contraction of the fleet enabled the Works to dispose of most of the remaining pre-war non-standard trucks – Brush AA and 21E, Mountain and Gibson, Peckham and ex-Mid Yorkshire – so that all top-covered cars now ran on 1914-1921 vintage 7ft wheelbase Hurst Nelson, Boving or Dick Kerr units. In March 1930 new car No. 60 was the last to receive the modern frameless upper-deck windows; subsequent construction reverted to oak-framed sheet glass, possibly reclaimed from withdrawn trams. Car No. 87 entered service with up-to-the-minute chromium plating on its controller top and brake handle, but daily wear and tear eventually caused the underlying brass to reappear.

Sharply increasing competition on the longer routes produced a Departmental loss of £29,963 while £38,403 had to be invested in new track; nevertheless the Rate Fund confiscated its usual short-sighted £10,000, so that within a year the vital reserves were reduced from £123,729 to a mere £45,363. The situation was not helped by the incorporation of Clayton into the city, as the 2½d stage on the Queensbury route had to be extended from Horton Bank Top to the new boundary at Calder Banks.

One resourceful passenger avoided farepaying altogether: a Great Horton dog had become so accustomed to accompanying his owner on visits to friends at Queensbury that eventually he 'took the lead' and made the journey unaccompanied, travelling by tram in both directions and enjoying a hearty meal at the home of his surprised hosts.

The passing of the Corporation's Trolley Vehicle Order 1930, formally authorised the abandonment of the tramways. The Chairman stressed that the powers would not necessarily be used in full, as the Committee had as yet no idea what course of action would be followed on any particular route. The Manager had no doubts about the issue; he was adamant that trams would be replaced by trolleybuses.

But events were swiftly moving to a climax. Alarmed by the serious loss of traffic, worsening finances and continual criticism of the management, the Committee voted on 1st September 1930, to reorganise the Department. A fortnight later Mr Wilkinson resigned, aged only 56.

Promptly the Committee appointed the Traffic Superintendent, Mr Stirk, as acting manager, and persuaded Lord Ashfield, chairman of the London company tramways, to allow Mr Spencer to investigate the Department and advise how its fortunes could be restored. For the next six months Mr Spencer paid regular visits while the Chairman, his deputy and Mr Stirk studied conditions in London, and the Works Superintendent, Mr N. A. Scurrah, inspected London's North Finchley and Stonebridge depots, Hendon and Chiswick works and the AEC factory at Southall.

Meanwhile many of the councillors were naively musing how the Department 'could have drifted so badly' since Mr Spencer left in 1918 – a trend of thought which did them little credit. Labour disputes, the fatal consequences of the General Strike, demands for lower fares as well as maximum profits, and the outflow of hard-earned reserves to subsidise the Rate Fund, had stifled the tramways' ability to operate profitably, while Mr Wilkinson's persistent advocacy of tracklesses had alienated him from the public. In November the Chairman, Councillor Irvine Smith, also retired, leaving the way open for new leadership.

On 13th December Mr Charles Richard Tattam, M.Inst.T, was appointed General Manager with effect from 1st April 1931. He had been operational manager of the Balfour Beatty group whose transport subsidiaries included Cheltenham and District, Leamington and Warwick, Llanelly, Mansfield and Notts. & Derby. As he was not an engineer Mr H.J. Troughton, A.M.Inst.,C.E., was appointed Rolling Stock Superintendent. Their new chairman was Councillor Walter Hodgson, a well-respected native of Thornton.

Mr Spencer's report, published in August 1931, made drastric comparisons and recommendations. Although the London companies' fleets were 41% larger than Bradford's, the Tramways Department's expenditure on wages, superannuation, workmen's compensation, sick pay and holiday pay was substantially higher than London's. Electricity charges were 33% higher than in Sheffield, while London's repair workshops achieved double Thornbury's output despite employing 33% fewer staff. Car washing took two hours by hand in Bradford but only three minutes in London with a high pressure jet. Track costs, 31% more expensive in Bradford, could be largely avoided if no further tramways were relaid, provided of course that trolleybuses or motor buses could give a more economical service. The practice of raiding the reserves and renewals fund was rightly condemned, as was the availability of workmen's fares and weekly passes at holiday times. Since only nine services now paid their way, fare evasion and the over-riding of fare stages called for greater vigilance. Tramcar speeds and lighting warranted further improvement, but seating capacities should revert to their pre-upholstery levels.

Local residents' suspicions that Thornbury Works was a 'convalescent home' were duly confirmed when over-age employees, 100 temporary workmen and foremen's deputies were dismissed without any visible effect on efficiency – indeed, overhauls were speeded up and failures on the road halved. By agreement with the unions wages were reduced by 2s 0d and holidays cut from twelve days to eight for the space of one year, and the Corporation Electricity Department volunteered a price reduction worth £11,500 per annum. Layover times at termini were reduced (a long overdue measure in many cases) with a saving of fifteen trams per day and £9,000 a year in wages, and hundreds of tram standards were filled with reinforced concrete to prolong their lives, unfortunately sacrificing their ornamental finials in the process. Not all Mr Spencer's recommendations were accepted: the old, cramped seating arrangements were not revived, and the bus services were pruned but not purged.

Mr Tattam's first public appearance was at the formal opening of the Greengates (via Idle) trolleybus route on 20th March 1931. When the last Idle (31) tram left the now-repaired Alexandra Hotel the following night for the ascent to Five Lane Ends and the depot, the last of the 30 year-old Demerbe rails passed into history, and the Bolton-Five Lane Ends section, relaid so controversially only six years previously, lapsed into peak-hour and bad-weather use until Mr Tattam ordered its discontinuance on 7th September; six years later the rails were removed for re-use.

Bolton depot was handed over to the trolleybuses, and its last remaining tramcars serving the Eccleshill route migrated to Thornbury depot. In order to provide off-street 'shunting' ie parking space for Peel Park 'specials' as well as all-year storage for snowploughs, a siding was laid alongside the Bolton shed. It was first used for the Bradford Pageant in July 1931, when 50,000 visitors to Peel Park travelled by tram and trolleybus. A special tram service was operated from Forster Square to a new crossover at Lister Lane, as the alternative route via Otley Road was limited by the capacity of Church Bank.

The trams were busy elsewhere too. In the first week of July they transported 1,573,080 passengers, ranging from 39,611 on the Baildon Bridge section to 419,186 on the Bradford Moor-Heaton and Crossflatts-Undercliffe cross-city services. With peak-hour frequencies such as one car every two minutes in Manchester Road there was an endless, purposeful procession of smart, dignified vehicles along all the principal thoroughfares where passengers rarely troubled to sprint for a car, as the next was usually in sight.

West of the city, slum clearance and the creation of new Corporation estates at Whetley Lane, Rhodesway and the approaches to Thornton village had increased tramcar patronage to such an extent that the already improved Thornton (7) service had to be augmented by regular shortworkings to School Green (6) and Fairweather Green (5), necessitating a 950-yard extension of the negative feeder cable from Four Lane Ends. Although the last car at night from Thornton travelled back to Duckworth Lane depot, the preceding cars to School Green and Thornton retired to rest in the little Fairweather Green depot in readiness for the first trips to Thornton and City next morning. Sufficient 'high-speed' cars had been allocated to Duckworth Lane depot for these services, providing a fast, lively ride up and down the Thornton Road sleeper track, whereas the normal Duckworth Lane (8) service was maintained by 'slow' cars, as the stops were closely-spaced and the loadings so heavy that the conductors could not have collected all the fares had journey times been reduced.

Continuing tramcar improvements included modern circuit-breakers in place of fuses, new or modernised resistances and greatly increased interior lighting: commencing in November 1930, the maplewood ceilings were overpainted pale cream and the dim bowl-type lighting gave way to 'floodlighting' ie bright 'Seagull' enamel lampholders as fitted to the latest trolleybuses. Plans to equip two of the 'high speed' cars with modern pneumatic and magnetic brakes at a cost of £250 per car were parsimoniously disallowed by the Finance Committee.

The long-term implications of Mr Spencer's report were beginning to affect the permanent way. Whereas in 1930 the track in Bridge Street (Union Street-Croft Street), Godwin Street and Westgate (to John Street) and the Easby Road/Laisteridge Lane junction had been carefully renewed, the 1931 programme was restricted to the St. Enoch's Road/Fair Road curve only.

Tramcar construction had quietly ceased as soon as Mr Tattam was appointed. Car No. 205, last of the long production line, entered service in January 1931, on a fully-reconditioned Boving truck, and like its predecessors Nos. 178, 125, 82 and 60 incorporated a modest touch of luxury in the form of brown grained leathercloth lining panels in the lower saloon, in place of polished wood.

Little-used rolling stock was now due for elimination. First to go was the unfortunate 'Leeds Road Flyer', on whose record card was written the unsentimental entry: 'To Works, Apl. 11, 1931 – breaking up' – a sad day for the craftsmen whose combined skills had reached their finest expression in the magnificently-constructed vehicle only four years previously. Its body survived 50 years as a seaside bungalow at Reighton Gap. Last of the condemned cars was the final open-top ('low deck') car, No. 168; still on the Peckham truck which it had 'borrowed' from a Brush car in 1917, it entered the Works for dismembering in August, after which the passenger fleet consisted solely of double-deck top-covered vestibuled and 'temporary front' cars.

Meanwhile the Works body-shop had been found to contain a surplus of timber and body parts, and the craftsmen were allowed to use them for the construction of one further body which was mounted on a Hurst Nelson truck, completed in June, 1931, and numbered 14. To emphasise the break with the past the new car did not receive the artistic rose-shaded gilt fleet numerals of the Wilkinson era which had last been applied to a freshly-repainted car (No. 235) a week earlier; No. 14 was the first to display the plain modern Gill Sans numerals of a soberer, simpler decade. Allocated to Thornbury depot, the newest car began life inauspiciously, suffering three minor collisions before the end of the year.

The tiny four-car depots at Lidget Green and Fairweather Green closed in the last week of March 1932, as the cost savings outweighed the 'dead mileage' thus incurred when the trams returned to their parent depots. On 5th May the Committee accepted in principle a proposal that the unprofitable outermost sections of certain tramways (ie Bingley to Crossflatts, Odsal to Shelf and Tong Cemetery to Birkenshaw and Drighlington) should be handed over to minimum-fare motor bus services. On hearing this, a resentful Drighlington tramcar jumped off the track at Westgate Hill and caused a van to ricochet into a house, with dire results for the van but not a scratch for the tram!

However, the Traffic Commissioners rejected the Bingley-Crossflatts bus licence application, and the trams survived, assisted by a competitive series of 1½d stages from City to Saltaire and Baildon Bridge, and later, a bargain 2d fare all the way to Baildon Bridge and Bingley. Christmas shopping was boosted by a maximum 1d fare within the City; 127,000 extra passengers were carried, the traders were delighted, and the tram revenues bore up well.

In February 1933 demands arose for the restoration of a full-time tramcar service beyond Wyke as far as Shirley Manor, but as the average number of passengers on the Bailiff Bridge cars prior to their curtailment had been only eight, no action was taken. Looking to the future, Mr Tattam forecast that the Department would be profitable once more within four years when the capital debt decreased.

There were indications, however, that the Tramways Department was not as firmly in control of events as it thought it was. On 15th February 1933, unsettling reports of a ghost tram travelling through Frizinghall towards Saltaire at about 3am were received from a councillor whose friends had often heard it but never managed to see it when they clambered out of bed and looked out of the window. A second councillor confirmed the story, while a third recalled that a well-known driver had vowed shortly before his death that he would come back and take his place on a tram from time to time. Reassuringly Mr Tattam suggested that these nocturnal noises were probably caused by a tramcar taking sand to Saltaire depot. But were they? Waiting at the Frizinghall fare stage one misty day Mr F. Hartley espied a 'Preston' car approaching through the swirling haze, but to his mystification it never arrived .....

Bradford's last new tramcar was No. 14, glimpsed here at Eccleshill in 1931.   *Photo: Mr F. Hartley*

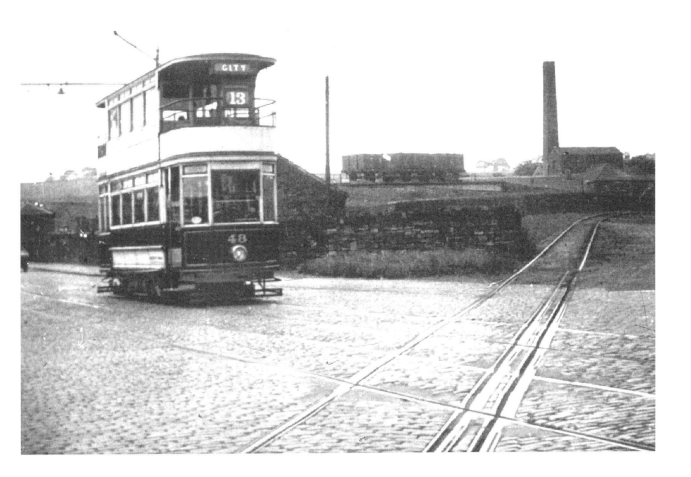

When this photograph was taken in July 1932 the Bailiff Bridge route on which tram No. 48 was working still enjoyed a full-time service. The car was about to traverse the mixed gauge level crossing in Huddersfield Road, Low Moor, which was used by the Low Moor Ironworks.

Photo: the late G. N. Southerden

The tram tracks in Commercial Street, Shipley (foreground) had been disused for two years when a Baildon Bridge tramcar (with medium-height canopy top and Boving or Hurst Nelson truck) rumbled across Fox Corner on its descent of Otley Road.

Photo: Mr S. L. Smith

13 - THE GREAT SNOWSTORM

'He giveth snow like wool and scattereth the hoarfrost like ashes;

He casteth forth his ice like morsels, and who is able to abide His frost?'

(Psalm 147)

On Friday afternoon, 24th February 1933, snow began to fall thickly and continued without abatement. During the evening the tramcars maintained the services with little difficulty, their tracks obliterated, windscreens continually obscured and the resolute rumble of their wheels unusually subdued and muted.

All night the snowplough cars travelled over every route as the depth of snow relentlessly increased, but despite their most valiant efforts the mounting drifts gradually defeated the service trams next day. One by one they struggled back to their depots; in lower Bolton Road, Eccleshill car No. 13 quietly slid off the ice-packed rails and parked neatly at the kerbside while its companions labouring uphill were halted in their tracks. Two trams were cut off altogether near Shelf and another beyond Wyke; only on the fairly level Crossflatts route was a regular service maintained. And still the snow fell.

When the blizzard reluctantly gave way to a slow thaw on Sunday evening a few skeleton services were attempted. That night every available employee including fitters from the Works set out with shovels; some toiled up to 24 hours without rest, while away from the tram routes a thousand men (half of whom were unemployed) worked to clear the 'highways and byways' of their vast accumulations.

On Monday evening one car reached Bolton Junction and another Lidget Green, returning gingerly on the same tracks, while the tortuous Heaton route was reopened in two sections with a single-line service to Buxton Street and a solitary shuttle car from that point to the terminus. But the exposed uplands of Thornton, Queensbury, Shelf, Wibsey, Drighlington and Birkenshaw remained inaccessible, and many tramcars were trapped inside Thornbury depot by hard-frozen points.

Next day snow-shovellers in Halifax Road removed a 4ft-depth of snow as far as Furnace Inn, where the two stranded trams were dug out, jacked up on to emergency bogies and towed back to Bankfoot depot. Meanwhile at Little Horton a rapidly-tiring snowplough car was vainly attacking the hard-packed bank of snow which barred the way to St. Enoch's Road, achieving nothing but a pair of deep grooves in the rail surface, ground by the helplessly spinning wheels. Not until a train of three tramcars was coupled up behind the plough could any impression be made upon the drifts; as they strenuously forced their way uphill a team of men shovelled hard to disperse what the plough had cast aside. Forty-five tons of salt were used by BCT during the long storm.

At Bolton depot where the trolleybuses were unable to venture forth until Thursday, the staff were secretly amused to observe that the snowplough car had turned into Idle Road to clear the disused tram tracks, with the pleasing result that Five Lane Ends (31A) tramcars returned after more than a year's absence for a few last triumphant days of service.

By the time that the Drighlington, Birkenshaw and Shelf workings had resumed on Thursday 2nd March, all Corporation routes were operational again, although for six further weeks the Queensbury trams were still venturing between high banks of smoke-sullied snow.

The emergency over, each of the battered snowplough cars was examined at the Works, where Nos. S1/2/3/7/8/10 were found to be unfit for further service and were replaced by withdrawn 'temporary front' cars – lower-deck and truck only, with second-hand trolley mast – whilst S9/12/14/16 retired without replacement. Then, thoroughly renewed, the little fleet was redistributed between the depots, ie Saltaire – S1, Horton Bank Top – S2, Bankfoot – S3/6, and Duckworth Lane – S7/8, whilst

The tram must get through .... when tramcar No. 42 returning from Bingley on Monday, 27th February 1933, found its path blocked by a snowbound lorry on the approach to Cottingley Bridge, the staff and passengers joined forces to push the obstruction aside. *Photo: Yorkshire Observer*

Recommending the closure of the Drighlington (16) section earlier in the year, the manager had stressed "the unsatisfactory nature of the permanent way", surely the understatement of the decade. The 30 year-old track with its many passing-places and obsolete narrow-tongued points had been severely pounded by the heavy 'Preston' cars and had, in turn, wrought its revenge on them. On one particular 'Preston' tram passengers could glimpse daylight between the upper-deck ceiling and the bulkhead framework as the sorely-tested vehicle swayed, lurched and jolted its way down the hawthorn-flanked country road. The last car was cheered by a small crowd which had gathered to pay an affectionate farewell when it left the terminus at 11.20pm on 8th August 1933. After its departure Drighlington crossroads relapsed into rural darkness when the electric current which fed the large overhead lantern from the tram wires was finally switched off.

Next day the Tong Cemetery (18) service, a peak-hour only facility since 1903, was revived to maintain an unaltered frequency of tramcars as far as the bottom of Westgate Hill, operating alternately with the Birkenshaw (17) service.

Interest in innovation was not quite dead. In June 'Preston' car No. 231 had been fitted with new English Electric controllers embodying quick-break elements on the series and final parallel notches, as well as regenerative braking which could be used in conjunction with the hand-applied mechanical track brake – a popular feature on long descents such as Huddersfield Road. However, they were replaced by standard Dick Kerr DB1 controllers within five years, and when catalogues proclaiming the virtues of modern Westinghouse air braking were received, they were cursorily studied and then filed.

S4/5/10/13/15/18 were shared between Thornbury and Bowling.

Before the next winter ten passenger tramcars (Nos. 2, 27, 31, 43, 55, 79, 93, 103, 105 and 119) were fitted with brackets on their fenders to allow them to carry snowplough blades if the need arose, but in normal winters the special plough fleet sufficed, and after a few years Nos. 2, 55 and 105 lost the fittings.

The great blizzard delayed the renewal of the 'Cock and Bottle' junction where a new curve was laid from Barkerend Road into East Parade for emergency use by city-bound Bradford Moor cars, and when summer returned, kerbside loading facilities were constructed outside the 'Cosy Cinema', Wibsey, thereby removing trams from the narrow entrance to High Street. Similar improvements were contemplated for Stanningley terminus where the road was being widened and a trolley reverser erected at last, but the necessary trackwork was never laid.

Blizzards of a different kind affected Departmental finances in 1933 to the extent that the Rate Fund which so often had raided the tramway reserves now had to refund £40,000. In addition to the effects of industrial depression, the tramway abandonment process was taking its toll of the profits, as there were fewer revenue-earning trams to repay the loans and interest on track renewals carried out in past years.

In the last days of the Drighlington route car No. 140 – originally No. 240, one of the first Bradford-built trams – was photographed battling its way down the 30-year old track near the city boundary.
Copyright: Yorkshire Post

14 – GETTING ON AND MINDING THE TRAMS

(Local saying indicating progress tempered with caution)

In the Spring of 1933 attention turned to the Duckworth Lane tramway – a route so heavily used that services operated from 5.30am to midnight with cars every five minutes mid-morning, every three minutes at the morning peak and from midday to 6.30pm, and every four minutes thereafter until 11.10pm, followed by five late depot journeys. The White Abbey Road (City Road-Arthington Street) section was now in need of renewal, and contrary to all its recent decisions the Tramways Committee accepted the manager's recommendation to relay it

A study in Bradford tramcar design, July 1932. Thornbury-built No. 43 at the Crossflatts queue barrier in Forster Square has a 'wide', four-window body, medium-height canopy top and DK21E truck while 'modern six-window' car 204 (left) waiting to proceed to the Heaton barrier has a taller bottom deck, a high canopy top and a Boving truck.

and seek competitive tenders for the work. The decision was sound, as most of the other track was relatively new:–

City to Godwin Street 1929, Sunbridge Road to John Street 1931, Arthington Street to Ashwell Road 1929 and Toller Lane to terminus 1924.

The decision was challenged by the Deputy Chairman (Councillor Carter) who successfully argued that the work should be carried out by the City Engineer's staff who were fully conversant with the tramways and whose assistance would be needed in any case with the laying of temporary track. For the first time for years loan sanction, for £8,100, was sought.

Despite these promising signs, the abandonment policy was still being pursued elsewhere. On 13th December 1933, the Committee decided to convert the Eccleshill, Thornton and Lidget Green routes to trolleybus operation, as the trams already ran under trolleybus wires for part or all of their route. However, there was still an outstanding debt of £32,000 for the permanent way on the three routes, and if their trams could have been permitted to survive a few more years they could possibly have redeemed it, as the routes were profitable and the tracks not worn out.

Next, the life-expired condition of most of the track on the Shelf, Heaton and Birkenshaw sections led the Committee to approve the use of motor buses, and discussions on the future of the Baildon Bridge service were opened with the tramways' inveterate competitor, the West Yorkshire Road Car Company.

Through all the minor changes that had taken place in the fleet livery over the preceding fifteen years, the basic colours of Prussian blue and ivory had never varied, but despite their undoubted durability and smartness, Mr Tattam considered them somewhat sombre. Possibly also suspecting that painting costs in the Works were excessive, he arranged for one tramcar to be painted in experimental colours by a private contractor, for which reason the work was carried out at Duckworth Lane depot. The selected car, No. 34, reappeared in Oxford blue and deep cream, with conventional lining and numerals but with the underside of the balcony roof canopies painted in a curious milk-chocolate hue. Garish and avant-garde, the trial colours found no favour.

A disturbing note was sounded on 13th February 1934, when Alderman Louis Smith expressed the (exaggerated) view that as the Duckworth Lane route suffered from 'the oldest cars and the most disgraceful and dangerous track', it should be handed over to trolleybuses instead. In reply the Chairman revealed that road-widening was being planned for White Abbey Road, necessitating the re-siting of the tracks and increasing the cost; nevertheless the Committee wished to retain the trams, as Duckworth Lane was the best route, and 'it was a pity to risk anything there' when the trams were giving satisfaction. As for the 'temporary front' and vestibuled six-window cars used on the route, they would be replaced by 'the very excellent cars always retained on the Thornton route' as soon as the latter closed.

A unique photograph taken in July 1932, at Stanningley terminus, where Bradford and Leeds cars numbered 224 were briefly glimpsed together. The Leeds tram, a 'Horsfield', is probably about to reverse at the bottom of Richardshaw Lane, while at the front of the Bradford 'Preston' car a passenger is wondering how a roll of carpet can be manoeuvred on to the platform.

Photo: the late G. N. Southerden

When photographed in 1932 ascending Wakefield Road (between Foundry Lane and Bowling Church), Birkenshaw-bound tramcar No. 34 still carried ornate Wilkinson-type fleet numbers with its otherwise modern livery. Its next repaint, possibly in March 1933, did not appeal to contemporary taste.

Photo: Mr M. J. O'Connor

The agreed series of abandonments began with the closure of the Eccleshill (33) route on 29th May 1934. On the final evening the service was maintained by cars Nos. 107 and 197, and when Driver Arthur Money piloted No. 197 from Eccleshill village, down Stone Hall Road and Bolton Road and then away via Well Street to Thornbury depot, Bradford's original 1898 electric tramway closed apart from a few yards in Forster Square retained for shunting.

During the preceding year the number of trams overhauled in the Works had shrunk to 72, as the trolleybus fleet was in more urgent need of attention.

On 31st March 1934 Bingley UDC ceased to buy electricity for the trams (and other uses) from Keighley Corporation, whose own trams and tracklesses had been discontinued previously; subsequently their supplies were derived from the Yorkshire Electric Power Company. On the same day the Bradford tramwaymen's wages returned to their 1932 level at a cost of £4,000.

In the interests of safe tramway operation in fog or bad visibility the Department had always operated a strict system of rules. Drivers of outward-bound cars were to give three periodic rings on the footgong and their inward-bound colleagues two, and none should enter a single line unless the conductor had obtained from the nearby fog-box ('bat box') the appropriate 'bat' or staff which should then be handed to the next driver travelling in the opposite direction. Failure to do so caused a violent collision between outward-bound car No. 125 and city-bound car No. 67 on the single line near Thornton Church in dense fog on 1st May. The platform of No. 67 was wrecked, and as it was one of the 1919 low-height 'Greengates' cars no longer needed for its original purpose, it was taken out of service (the first postwar car to be withdrawn), whereas No. 125, only five years old, 'lived to fight another day'.

Further downhill the modern, scenic reservation had by this time acquired the title of 'the rocking-horse track', as the resilience of the sleepers, the open rail-joints and the speed of the trams had combined to produce a lively motion which on one occasion caused an unsteady upper-deck passenger to put his elbow through the window. One of the first public appearances of Alderman Hodgson in his year as Lord Mayor was at the official opening of the Thornton trolleybus service on 20th November 1934, a few hours before the tram service ceased. Ironically, insufficient trolleybuses were available next day, and at the peak-hour a few trams had to help out, possibly to Fairweather Green or School Green only.

To the indignation of Duckworth Lane travellers all the promised 'high-speed' cars (with the possible exception of 73/ 75) were instantly despatched to Thornbury depot, as the Duckworth Lane route was also now doomed to lose its trams before long: the cost of the major relocation of the tracks in the soon-to-be widened White Abbey Road had caused the reluctant committee to change its mind on 21st September. Eleven surplus Siemens-motored trams were offered – vainly – to other 4ft 0ins gauge operators.

Lidget Green (4) also lost its trams on 11th December, provoking complaints that the replacing trolleybuses were less comfortable than the well-upholstered 'high-speed' cars which they had replaced.

The last day of the old year saw the inauguration of Bradford's first traffic roundabout in Victoria Square. Initially it consisted of a white circle painted on the carriageway, but even when it was made permanent, the tramcars continued to travel through

The Lidget Green route did not always enjoy a monopoly of 'high-speed' trams, as demonstrated by Maurice O'Connor when he photographed 'slow' Siemens-motored 'modern six-window car' No. 198 in the Thornton Road kerbside loading bay. The neat, stylish fleet numbers were an experimental breed tried in 1932.

Forster Square in 1932: elegant 'high four-window' car No. 156 on a cross-city journey from Bradford Moor waits at the Heaton 'sheep pen' with its glazed awning while the late-Victorian Post Office and the mediaeval Cathedral provide an imposing background.

it; indeed, the Victoria Square crossover was sited partly within the charmed circle. Similarly the introduction of a gyratory traffic system in Forster Square in August 1932, had not affected the trams which mostly kept to the perimeter of the island when running against the flow.

The Shelf (12) tramcars, lonelier now since the withdrawal of their Halifax colleagues (also numbered 12) in 1933, made the final runs along their level route with its long vistas and 32-year old track on 19th February 1935. As the Halifax Road reserved track was barely ten years old, it was retained as far as Horsfall Playing Fields for 'sports specials', though normal services terminated at Odsal (15).

The occasional pre-1929 practice of equipping newly-built lower decks with the renovated top deck of their predecessors sometimes led to later problems, including premature withdrawal. In August 1935 passengers on car No. 102 complained that the 'top saloon was creaking badly', with the glass in the bulkheads 'floating about in the frames.' The 23-year old top deck was therefore parted from its nine-year old lower half and replaced by a sound unit – only 22 years old! – from withdrawn car No. 140. As the salvaged structure was not rebuilt to modern dimensions it retained its 5ft 3ins roof canopy length which did not match the 6ft balcony length of No. 102. A few cars such as Nos. 13, 164 (and in later years 79, 86, 195 and 239) suffered from 'Hollingworth Droop', ie their balcony canopy roofs had to be propped with tubular stanchions, similar to those fitted to all the 'Preston' cars, when they sagged beneath the weight of ponderous shedman Hollingworth who hopped from roof to roof when greasing the trolley heads.

The Heaton (28/29) and Undercliffe (20/22/23) tramcar services ceased simultaneously on 7th April 1935. At Heaton the event aroused considerable interest; a ciné-photographer recorded cars Nos. 128 and 202 approaching the picturesque terminus (probably on 6th April), and a small group of locals watched as car No. 210 with Driver Railton at the controls commenced the last cross city journey to Bradford Moor. The North Park Road (Oak Lane-St. Mary's Road) section of the route continued in use for the 'shunting' of football specials, which were duly labelled 'Park Gates' whilst those which reversed near the stadium displayed 'Valley Parade'.

As the cross-city links with Bradford Moor (29) and Saltaire (22)/Bingley and Crossflatts (23) were now severed, the Bradford Moor cars commenced a new through service to Saltaire and beyond, displaying different route numbers in each direction

Not long to go: the Heaton service was due for closure when 'Preston' No. 249 was seen descending Wilmer Road on a cross-city journey to Bradford Moor. The dark patch on the tram standard reveals that the tram stop had been moved elsewhere for improved road safety.
Photo: Woods of Bradford

ie Bradford Moor – 30; Saltaire – 25; Bingley and Crossflatts – 24, with peak-hour and Saturday afternoon extras from Killinghall Road (16) to Frizinghall (27).

Uniquely, although Undercliffe had now disappeared from the BCT tram timetable, the suburb continued to enjoy a ghost service more substantial than its Frizinghall counterpart. Each weekday morning at 7.50am a solitary passenger-carrying car made its unobtrusive way up to the terminus and back, leaving the route to the buses for the rest of the day. Mr Tattam later claimed that the line could not be wholly closed because the tracks, relaid in 1924, were not debt-free – but neither were the much newer Duckworth Lane metals. Nevertheless, the retention of the installations proved useful – impenetrable fogs which vanquished the buses allowed brief reappearances of the trams; 'specials' worked as far as Peel Park on gala days, and when the St. Enoch's Road feeder cable gave intermittent trouble, the Wibsey trams and Undercliffe buses exchanged duties.

When the Silver Jubilee of TM King George V and Queen

Mary was celebrated in Bradford on 4th-6th May 1935, fourteen decorated trams and the illuminated car operated on all the surviving routes; the tramwaymen received a day's holiday, and takings on 4th May were higher than on any previous Saturday.

Recognition of the changing nature of the Undertaking came on 15th July when the Tramways Committee decided on a more comprehensive title which was thenceforth displayed on the tramcar rocker panels as 'Bradford Corporation Passenger Transport' otherwise BCPT.

Work on the unsought conversion of the Duckworth Lane (8) route to trolleybuses had been proceeding for some time, making use of numerous poles recovered from the Thornton sleeper track as well as a few bought from the Burnley tramways. For several days in June 1935, the first and last journeys were made by motor bus to allow the overhead linesmen more time for the erection of complex junctions at the depot and termini. A strike at the English Electric Company's Preston works delayed the delivery of the new vehicles, and the trial run was postponed until 24th September. On the afternoon of 1st October Duckworth Lane depot was cleared of all its trams (five-window cars Nos. 146/8 stored there since Spring had already been scrapped), leaving the service to be maintained by 'slow' cars such as Nos. 113, 158, 163, 198, 211 and 212 and possibly 'high-speed' Nos. 73 and 75. The last tram – the staff car driven by Joe Rushworth and conducted by J. Alvin – slipped away un-noticed and unrecorded, as the shedmen, their backs turned, were busily 'kalling', ie wholly absorbed in discussion.

A week later the Chairman announced that the now-redundant tracks in Sunbridge

Although Duckworth Lane was always served by 'slow' trams like 'modern six-window' car No. 211, the replacing trolleybuses such as No. 600 (newly in service on the Allerton route) were so swift that elderly conductors found themselves overworked. Jackson's china shop removed from the Mechanics' Institute before its demolition in 1974; George Newby (right) was a high-class purveyor of fish, poultry and game.
Photo: AEC Ltd

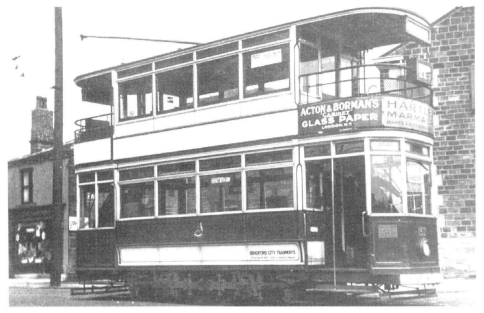

save for the double track on the railway bridge at Bierley Bar, which Bradford had agreed in 1903 to maintain in perpetuity; complete with granite sett paving, it remained undisturbed until 1951.

The rapid pace of route closures in 1935 spelt the doom of nearly 40 tramcars, including the remaining 'temporary front' cars (all Milnes) of which Nos. 110, 172 and 177 had once been dual-gauge trams. Gone too were all the 'five-window' cars, several of the earliest Thornbury-built cars (Nos. 162 ex 229, 140/1/3 ex 240/1/3 and 153 ex 198), nine vestibuled six-window cars including Nos. 128, 170, 190/1 and 203 which bequeathed their 'high-speed' equipment to luckier trams, and No. 183 whose aged bones had not been able to withstand the excitement of a 'high-speed' life. Two of the elegant 'high four-window' cars, No. 156 ('high-speed') and No. 159 ('slow') also bade a dignified farewell. All the above, except the Milnes cars, were fit for many more years of service.

Significantly they were joined by seven 'Preston' bodies, of which three were barely fourteen years old, and one (No. 249) had been upholstered only six months previously; a full ton heavier than the Thornbury-built products, they had developed structural movement on both decks which, in normal circumstances, would have been cured by a visit to the body shop. As they were not yet debt-free, for book-keeping purposes their fleet numbers were transferred to the BCT-built bodies which inherited their 'high-speed' Dick Kerr 21E trucks.

Road, Godwin Street and Westgate as well as John Street, Rawson Square and North Parade were to be retained to allow access to Valley Parade for football specials from the south and west of the city. Whether they were ever used again no one can recall; for rating purposes they were declared disused, and by March 1936 they were officially closed; nevertheless the tracks and overhead wires remained available until 1939.

Negotiations for a Bradford-Dewsbury bus service to supersede the Birkenshaw (17) trams had been concluded with Yorkshire Woollen, whose own trams to Birkenshaw had ceased in March, 1932. Accordingly at about 11.15pm on 29th October 1935, a small knot of onlookers gathered to watch the last car, No. 150, as it rumbled down to the terminus in a light shower of rain. Next morning the Tong Cemetery (18) service was further augmented to maintain an unchanged tramcar frequency to that point, as the new Dewsbury buses were operating at a higher protective fare. Later the abandoned Birkenshaw track was removed by the County Council at the Corporation's expense,

Next for sacrifice was the Baildon Bridge (26) route, originally envisaged as the springboard for long extensions to Baildon and Ilkley but long since swamped by private buses; despite providing a regular and reliable service to Shipley town centre and the woolcombing mills alongside the river (fastidious drivers disliked the smell of wool-grease which pervaded the saloons at the end of shifts), it worked at a loss. The West Yorkshire company agreed to surrender their Lister Park-

Bankfoot bus service provided that BCPT withdrew from Baildon Bridge altogether. On the final day of operation, 4th February 1936, tramcar No. 3 was photographed at the bridge and No. 99 surmounting the crest of Otley Road (Shipley), to which point a new service, City to Branch (26 or 27) was introduced next day to avoid any diminution of tramcar services along Manningham Lane.

A well-attended Rugby match on 22nd February called for twenty trams to and from Odsal in addition to the Wyke tramcars and Oakenshaw trolleybuses. Vainly the automatic circuit-breakers registered protests at the gross overloading of their capacity; every time they blew open they were promptly reset by hand.

Two days later the entire distribution system 'came out in sympathy' when a major short-circuit at the Valley Road power station started a blaze which destroyed the main high-tension switches and plunged the city into darkness at 6.18pm. Only in the Shipley and Bingley districts was any tramcar movement possible, and apart from eleven cars about to re-enter the city at Frizinghall the remainder sought shelter at Saltaire depot overnight while within the city staff armed with oil lamps kept vigil in the darkened trams and trolleybuses. Early next morning a long-disused turbo-generator was revived to provide a limited traction supply until full power was restored on 2nd March.

Brighter days returned with Shopping Week (14th-21st March) for which cars Nos. 24, 42 and 71 were decorated and illuminated. 'During Shopping Week', Gerald Brailsford recalled 50 years later, "the whole city was alive – window-spotting, competitions for the public and prizes for the best display – and that glittering tram with the thousands of glowing bulbs was a jewel rolling along through the darkness like a swaying showboat straight out of fairyland." Once again an off-peak penny fare attracted phenomenal patronage, encouraging Shipley to hire four similar trams for their Carnival Week.

One of the four, No. 248, had been car No. 21 until a few days previously, when together with some of the earliest postwar products – Nos. 11, 39, 63, 'Greengates' 69 and 'high four-window' Nos. 158 and 164 it had inherited a truck and fleet number from a contemporary but less robust 'Preston' body

– a fine tribute to the standard of body construction at Thornbury. Stout bodywork was needed now to withstand the effect of deteriorating tracks; journeys along Keighley Road past the 'Spotted House' were said to produce sensations akin to a voyage across the Bay of Biscay, and partly-worn rail had to be laid to quell passengers' queasiness. Not that substandard track was without its usefulness: Dr Hainsworth used the Queensbury trams as a means of solving the problem of prolonged pregnancies. A journey to Bradford and back usually sufficed.

Requests from Queensbury UDC for a more frequent tram service were neatly sidestepped by BCPT who merely increased the seating capacity of various 'wide' cars and (less comfortably) two 'intermediate' cars by the expedient of providing 2 and 2 seating in the upper saloon, as on most of the 'Preston' cars, producing a total of 19+43=62. Nine of the re-seated cars, Nos. 23, 42/8/9, 52/3, 79, 103 and 104 then took up residence at Horton Bank Top depot.

For the Coronation of King George VI and Queen Elizabeth on 12th May 1937, tramcars 71, 90 and 239 were colourfully decorated at a cost of £61 14s 5d, but the old, much-admired

Illuminated Tram was kept indoors and never used again, its place being taken (inadequately) by a bus. When the newly-crowned sovereigns visited the area on 20th October, travelling from Saltaire via Lister Park and Manningham Lane to a reception at the Town Hall before departing for Halifax, the City-Saltaire trams were suspended from 10.30am until midday, with a shuttle service between Saltaire and Crossflatts, while Manchester Road services did not operate from 11.30am to 12.30pm, so dense were the crowds.

Meanwhile tramcar No. 239, one of the 'stars' of Coronation Week, had 'come down to earth with a bump'. Until a few months earlier its fleet number and truck had belonged to a Bowling depot 'Preston' car, and memories were long. Following an overhaul in the Works on 4th October it was despatched to Bowling, but whereas for the truck the tracks were familiar, for the 'high four-window' body they were forbidden territory. The outcome was unhappily described in the Works records:–

'Roof, trolley-base and boom damaged and 2 upper-deck windows broken by Bowling Bridge.'

The management, however, did not blame the bridge. Instead, they angrily pointed out that since No. 239 lacked the essential letter 'B' on its staircase, the tram should not have been sent there. However, the days of low bridges were drawing to an end, as in February the Committee had voted £49,000 for trolleybuses as replacements for the Dudley Hill (19) and Tong Cemetery (18) trams which passed beneath Bowling Bridge. In anticipation of 'redundancies' within two years two dozen cars were withdrawn from the normal full overhauls schedule, though not at the expense of smartness – six-window car No. 209 was repainted as late as 21st May 1938.

In March 1937 No. 161, last of the original batch of cars built by BCT before the war, and the last reversed-stairs car in the fleet, retired after a working life of 25 years, by no means worn out.

When traffic lights at road junctions were first introduced, many of them could be activated by means of rubber pads embedded in the carriageway; for the trams a 'skate' on the overhead wire performed the same function. The installation of the Great Horton Road/All Saints Road traffic lights understandably brought about the removal of the Board of Trade compulsory tram stop at that point, even though the Corporation had no power to do so.

An unusual transformation occurred on 28th May 1938 when 'Preston' car No. 221 and BCT-built No. 125 exchanged trucks and fleet numbers. Predictably the carriage springs of the Boving truck beneath the 'new' No. 125 sagged under their unaccustomed burden, and the car went for scrap on 11th July.

During the last weeks of tramcar operation up Wakefield Road the conductors had to swing the trolleys manually at the Dudley Hill and Tong Cemetery termini where the automatic reversers had been removed to allow the erection of new trolleybus wiring. Leaving Tong Cemetery for the last time on 5th July 1938 'Preston' No. 226 passed the now-empty Bowling depot whose constricted site made it unsuitable for trolleybuses. The replacement vehicles as well as the former Bowling contingent of trams needed for the Wibsey route were to operate from Thornbury, and on 7th July the newly-dispersed depot staff held a farewell supper.

However, although removal of the rails in Tong Street and upper Wakefield Road soon followed, the tracks to the closed depot and Bowling Hill were retained so that redundant trams could be dismantled there, as final tramway abandonment was envisaged within about four years. Condemned cars were therefore deprived of their trolley equipment and towed by tram up to Bowling depot where (to quote the Rolling Stock Engineer) 'the yard provides a convenient place for the dismantling of trams which have been sold' – a sentiment not necessarily shared by

(Upper) Of this once-familiar scene nothing remains except Bowling Bridge (behind 'Preston' car No. 253 which is returning from Tong Cemetery) and the distant spire of St. John's Church, although much of Dudley Hill-bound No. 251 survives at the National Tramway Museum in the guise of Sheffield railgrinder No. 330.
Photo: H. B. Priestley

(Lower) Against a background of tranquil farmland – as well as a police call box and the remains of the abandoned Drighlington tramway – 'Preston' car No. 244 stands underneath the newly-erected trolleybus turning-circle at Tong Cemetery. *Photo: H. B. Priestley*

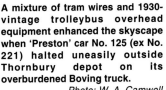

A mixture of tram wires and 1930-vintage trolleybus overhead equipment enhanced the skyscape when 'Preston' car No. 125 (ex No. 221) halted uneasily outside Thornbury depot on its overburdened Boving truck.

Photo: W. A. Camwell

(Below) Surrounded by the wreckage of discarded controllers, resistances and wheelsets, the lower deck of 'high four-window' car No. 163 blazes in Bowling depot yard.

Photo: Bradford CPTD.

householders, as car bodies not sold for further use as bungalows or huts were actually burned not many yards from their front windows!

Although the adjoining permanent-way yard continued to store rails, poles, ballast and setts, the railgrinder (No. 11) previously kept there had departed for Bankfoot depot. And following the withdrawal of fifteen more tramcars including No. 204, the last wooden-seated car, the 135-strong all-'high-speed' fleet was for the first time outnumbered by the trolleybuses but not, as yet, by the motor buses.

A little extra colour entered into the life of the tramcars when No. 52 entered the paintshop in search of a fresh coat of Prussian blue and ivory and, instead, reappeared on 10th July 1937 in what was described as 'blue-black and cream', a new combination which was superseded on 3rd September 1938, when car No. 34 (victim of the earlier 'Oxford blue' trial) was treated to a more pleasing blue-black variously termed 'dark blue' or 'ultramarine', also with pale cream, which was adopted for the whole fleet.

Bradford and Leeds tramcars bade their final farewells to each other on 3rd December 1938, when the LCT cars ran for the last time to Stanningley (foot of Richardshaw Lane), after which they withdrew out of sight across their city boundary a few hundred

yards away. Three of the LCT poles were then 'commandeered' by BCPT as anchor-poles for their now-isolated overhead wires.

The fate of the seven-mile long Crossflatts tramway had been decided in December 1936 when Mr Tattam recommended that trolleybuses should be installed in preference to motor buses, as their longer life would ensure an annual saving of £7,124 despite capital costs of £115,103. Agreement with Shipley and Bingley having been reached, work began at the outer end of the route on 25th May 1938 as soon as the Wakefield Road alterations were complete.

Good quality 'A' type poles retrieved from Bingley during the conversion were used to rejuvenate ageing installations elsewhere. Some took over the bracket arm suspension in Horton Bank and below Arctic Parade where the 1898 Blackwell poles were so slender that they flexed continuously like saplings in a breeze; above Arctic Parade and in All Saints' Road they were used for modern span-wire construction. At St. Enoch's Road some of the 1907 poles which had weathered badly in their exposed position were displaced by stouter 'B' poles probably taken from the Canal Road or Rooley Lane trolleybus routes. All these, together with many of the Blackwell poles and the pre-1907 bracket-arm poles which had been filled with reinforced concrete, were crowned with modern domed copper cowls to keep the rain out. Worn-out round-section copper wire was replaced by new cadmium-copper grooved wire in St. Enoch's Road, Barkerend Road and down the Huddersfield Road reserved track.

When the formidable and complex task of installing the new trolleybus overhead equipment between Forster Square and Crossflatts was nearing completion, the Transport Committee resolved to perform an official opening of the new service, but in the event they also decided to mark the closure of their longest and most important tramway.

And so on Saturday 6th May 1939 spare drivers and shedmen were busily employed in the ferrying of new trolleybuses to Saltaire depot, returning to Thornbury with tramcars not needed for service. The throng of cars which rolled elegantly along

Manningham Lane that day did not include any 'six-window' cars, as the last of that long-lived breed, Nos. 201/209, had been sent to the Works during the morning for scrapping.

The last Frizinghall (27) to Killinghall Road (16) extras ceased their shuttle service at teatime, and as night fell brightly-lit cars continued as usual to speed along Bradford Road and nose their cautious way round the blind approach to Cottingley Bridge before beginning the gentle ascent to Bingley where the tracks, laid in 1913, now veered from one side to the other of the new realigned 80ft-wide highway.

'Trams for Bradford Start Here' – but not for much longer, as the overhead wires in Bingley Main Street from which 'Preston' No. 236 is drawing power are now attached to new trolleybus poles. Although it is a cool day, the rear balcony is well filled with youthful passengers. *Photo: W. A. Camwell*

Saltaire terminus, 1938. Handsome 'high four-window' car No. 239, newly-escaped from its brush with Bowling Bridge, has just traversed the crossover for a journey to Bradford Moor, although its destination still displays 'Saltaire'. The single line curving into the depot yard is intersected by the long-disused Saltaire Road (route 32) tracks. *Photo W. A. Camwell*

The new trolleybus overhead equipment had already been thoroughly tested when tramcar No. 111 was photographed at Crossflatts terminus on 1st May 1939, by Mr E. Thornton.

On a normal Saturday evening the last Crossflatts (24) car left Forster Square at 10.32pm, followed by Bingley (24) trams at five-minute intervals until 11.02pm with Saltaire (25) cars also at five-minute frequencies until 11.32pm – but this was no normal evening. The last service tramcar to Crossflatts was No. 241, and car No. 2 on its final departure from Bingley at 11.34pm encountered an infinitely more magnificent tram travelling in the opposite direction.

Tramcar No. 88 which had been sent to the Works on 12th April from its normal habitat at Bankfoot for a full overhaul and repaint had been subsequently detained there and bedecked with bunting and festoons of coloured lights for the civic safari.

Thus, at about 11.20pm, its illuminations outshining the eerie new mercury-vapour street lighting, and manned by the longest-serving staff, No. 88 performed a last circumnavigation of Forster Square island to take on board the Transport Committee and officials. Then, determinedly rounding Cheapside corner at a much more rapid pace than Holroyd Smith's little experimental car of 1892, it headed north, and when it clattered over the points at distant Crossflatts terminus there were many present who had witnessed the first car less than 25 years earlier.

The Bradford contingent was now joined by the Chairman of Bingley UDC (Councillor Newhill) and his Lighting and Tramways committee chairman (Councillor Bentley) as well as Mr Tom Snowden who had addressed the crowds from the balcony of Bingley's first tram. A throng of 300 people – almost the entire population of Crossflatts – raised a cheer when on the stroke of midnight Conductor Smith gave the departure signal to Driver Farrer.

Confidently entering the empty single-line sections with their twinkling signal lights, the car arrived back in Bingley Main Street where another crowd of admirers gathered round the resplendent vehicle. They had plenty of time to admire it, as the civic parties retired to the 'Ferrands' Arms' for coffee and sandwiches, being joined by dozens of 'gate crashers'. On rejoining the car they removed some of the coloured bulbs as keepsakes, plunging it into partial darkness. At the Nab Wood boundary the Bingley members were replaced by their Shipley UDC colleagues led by the Chairman, Councillor Horne, who drove the car through Saltaire (where a track gang was waiting to lift the rails so that the new roundabout could be completed) to the city boundary at Frizinghall. There all the invited guests departed, taking with them so many small souvenirs that by the time No. 88 reached Thornbury it had to return to the Works for attention. As soon as it had travelled through Forster Square into Well Street a second track gang

commenced to alter the tracks in readiness for the morrow.

Next day Forster Square was transformed, with an endless stream of sleek new trolleybuses circling the island. Only the Bradford Moor (30) trams on their truncated siding represented the glories of yesteryear. Even the spectral driver of the ghost tram had adapted to changed circumstances, as he was not heard of again. Perhaps he, too, had 'gone trolleybussing'.

Meanwhile the sad procession of redundant tramcars to Bowling depot yard continued, the latest recorded journey being made by 'Preston' No. 253 which was towed there on the discarded truck of No. 15 on 13th May.

The fleet was now reduced to 112 vehicles:–

Greengates 70-75, 80, 90/92, 222	10
High four-window 107, 232/239	3
'Preston' 214-7, 219, 220/4, 234/6-8, 242/3/6, 251/6-8	18
BCT narrow cars with medium height canopies	
24, 50/6/7, 77, 86, 223/8, 241/7/8	11
BCT wide cars with medium-height canopies	
26-29, 30/1/7, 40/42-5, 47-9, 51-3, 83	
93/7, 103-5/8/9, 111, 130, 195/6, 226, 230, 240, 253	34
BCT wide cars with high canopies	
19, 34/5, 79, 89, 94/5/9, 102, 119, 189, 218, 231,	
244/5, 254	16
BCT intermediate-width cars with medium-height canopies	
17, 20/3, 55, 61, 81/8, 178, 181, 213	
221/5/7/9, 233/5, 249, 250/2/5	20
	112

Altogether a pleasing miscellany of smart, sturdy cars – but Mr Tattam did not propose to prolong the pleasure, as his attention had already turned to the heavily-laden Wibsey tramway which was clearly suitable for trolleybuses. Nevertheless on 15th June he induced the Committee to agree (contrary to their May 1932 policy, although he did not mention it) to use motorbuses, and eighteen were duly ordered. But the international scene, increasingly ominous since 1935, was suddenly reaching a crisis – a crisis for which Bradford Corporation had been quietly preparing for more than a year.

Contrasting styles at Trinity Fields, 2nd July 1938. Car No. 214 (left) entering Easby Road from Dirkhill Road is a Horton Bank Top-based 'Preston' car returning from White Horse, while car No. 222, caught in the act of operating the automatic points for entry into Laisteridge Lane (right) on its way to Wibsey, was originally 'Greengates' car No. 69 and is on loan to Bowling depot. The old Blackwell pole (left) cannot match the girth of the newer pole (right) with its typical BCT base.

Photo: H. B. Priestley

By 1938 many of the 31-year old tram poles in St. Enoch's Road had been replaced (left) by second-hand trolleybus poles, and new overhead wire with modern fittings permitted fast downhill running. Car No. 70, on its way to Wibsey, had been the last Greengates tram a decade previously.

Photo; H. B. Priestley

(Below) When the Wibsey tramway was curtailed by a few yards in 1933, a new kerbside loading bay (with trolley reverser) was installed outside the 'Cosy Cinema' in Fair Road. An unidentified tram (probably No. 103) waits for former 'Windhill Bridge' car No. 57 to reverse over the points

Photo: H. B. Priestley

15 – BOMBS AND BLACKOUT

**"Don't know what's coming tomorrow;
Maybe it's trouble and sorrow ...."
(Flanagan and Allen, 1939)**

Early in the morning of Friday, 1st September 1939, the depot telephones rang urgently. German troops had invaded Poland; war was imminent; blackout precautions must be implemented by nightfall, and extra trams and buses were required to convey local schoolchildren to Exchange and Forster Square stations for evacuation to safer havens.

Detailed plans laid many months earlier fell swiftly into place. During the day all tramcars received blackout masks on headlamps and interior lights; destination indicators were shielded from the prying eyes of enemy airmen, and gleaming white paint was hurriedly applied to fenders, platform step edges, tramway standards and the tips of trolley booms to assist visibility, as the street lights would not be in use that night or as long as the emergency lasted.

Thereafter normal routines continued for a while. Up at Horton Bank Top the depot doors swung open next morning at 4.23am to allow tramcar No. 105 to roll out for duty on the Queensbury (3) service. Forty minutes elapsed before No. 49 followed, but then the pace quickened. In stately succession cars Nos. 217, 107 and 52 set out for White Horse (2) and Nos. 28, 56, 214, 23, 86 and 81 for Queensbury; later, car No. 218 swelled the White Horse ranks and Nos. 109 and 23 provided a supplementary service to Southfield Lane (2) while tramcars Nos. 77, 104 and 102 mingled with their Thornbury-based brethren on the jointly-served Wibsey (1) route. By mid-morning Nos. 24, 79 and 252 were working an intermediate turn to Wibsey, and early afternoon brought schedule changes for cars Nos. 52, 53, 109 and 81. Only trams Nos. 108, 216, 92, 57, 232 and 258 remained inside for washing. Similar routines were enacted at the other depots.

Domestic radios were the focus of attention that day as the last hours of peace slipped away, but the prevailing attitude was one of philosophical cheerfulness. Emerging from a city centre cinema that evening into the misty, darkened streets a young man was heard to comment, hopefully, "It's a reight courtin' neet!"

The dimming of the tram and bus interior lights proved to be highly successful, as the bulbs had been painted blue and shielded with thin black cardboard cones, so that from a distance of twenty yards only a faint glow could be discerned. Within a week or two, however, the effect was judged too eerie for comfort, and blue was replaced by a more cheerful red.

Although the task of the tram drivers was somewhat easier than that of their bus and trolleybus colleagues who had to steer their vehicles as well as peer through the darkness ahead, intending passengers had to be warned to signal them by shining a torch towards the ground and not into the drivers' eyes.

War was duly declared on Sunday, 3rd September, and on Monday Mr Tattam and Alderman Hodgson were given

Car No. 253 stands triumphantly at Undercliffe terminus on 30th October 1939, six weeks after the route re-opened. On the right passengers are waiting for the tram to reverse over the crossover and negotiate the trolley reverser.
Photo: H. B. Priestley

emergency powers.

Overnight the tramcars, independent of imported fuel and raw materials, became a valuable asset, and were soon seen as part of the national drive for self-sufficiency made popular by the famous 'Dig for Victory' campaign.

An immediate response was made to official edicts that in order to conserve essential oil supplies all passenger transport must cease at 10.0pm each night and that motor bus services should be curtailed. On the morning of Monday 11th September the full tramcar service to Undercliffe (20) was resumed, employing up to seven cars at peak hours. The automatic point mechanism at the 'Cock and Bottle' junction was soon reinstated, but as the tram stop signs had all been removed in 1935, cars temporarily observed the bus stopping-places.

Simultaneously the sleeper track in Halifax Road, retained for 'sports specials' as far as 'Horsfall Playing Fields' when the Shelf service ceased in 1935, came back into use for a teatime extension of the Odsal (15) service. Although the inventive Thornbury Works signwriters managed to squeeze the new, lengthy destination name into the wide front and rear destination screens, they had to admit defeat with the much smaller side-screens.

As it was obvious that the tramcar scrapyard at Bowling depot would not be receiving any more victims for a long while, the remaining tracks from City to Foundry Lane were quietly lifted for scrap or re-use, and a new modern design of double-sided tram-stop sign was ordered in August, 1940. In order to minimise overhead sparking and flashing during the blackout, lengths of new grooved wire with flush-fitting suspension ears were erected in various places, and the covered passenger shelter in Forster Square was lengthened in order to reduce overcrowding.

101

Bradford Northern were billed to play Keighley at Odsal Stadium when tram No. 240, on temporary loan from Thornbury depot, battled its way past snowdrifts at Littlemoor on its way to Queensbury in late January 1940
Photo: N. A. Scurrah

Overcrowding was affecting the trams too. With the virtual cessation of private motoring and the mushroom growth of the munitions industry, tram queues lengthened endlessly. The Stanningley (10) cars had to be supplemented by extras to Pudsey Lane End (12), and full standing loads on both decks became commonplace. Sturdy and undaunted as a British bulldog, the Bradford Tram was making its own contribution to the War Effort.

Heavy snow and bitter weather on 27/28th January 1940 added to the mounting hardships, but the trams battled through the drifts to lofty Queensbury without interruption, whereas no bus from Halifax reached the village for a week. Partial relief was obtained from Ministry sanction for the extension of tram and trolleybus services to 10.30pm on 1st March and to 11.00pm (as pre-war) on 6th May.

New blackout regulations kept the Works staff busy in March when signal lamps had to be fitted to the tramcar platform dadoes, above the headlamps, displaying a discreet white light at the leading end and red at the rear. New regulation masks comprising grey-painted canisters were fitted over each interior lamp, allowing a narrow beam of clear light to be directed downwards.

The new precautions were put to the test on the evening of 31st August when air-raid sirens sounded as the city centre theatres and cinemas were beginning to empty. Air-raid wardens urged the crowds to take shelter, but various Queensbury residents, conscious that their last tram was due to arrive at any moment, rejected their advice and joined the waiting queue in Tyrrel Street. Almost immediately the whistle of a bomb was heard, followed by explosion and shrapnel. The tram rails reared skyward to meet the falling wires, and if there was a last tram to Queensbury that night, it did not depart from the city centre.

For four hours hundreds of people huddled in the shelters while high-explosive and incendiary bombs rained down, killing two people and causing fires which could be seen far and wide. Then, in the half-light of early morning, they walked wearily home, glad to escape.

For the next day or two the Wibsey, Great Horton and Queensbury services used the Victoria Square crossover as a temporary terminus which Thornbury-based cars reached with difficulty, being obliged to negotiate the seldom or never used westbound tracks in Town Hall Square, their conductors seeking a live wire for the trolley wherever they could find one. Damage at Laisterdyke caused a brief diversion of the Thornbury and Stanningley cars via Harris Street and Bradford Moor, but the Undercliffe tramcars disdainfully ignored a neat bomb crater between their tracks near Butler Street. No tramcar was damaged, and although other minor raids followed, services were not interrupted again.

Increasing breakages of the obsolescent Oakenshaw trolleybus wiring beyond Odsal led to the withdrawal of the service on 31st July 1940. Unusually, the much-newer wiring in Manchester Road which the trolleybuses had shared with the trams was retained almost intact, and was cross-bonded to act as a voltage booster between Croft Street and Odsal. In the event of a trolley de-wirement in the blackout, conductors had to ensure that they replaced the trolley on the correct (inner) wire, otherwise they suffered a second de-wirement where the outer (ex-negative) wire terminated!

Economies and shortages multiplied. An appeal to the

In this 1940 view car No. 30 on a return journey from Wyke is making its way across Town Hall Square with the 'New Inn' on the left and Tyrrel Street on the right. Blackout masks shield the destination indicator and headlamp, and the gold lining above the fleet number circles the new small 'signal lamp'.

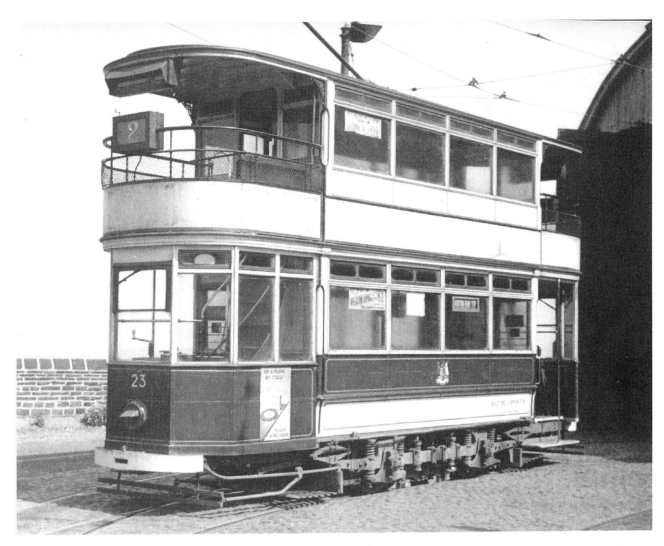

A fine study of car No. 23, one of the two cars built in 1929 with sheet metal vestibule panels. Mounted on a Boving truck – a sturdier BCT version of the Hurst Nelson 21E – and with windows coated with anti-blast cellophane, the tram is seen in 1941 at the entrance to Horton Bank Top depot, high above the city.

Photo: E. Thornton

Ministry of War Transport for delivery of the hoped-for new buses as replacements for the Wibsey trams was firmly rejected; paper scarcity led to thinner tickets, and a demand for scrap metal for armaments brought about the sacrifice (by dint of strong arms and sledgehammers) of all but ten of the handsome ornamental cast-iron pole bases. More pleasingly, conductresses made a welcome return on 31st March 1941 although in view of the somewhat strenuous nature of tramcar duties – swinging the seat backs over at termini, changing points and manhandling the trolley – most were allocated to trolley and motor buses. Increasingly, therefore, the tramway staff tended to include the older, longer-serving employees, a few of whom additionally manned the Home Guard post at Thornbury Works.

Following protests that users of the much-curtailed Shelf bus service were being crowded out by short-distance travellers, the part-time Horsfall Playing Fields (15) trams began on 14th April 1942, to operate at all morning and evening peak hours as well as Sunday mornings.

By Ministerial request the motor buses began to receive a drab, overall khaki-grey livery as a form of camouflage in case they had to visit aerodromes or munitions factories.

Coincidentally, however, Mr Tattam, who had already made three attempts to lighten the shade of blue traditionally used by BCPT, had been so impressed by the powder blue livery of Southend trolleybuses currently on loan to Bradford that in mid-June 1942 two BCPT trolleybuses were painted in a not dissimilar colour which is believed to have been a gloss version of the normal Bradford undercoat, with a primrose contrast. Officially termed 'Bradford Blue and Broken White' but usually known as 'South Sea Blue and Primrose', the new colours were promptly adopted for the trolleybus fleet.

However, when tramcars 29 and 245 emerged from the paint-shop some weeks later in the now-superseded dark blue and cream, sinister rumour whispered that the tram fleet would shortly share the dismal fate of the motor buses. Fortunately, timely intercessions saved the day, and on 25th July tramcar 213 duly received the new colours in the traditional proportions. The overall effect was unsatisfactory, as the new, cheerful light blue was overwhelmed by the large expanse of primrose. Car No. 26 therefore appeared a month later with blue-painted upper-deck panels to redress the balance, but it was not until September, when car No. 19 received blue rocker panels also, that departmental aesthetics were satisfied.

In view of the prevailing shortage of pigments the new livery was an impressive achievement, as No. 19 was in fact more elaborately painted and lined out than any tram since the Wilkinson era. With chrome-yellow lining on the blue, blue lines on the primrose, gold leaf numerals and fleet name, red oxide roof, lifeguards and truck, and black fender, trolley, axle boxes and panel edges, the tram presented a colourful picture, even

but for the Stanningley and Wibsey routes nothing short of complete renewal would now suffice. Reluctantly the Ministry conceded that Stanningley was beyond redemption, as the fast, straight run from Gipsy Street, Thornbury to Woodlands Terrace, Farsley was (to say the least) lively, especially on the slight downward gradient past Pudsey Lane End where the trams often outpaced the Leeds buses.

The route managed to survive long enough to glimpse a few more cars (Nos. 239, 42 and 80) in the new livery, but 'the last of the gallant old steeds' which 'rocketed down there for the last time' on 18th October 1942, was dark blue No. 223. Borrowed buses took over next day, and with the removal of the rails and overhead equipment the forgotten fragments of the historic taper-track disappeared at last. The short section between Thornbury depot and the junction with Leeds Old Road was retained for depot access for the Forster Square services and for peak-hour specials (via the Thornbury route but labelled 'Bradford Moor') for the English Electric employees at Phoenix Works.

Ten of the 'Preston' cars were offered for sale, being quickly acquired by Sheffield Corporation whose fleet had suffered air raid damage. Accordingly Nos. 214-7, 219, 237, 242/3 and 251/7 departed for a new life by courtesy of the LMS Railway, and on arrival their open balconies were neatly enclosed with the help of the drawings prepared by their previous owners twenty years earlier!

The Wibsey route survived once again, despite Mr Tattam's protestations; indeed, he was ordered to 'patch it up' for a few more years, which he did by means of odd lengths of good-quality rail and short pieces inserted into worn rail joints. Although the result was far from perfect, it undoubtedly allayed the anxieties of Bradfordians concerned about the need to conserve rubber and oil. The authorities were concerned too. The Regional Traffic Commissioner (Major Eastwood) had put forward proposals for eliminating all bus services which ran along tram routes, but as (in Bradford at least) the

Gleaming with fresh paint and varnish, car No. 19 proudly exhibits its new 'South Sea Blue and primrose' livery at Wibsey terminus in September 1942, with windows obscured by anti-blast netting. The high-type canopy top, inherited from the original No. 19, was fourteen years older than the lower deck, and had recently been rebuilt and braced up.

Photo: E. Thornton

though the windows had to be disfigured for a while with regulation anti-blast netting.

Connoisseurs of the tramways speculated how the new livery would suit the different proportions of the 'Preston' cars, but, alas, they were doomed to disappointment. Creaky No. 246 had already retired to an easier life as a garden shed, bequeathing its DK truck to snowplough S4 which thus acquired 'high-speed' status, unique among the ploughs, as well as the name 'Norman' in unofficial honour of the Rolling Stock Engineer (Mr N. A. Scurrah) who had sanctioned the conversion. Other retirements were threatened too, as the pre-war policy of minimum track maintenance had produced a crisis.

In January 1942 the permanent-way engineer (Mr C. F. Clyne) had visited Southend and other towns in search of salvaged rail,

Here snowplough S4 (formerly Milnes six-window car No. 133), nicknamed 'Norman', proudly displays its newly-acquired DK21E truck in the windswept yard of Horton Bank Top depot.
Copyright Mr E. Thornton

Predictably the existence of modern streamlined cars on Darwen Corporation's 4ft gauge lines was pointed out to him by a well-informed correspondent who recommended the introduction of an experimental luxury tramcar as soon as circumstances allowed. Others hastened to join the debate, emphasising that,

'Bradford is above all things a city of long, steep gradients, and it is on these that the trams really do score over the buses. In addition, a tram is a much safer vehicle, particularly on hills, as it uses its tracks as well as its wheels for braking. Also, the tram is able to continue operating in severe conditions of fog, ice and snow long after rubber-tyred vehicles have been brought to a standstill.'

Meanwhile the permanent-way gang had removed to the Wyke route, where they re-laid the reserved track between Odsal and Low Moor with new rail, sleepers and ballast. But the adjoining section of street track, from Low Moor to Wyke terminus, officially 'worn out' even before the war, was now in a perilous condition. Clinging to the balcony rail of storm-tossed No. 47 as it staggered round the long curve past St. Mark's Church, its trolley gyrating wildly beneath the heaving wires, the author felt himself only slightly less endangered than his colleague Mr J. A. Pitts who, voyaging over the same tracks on extra-tall car No. 232, was so convinced of imminent shipwreck that he retired to the lower deck. On one memorable length of rail the tread had worn paper-thin and had to be beaten back into place with a point-iron.

Unfortunately visits to the Sheffield steelworks in search of further supplies drew a complete blank, and Ministry inspectors, hurriedly summoned, had to condemn the track and authorise replacement of trams by buses on the entire route beyond Odsal. The public, still delighting in the newly-rediscovered pleasure of floating down the Low Moor sleeper track as if on a feather bed, were naturally amazed and scandalised, especially as the apparatus of track renewal – wheelbarrows, watchmen's huts, red warning lamps and heaps of ballast – were still on site.

extra pressure on the already overburdened tramcars would have been intolerable, the idea was not pursued.

As the war progressed, small quantities of new rail occasionally became available. In April/May 1943 Church Bank and the Forster Square siding were completely relaid, allowing the Undercliffe and Bradford Moor trams a brief respite from normal routines: they loaded in Well Street and proceeded via Harris Street. Then the permanent-way engineer succeeded in making a much larger purchase from the Skinningrove Iron Company which allowed him to re-lay the Manchester Road line from Croft Street to Bankfoot, employing temporary track and single-line working where necessary, as the work had to be carried out in daylight.

Nevertheless the manager felt the need to remind the public that as soon as new vehicles became available the tram replacement programme would resume. In response to pointed queries as to why modern tramcars could not be used, he answered that,

'In Bradford it is impossible to introduce modern cars of large carrying capacity owing to the narrow gauge and the restricted radii of curves where junctions of adjoining streets have to be negotiated.'

Nevertheless car No. 37 duly made the final descent to Bailiff Bridge at midday on 10th June 1944 (only four days after D-Day), being greeted by cries of "Last old jigger!" – not that the Wyke to Bailiff Bridge track ever gave anyone a jigging, as it was in perfect condition. The last tempestuous journey to Wyke followed the next evening, after which the new rails from the sleeper track were shamefacedly retrieved for further service in Leeds Road (Harris Street-Laisterdyke).

Fortunately, for the well-worn 'Cock and Bottle' junction a good supply of 'special work' – manganese steel points, crossings and curves – was available, and the tracklayers took possession in October. The Undercliffe service was temporarily bus-operated via North Wing while the Bradford Moor trams traversed the full length of Harris Street in both directions; inward bound cars descending Barkerend Road had to 'reverse' into Harris Street, thus obliging saloon passengers to complete their journey facing rearwards. In order to restore their dignity the Department renewed the Barkerend Road-East Parade curve first, and as soon as the rest of the complex jigsaw had been re-laid, paved and tested, normal services recommenced.

Despite the recent route closures not many cars could be dispensed with. In the autumn of 1944 a survey of Friday teatime (4-6pm) requirements showed a need for 94 trams, ie Wibsey-15; Great Horton and Queensbury-19; Thornbury-10; Undercliffe-7; Bradford Moor-16; Odsal and Horsfall Playing Fields-21 and Bowling Old Lane-6. Nevertheless 'Preston cars Nos. 224, 236, 256 and 258 were sent to Bankfoot (and later Horton Bank Top) for 'special workings' only; No. 234 was scrapped altogether, bequeathing its truck to No. 77, while tram No. 119, stripped of its motors, gathered dust in Thornbury depot for a year, the first conventional post-1919 Thornbury-built car to retire.

The war in Europe was visibly drawing to an end now; blackout restrictions on tramcar headlamps, destination indicators and interior lighting had been relaxed, and the Ministry had finally agreed that the Wibsey route could close as soon as sufficient buses could be mustered.

No one could deny the condition of the Wibsey track. In Laisteridge Lane the rail surface corrugation was so acute that whenever cars halted at the Little Horton Green stop the sudden silence hurt the ears – as did the conductor's whistle when he leaned over the balcony rail to give the starting signal. Ascending St. Enoch's Road the wheels pounded rhythmically over the worn joints, and on the descent – always much swifter than on any other Bradford hill – the bodywork creaked and the sliding doors opened and closed continuously as the cars swayed from side to side, whilst the passengers, unperturbed, enquired, "Is this the new world we have been promised, or do they mean the next?" Tram No. 253, the last to bear the proud route number 1, provided the final, well-patronised journey on 7th January 1945.

Remaining blackout restrictions were lifted on 23rd April and the European conflict ended a fortnight later. Possibly the

(Top) Renewal of the Church Bank and Forster Square tracks in April/May 1943, caused temporary diversions. Here Undercliffe car No. 50 has turned from Leeds Road into Harris Street and is passing Sion Baptist Church (left). Today the six-lane Shipley Airedale Route crosses the scene diagonally left to right, but upper Harris Street (with tarmac-submerged tram-lines) still survives.
Photo: the late J. A. Pitts

(Above) Following the successful 'D-Day' landings in Europe, blackout restrictions were eased, enabling tram destination indicators to be uncovered, though headlamps remained masked. The end of hostilities in August 1945 was also the end of the line for the remaining 'Preston' cars such as No. 220, seen here on a rare visit to Bowling Old Lane terminus.
Photo: the late J. A. Pitts

general rejoicings were not shared by the remaining 'Preston' cars No. 220/4, 236/8 and 256/8 and Bradford-built Nos. 95, 119, 231 and 245, all still in the old colours, which were sold for scrap shortly after the Hiroshima and Nagasaki bombs ended World War II.

16 – RETIREMENT

"I have fought a good fight; I have finished my course" (2 Timothy 4)

Hopes that the return of peace would bring an early abundance of new buses were quickly dispelled, as the cost of waging a six-year war had drained the nation's finances, and industrial output had to be directed towards an export drive.

For the 89 Bradford tramcars life therefore continued as usual, although the Southfield Lane shortworkings ceased, and all Great Horton cars thenceforth reversed at White Horse except on Sunday mornings when the Horton Bank Top crossover was used. Improvements to the Shelf bus service limited the Horsfall Playing Fields service to weekday teatimes and evenings and Sunday mornings only.

When the Dirkhill Road and All Saints Road permanent way was renewed in May 1946 the Great Horton and Queensbury trams were diverted via Laisteridge Lane and Park Avenue, with a temporary tram stop at Horton Park Gates. A more modest track renovation in Leeds Road (Hall Ings to Well Street) coincided with a major overhaul for 'Greengates Bridge' car No. 92, which as it glided along the new rails on its new tyres provided a vivid reminder of the quality of travel which trams could still provide.

These proved to be the last significant track renewals, although individual lengths of rail were replaced from time to time. Thus,

The drabness of early postwar Bradford can be seen in this 1947 view of Manchester Road, where 'Greengates' car No. 90 is emerging from Bowling Old Lane. A disconnected remnant of the former Oakenshaw trolleybus overhead equipment is visible in the top right hand corner of this photograph by the late Mr J. A. Pitts.

The unhandsome railgrinder, No. 11, comprised an open waggon used for transporting permanent-way materials, a tall trolley mast from the Phoenix Munitions Tramway and cabs from the two 'railless' lorries, Nos. 501/2.

Copyright: Mr J. Copland

while the Permanent Way Department retained their ancient welding van and even purchased a new Bedford tipping-waggon (EKU 366), the redundant railgrinder (No. 11) had to find new employment as a snowplough.

The conductresses gracefully withdrew at the end of the 1946 Bradford holidays ('Bowling Tide'), their job supremely well done. A few weeks later the worst floods for 30 years swept into Bradford on 20th September, swamping the central area, disrupting railway services and ripping up paving. The Manchester Road (11/15) tramcars had to reverse at the 'Blue Lion' and the Great Horton and Queensbury (2/3) cars in Victoria Square, but in Forster Square the Undercliffe and Bradford Moor (20/30) drivers blithely ferried their passengers through the swirling waters, risking short-circuited motors, until espied by Mr Tattam who bade them cease.

Worse weather was to come. In the Spring of 1947 two severe blizzards – which briefly defeated the best efforts of the veteran snowplough cars – were followed by 53 days of continuous frost. Even in a normal winter travel on public transport was a chilly affair; and Bradford's trams – totally unheated like their rubber-tyred colleagues – required their passengers to be warmly clad. Rebuked by the conductor for travelling on the front balcony of a Horsfall Playing Fields tramcar on a freezing, foggy day, the author had to point out that if there were a difference between inside and outside temperatures, he had not detected it. Nevertheless, out of consideration for the conductor's chilled fingers, he rode on the rear balcony for the return trip!

The ability of the trams to cope with exceptional demands was amply demonstrated on 4th October 1947 when in the afternoon 21,000 football supporters flocked to Park Avenue, and in the evening so many speedway enthusiasts wished to travel to Odsal that the tram queue encircled the Town Hall twice. All were accommodated, and at the end of the match the crowds were cleared within 30 minutes. Part of the secret of the trams' success was their robust construction and the cheerful willingness of the staff to allow unlimited standing passengers (the staircases and driver's platform only excepted), an entirely unofficial but greatly appreciated practice, typical of an era which would have viewed today's intrusive Brussels 'directives' and over-protective Health and Safety quibbles with amused, hearty British contempt and disregard.

Meanwhile the Transport Department's planners were pursuing their quest for a tramless Bradford. In March 1946 they had announced that preparations for the conversion of the Bradford Moor (30) tramway to trolleybus operation would begin soon. Begin they did, but completion was to be long delayed, and when the new trolleybus wires were eventually erected, they were burnished by tramcar trolley wheels for many a long month. Similar plans for Undercliffe (20) were publicised a year later, but the vehicles required for the conversion were not delivered until the next decade, by which time rising inflation and nationalisation of the Corporation Electricity Department had made electric traction uneconomic.

Increased wage bills inevitably entailed fare rises, a factor not always accepted by the public. In September 1947 the 1d, 2½d and 3½d fares rose by ½d and the 3d fare by 1d, to the displeasure of Queensbury residents who now paid 4d to travel to and from City. Even more strongly resented was the 50% increase – from 1d to 1½d – suffered by Bowling Old Lane residents, but their tram conductors collected the offending fare for less than three months, as the Bowling Old Lane (11) service ceased on 13th December 1947, when for the last time car No. 88 ventured between the tall mills and the densely-populated terraces of 'back-to-back' housing to the quiet terminus at Gaythorne Road.

Road on the 'wrong' side of the shelter and invite people to board.

Two notable links with the past were snapped in July 1948, with the deaths of Inspector W. G. Railton, an employee since 1903 and Chief Inspector since 1934, and of Mr George Seniour, driver of the first Corporation tramcar 50 summers previously. Subsequently promoted as foreman at Bankfoot depot, Mr Seniour's career had embraced the distant past as well as the beckoning future, as he had begun his career as a steam-tram driver and ended it as a garage-owner at Odsal. The eventful half-century of Corporation transport which he had inaugurated and which had bestowed immeasurable benefits on the public of Bradford, was ignored by the City Council, who rejected Transport Committee plans for a £1,000 celebration.

A few days before the uncelebrated Jubilee the arrival of new Leyland buses brought about the closure of the Undercliffe (20) tramway for the second and, sadly, the last time on 17th July 1948, with the departure of car No. 93 – normally a Manchester Road tram which chanced to be visiting Thornbury Works that week, Next day the automatic warning lamp which had presided over the safety of Church Bank trams since the 1907 'smash' was finally switched off in recognition of the reduced volume of tramcars making the steep ascent.

At the same time the planned expansion of the trolleybus fleet led to an exchange of accommodation at Thornbury depot where the trams vacated the 'new' (1902) section of the shed and returned to the 'Far West' with its warren of tracks, disused since 1930, which were now reconnected to the Leeds Road lines. In order to avoid entanglement with the maze of new overhead wiring outside the depot, the Thornbury (9) trams began to terminate at the 'Works' crossover 50 yards nearer to Bradford Moor, receiving as a consolation prize an ingenious new trolley reverser which neatly intersected the trolleybus wires.

In November an eight-day fog caused collision damage to 30 Corporation vehicles as well as cars, lorries and other operators' buses. On several

The arrival of two smart Karrier 'Eagle' tower-waggons allowed the Overhead Lines Department to discard the last of the leisurely horse-drawn waggons whose motive power was put out to grass. Then, concerned at the somewhat shabby state of various vehicles repainted in the latter days of the war, the Works treated 23 trams to a one-coat repaint without lining, varnish or new transfers. Less attractive than the full livery which fully-overhauled trams continued to receive, the plain finish was nevertheless reasonably durable in normal circumstances, although not proof against the searching, diluted caustic soda shampoo administered each Spring to the Horton Bank Top cars as an antidote to winter grime!

Eloquent proof of the saying that, 'You can't please all the people all the time' occurred when Thornbury residents waiting in the Hall Ings shelter complained of seeing 'football specials' returning to depot via Leeds Road without halting to allow them to board. It transpired, however, that the cars actually proceeded only as far as Harris Street, where they reversed on the single line and thoughtfully returned to Hall Ings to collect the passengers in the normal manner. This practice, although unquestionably considerate, was also expensive, as the staff were being paid at overtime rates – hence even stronger complaints, following which the staff were instructed merely to halt in Leeds

Scheduled to be the final tram to Undercliffe. No. 93 enters Otley Road at the 'Cock and Bottle'. Traces of wartime blackout paint still disfigure the facade of Lloyd's Bank but a new trolleybus pole (right) is now in place. *Copyright: Mr R. Brook*

evenings the trolley and motor buses were withdrawn after dusk, and even the trams had to admit defeat on the evening of the 29th, so impenetrable was the smoke-burdened gloom.

But the gloom which had beset the transport planners for so long was beginning to lift: forty AEC buses were at last promised for delivery, seven years after they had first been ordered. As the impending growth of the motor bus fleet threatened an early conflict with the trolleybus fleet number series, it was decided

that for the new acquisitions a fresh start should be made at the expense of the dwindling band of tramcars. Accordingly on 31st March 1949 cars numbered below 50 (ie 17/19, 20/23/26-29, 34/35/37, 40/42-45/48/49) were renumbered with the addition of the prefix 1. For car No. 37 the transition to 137 was easy, as only one platform vestibule remained after a disastrous collision in Manchester Road, but for No. 30 the survival of sister cars Nos. 130 and 230 posed a dilemma which was only solved by the late arrival of the new bus!

Age never wearied the trams. When a collision between two motor vehicles held up the entire Bradford Moor service for twenty minutes, the first tramcar to be released from the blockage made up for lost time by returning to City at an astounding speed. Thundering down Barkerend Road with footgong clanging to deter hopeful passengers advancing out into the road, the car swept across the Harris Street junction with a rumbustious clamour and did not slow down until Church Bank was in sight. The sole passenger was, to say the least, exhilarated.

The overhauling of tramcars came to an end when car No. 86 entered the Works on 15th February 1949, and emerged on 8th

A wet night at Undercliffe: tramcar No. 93 was the last car to leave the terminus on 17th July 1948.

Photograph: Mr F. Hartley

The lower part of Bowling Yard contained railway sidings and a railway/tramway mixed gauge weighbridge which was still intact in 1950 though long-disused.

Copyright: Author

When the last Bradford Moor tramcar, No. 248, prepared to leave Forster Square, the neatly-dressed passengers (and Mr J. A. Pitts on the right-hand side of the balcony) were joined by a reveller who did little to enhance the photograph.

Copyright: Telegraph and Argus

April after exchanging its Boving truck for a reconditioned Dick, Kerr unit (ex car No. 254, deceased) and having been treated to a last, thorough repainting and lining-out, with Kearsleys' blue and Dockers' varnish as usual.

Following the municipal elections in May 1949, the Corporation made its annual appointments to the Municipal Transport Association's Tramway Traffic Sub-Committee; regrettably, these were to be the last such appointments.

Of the long hoped-for Bradford Moor trolleybuses there was still no sign, and against its will the Department had to order new track for the Forster Square siding. However, no sooner had the rails and pointwork been delivered to the permanent-way yard than the trolleybuses made their appearance. The trackwork was therefore retained at Bowling Yard and assembled for a highly-untoward use – the storage of redundant tramcars prior to their dismemberment. Accordingly a dismal procession of condemned cars, headed by No. 129 on 9th June, made its way from Thornbury by low-loader, the roofs having been sawn off to prevent premature demolition by Bowling Bridge. The dismantling process also destroyed the old tramway overhead wires in the yard, which since 1938 had transmitted power to the clinker-crushing plant from the Wakefield Road trolleybus wires; the demolition contractors allowed their crane to run amok one morning, and that was that.

Meanwhile, on the golden summer evening of 23rd July 1949, tramcar No. 248 had embarked, 'with all the usual clatter but no ceremony', upon the last, fully-laden journey from Forster Square and up Church Bank to Bradford Moor. With it went much of the character and atmosphere of the stately Square, never to be recaptured.

Local passengers had already commented on the change-over. 'At busy times in the present heatwave', wrote one, 'Hot and uncomfortable humanity squeezes in, jumps up when a stop is reached, flops back unintentionally on the nearest knees as the tram gives the usual jerk, then up again to squeeze out, jostling down the narrow gangway and taking a deep breath on the platform. It is much cooler 'on top', of course, but only the intrepid can face those stairs'.

Fortunately there was no dearth of intrepid folk in Bradford. Regret soon followed:–

'... at least they were reliable, and breakdowns were rare. The people who are going to miss them most are those mothers of young children who are obliged to make frequent trips to town. The tram driver's platform could accommodate almost every kind of pram, but there are not many that will fit under the steps of a bus.'

Similar sentiments accompanied the announcement that the Great Horton and Queensbury route would be next for closure:–

'....of late, parts of the track have become so worn that the journey is a hazardous one for passengers ... the trams rock and sway like ships in a heavy sea, and there are breathless moments, especially on the Dirkhill Road/Easby Road section, when one feels that the city-bound car will plunge into Trinity Fields. It is an everyday event for passengers to be forcibly acquainted through being shuttlecocked against each other – it is surprising that the Department has not been inundated with claims for bruised heads and damaged hats!'

Nevertheless there were plenty of Bradfordians happy to risk a bruise or two when on 'Plot Night' (5th November 1949), tramcar No. 149 was cheered on its final departure from Tyrrel Street, piloted by Reginald Laverack, a driver for 41 years, whose

conductor David Morton took a more detached view of the proceedings, having been demobilised from HM Forces only eight weeks previously. At Queensbury the Chairman of Queensbury and Shelf UDC joined his townsfolk in a fond farewell.

However, at the top of Horton Bank a loyal span-wire had decided to snap in a mute attempt to retain its old friends a little longer. For a while No. 149 lingered outside the now bus-filled depot with shortworking car No. 109 while staff debated whether to take them inside overnight, but emergency repairs having been made, the two cars journeyed together to Bankfoot depot where they joined ten of their fellow exiles, the remainder having been despatched either to Thornbury or, like No. 107, last of the dignified 'High Four window' cars, to the scrapyard.

A month later a Ministry of Labour ruling that Saturday work after 1.0pm should qualify for 'time-and-a-half' payment compelled the Transport Department to raise fares again. As only two tram services now remained, the new tramcar fare-table was easily summarised:—

City to Thornbury	2½d
City to Odsal	2½d
Pakington Street to Horsfall Playing Fields	2½d
City to Horsfall Playing Fields	3½d

The threat of nationalisation of the Transport Undertaking was debated by the City Council on 20th December, when, in reply to a motion supporting 'Transfer of Road Transport to the British Transport Commission', Alderman H.K. Watson protested that

"We should do all we can to prevent local transport from being run from Sheffield, Leeds or anywhere else. The abolition of local control should be resisted."

Mercifully, the question was academic for the tramcars,

Meanwhile at Bowling Yard the sad slaughter was gathering pace. An edict that trams which sustained any damage should no longer be repaired was carried out unquestioningly, to the extent that immaculate car No. 226 on new, expensive full tyres was condemned for trifling damage to a vestibule panel while No.

A stately view of 'high four-window' tram No. 107 ready to enter Horton Bank Top depot yard. Its trolley is just about to clear the reverser. *Photo: Mr F. N. T. Lloyd-Jones*

The youth of Queensbury deserted their 5th November bonfires to watch the departure of their last tram, No. 149. *Photo: Telegraph and Argus*

77 with its heavily-worn flanges and axle-box keeps continued to give passengers a jolting, tailwagging ride.

Since November 1949 it had been possible to traverse the entire Thornbury route from Hall Ings to the new Bradford Moor turning-circle by trolleybus, but economic circumstances had persuaded the Department to supersede the Thornbury trams by motor buses. Not that the public were clamouring for change. Late-evening passengers waiting in the Hall Ings shelter on 4th March 1950 spurned the opportunity of riding home on one of the sleek Karrier/Weymann trolleybuses returning to depot from Tong Cemetery – they wanted to travel for the last time on their Thornbury tram, and when car No. 229 drew alongside, it quickly filled with cheerful Bradfordians.

The last of the dark blue trams, No. 127, was photographed at Thornbury on the final day of the Leeds Road tramcar service.
Photo: the late Mr J. A. Pitts

After hurried photography at the outer terminus Driver Woodworth began a fast cross-city run to Bankfoot depot where No. 229 joined the cream of the fleet now gathered there for the remaining life of the tramways. Among the unlucky victims which went for scrap were No. 127, last of the dark blue trams, and No. 196, a serviceable car whose vestibule had been damaged that day by a lorry laden with Bradford wool, thereby allowing a brief respite for No. 70, whose departure from Greengates terminus 22 years earlier had begun the tramway abandonment process.

Destined to be the last service tram to Thornbury a few hours later, car No. 229 was photographed negotiating the almost-new trolley reverser whose apex was between the positive and negative trolleybus wires.
Photo: Mr J. Copland

However, Leeds Road had not seen the last of its trams, as its tracks needed to be kept in working order to allow the Bankfoot-based cars to travel to Thornbury Works for 'minor operations' such as motor changes. For a few weeks tramcar No. 247, retained in the 'Far West' as a reserve vehicle along with Nos. 52, 77, 109 and plough S4, made an unobtrusive daily journey to Hall Ings and back as though nothing had happened, but afterwards the duty was carried out from Bankfoot depot.

Bradford's tramways had been 'a long time a-dying', and few people could accept that the gradual process would soon be complete; the timeless tramcars had grown to be 'as much a part of Bradford as gondolas were of Venice or rickshaws of Hongkong'.

'When the last tram runs in Bradford', wrote Mr G. Hayward, 'memories will float back to the late 'twenties, when the city's squares seemed gayer and resounded to the sound of tramcars leaving for all parts. We shall no longer hear the deep hum of powerful motors, the ring of the wheels on the sharp curves, the shriek of the conductor's whistle or the squeal of the brakes down the last steep slope to the city centre.

Who would have paid 1s 0d for a ride on the dodgems when for 4d one could have a thrilling ride of 4½ miles to Queensbury, with wonderful air and scenic views as a free tonic?

On the tram one did not feel so confined as on the bus – there was the open balcony on which to linger, and the spacious platform with its fascinating array of brass fittings, wheels and controls. The eye was not bored with straight lines or streamlining, as there were interesting little carvings and much sturdy woodwork.'

Few Bradfordians could have expressed more evocatively their affection for the familiar vehicles which had served them so faithfully and so long.

The possible choice of a tramcar for the official last journey aroused speculation. Would it be No. 225, smart and exceptionally smooth-riding, No. 86 with its new paintwork, No. 102, elegant and recently re-upholstered, or even time-honoured No. 247? The question was answered towards the end of April when tramcar No. 104 was despatched to the Works in preparation for the ceremonial closure. The selection had been inspired by the wage-check number of the Bankfoot depot foreman, Mr 'Wally' Northrop, but fortunately his choice had fallen on a typical and acceptable car devoid of any uncharacteristic features.

Saturday 6th May 1950 was a busy, eventful and memorable day, and, appropriately for an English springtime, cool and drizzly. Morning strollers were intrigued to glimpse two unusual tramcars travelling down Leeds Road and passing in front of the Town Hall on their way to Bankfoot depot. The first was old No. 77 whose roof canopies, lifeguards and staircase had been removed for model-making purposes, while the second – the final tram to leave Thornbury Works – was No. 104, beflagged and adorned with the multi-hued lights and decorations last borne by car No. 88 on its historic journey from Crossflatts exactly eleven years previously.

On arrival at Bankfoot No. 104 was allowed out into the depot yard several times during the day for admiration and photography, whilst inside the depot the patient shedmen were permitting visitors to inspect the trams and remove modest souvenirs.

Meanwhile the usual Saturday routines were being carried out, although for the first time since the pre-war May Days all the trams in service flew bunting on their trolley booms. The 'teatime rush' from 4.0pm onwards was followed by a brisk

A familiar Bradford scene – for a few more hours. Flanked by wool warehouses, a horse-drawn cart carrying bales of raw wool and a 'British Olivetti Typewriters' van, tramcar No. 104 passes Station Court in Leeds Road on its way to Bankfoot depot, Saturday, 6th May 1950. *Copyright: the late J. A. Pitts*

demand for 'Speedway Specials' to Odsal, which absorbed no fewer than 21 cars, leaving only seven indoors for various reasons, ie hot bearings (No. 102), worn tyres (No. 255), motor damage sustained a few days earlier (No. 142), partial dismantling (Nos. 70, 77 and 247) and, of course, No. 104.

Then at 9.0pm the returning 'specials' moved off the Horsfall Playing Fields reservation for the last time, No. 109 bringing up the rear, and for the next half-hour every car to City ran fully laden, with a chain across the entrance to deter would-be boarders. However, when No. 248 backed into the depot at about 9.15pm, its working days were already over.

Time for one more trip to Odsal and back, and then, slowly, the crowds began to gather in Town Hall Street. By 10.55pm the tram queue already extended around the corner into Market Street, and despite the vigilance of the efficient inspectors, a few instances of 'queue-jumping' occurred when car No. 149 loaded for the last ordinary journey at 11.4pm, to Bankfoot.

No sooner had No. 149 departed than the reflected brilliance of the approaching illuminated car, No. 104, began to fill Town Hall Square, and turning into Town Hall Street the splendid vision halted at the Wyke barrier, Driver Laverack smiling broadly amid cheers and shouts of "Good Old Reggie!" As crowds gazed admiringly at the flags, the bunting and brilliantly-lighted decorations, No. 104 was boarded by its special guests, the Chairman of the Transport Committee (Councillor B. W. Berry), his deputy (Councillor A. S. Downey), the General Manager (Mr Tattam) and their colleagues. As in 1898, the Lord Mayor was not present.

The loyal public of Bradford had not been forgotten. For them Mr Northrop had chosen two extra cars – No. 140 which he considered the quietest, together with the lowest-numbered tram, No. 51. Both were quickly packed to capacity – and beyond –, the front balcony of No. 51 somehow finding space for eight standing passengers (the author and seven boisterous youths who shouted and sang to the crowds below) as well as the official quota of nine seated passengers.

Inside the saloon, looking through the haze of tobacco smoke to the polished brass and gleaming woodwork that they had known for a lifetime, the passengers found it hard to believe that in a few minutes' time they would have finished with its cheery familiarity for ever.

113

Promptly at 11.8pm the Chief Inspector signalled the moment of departure, and to an accompaniment of cheering and waving the historic cortege moved off, rocking and clattering up Nelson Street to where the Croft Street traffic lights, anxious to salute their old colleagues for the final time, allowed car No. 104 to pass but detained its companions.

In Manchester Road knots and groups of locals had gathered to cheer, and after the conductors had – with the utmost difficulty – collected all the fares, a few passengers alighted at the fare stage. Then at Smiddles Lane the electricity sub-station took its turn in prolonging the nostalgic farewell: pretending to have been overburdened by the extra current drawn by the illuminated car and by the amateur driving techniques of the Chairman and his deputy, it plunged the procession into darkness and immobility for ten minutes while householders standing at their doors drank tea and exchanged jocular quips.

Now the final parting could no longer be delayed. Ablaze with light once more, car No. 104 proceeded on its way to Odsal while its humbler brethren, No. 140 and last of all No. 51, took turns to unload their passengers outside the 'Red Lion', Bankfoot.

Then, cautiously negotiating the crossover through the dense throngs, they moved back down the road to reverse into the lower depot yard.

Meanwhile car No. 104 had returned from Odsal to the upper part of the depot, where the Manager, Rolling Stock Engineer and Chairman led the onlookers in the singing of 'Auld Lang Syne', after which the colourful lights of the illuminated car were switched off at 11.55pm and the officials and the drivers and conductors of the three last cars departed by bus for a midnight repast at the Town Hall.

For a few moments longer the cars in the lower yard stood with all their lights ablaze, and a farewell photograph was taken inside No. 51. Then, in the first minutes of the new day and with many a backward glance, the onlookers slowly departed. And one by one the lights went out for the last time.

(Above) Before the lights went out: tramcars Nos. 120, 140 and 51 in the lower yard of Bankfoot depot, with Driver Jacky Elam (car No. 140), Driver M. Dinsdale (car No. 51) and his conductor (centre, name not recorded).

Copyright: the late J. A. Pitts

(Below) The Bradford tramway fraternity gathered inside tramcar No. 51 for a final photograph. Left to right: Messrs R. Addy, M. Peck, J. A. Pitts and E. Thornton, the conductor, Mrs M. Copland, Mr J. Copland, the author and Messrs F. Hartley and A. Brooke.

Copyright: Mr J. Copland

17 – RESURRECTION

'We got rid of the trams years back and had trolleybuses, and then they bought the trams back – had to relay the lines and everything.'

('Sheldrake', by Michael Wharton, 1958 – a pipe-dream not yet fulfilled)

"All things considered", commented an Odsal lady after the closure, "we should be glad to see the back of them. Yet on Saturday, seeing them on their last day, flags flying from the trolley arm, they seemed gallant vehicles. It is a little sad to see something that has worked hard and bravely, outgrow its usefulness and be replaced by things more modern."

Evidently the trams thought so too, as they were in no hurry to disappear. On Monday 8th May car No. 51 happily consented to be driven up to Odsal for an official photograph, while on Saturday 13th May the shedmen readily allowed Mr J. A. Pitts and the author to take car No. 104 out into the yard for more photographs.

But fate was knocking at the door now – with a sledgehammer. Dismantling of the tramcars in the lower shed began on 18th May and was complete by 6th July, on which day the cars from the upper shed took their place. For the convenience of the workmen car No. 104 performed the final journey on the public highway on 12th July, being driven as far as the 'Red Lion', traversing the crossover and 'reversing' into a more accessible part of the lower shed yard where its truck and other equipment were removed.

Two days after the ceremonial closure of the tramways, car No. 51 was driven to Odsal for an official photograph. With Coll Mills in the background, the tram is standing on the Halifax Road single track between Odsal terminus and the beginning of the reserved track. *Copyright: BCPT*

Only tramcar No. 255 remained intact, the last, lone survivor of the once-mighty fleet. For a few more days it stood quietly inside the depot, but when Messrs Pickford called to collect the body of No. 104 on 17th July, No. 255, quickly divested of all electrical and mechanical items, departed a few hours later for a restful retirement on a Thornton allotment.

Current in the remaining overhead wires, from Smiddles Lane to Rooley Lane, was finally switched off, and the wires themselves were cut down in early August. Meanwhile, over at Bowling Yard the last, roofless remains of 'Greengates' car No. 72 had trundled down the breakers' siding on 28th July to be sawn asunder.

A few of the Dick Kerr tram controllers were despatched to Calcutta for further use, and Leeds acquired some of the comfortable leather-upholstered seats for use in their ex-Southampton cars and to improve the lot of their passengers who still had to endure hard wooden seating. Leeds was also the destination of some of the enamelled lampholders which not only improved the lighting in the 'Southampton' cars but also provided the finishing touches for their future railcar No. 600.

Within the next five years almost all the surviving permanent way was tarred over or removed, but where the former Horsfall Playing Fields route had crossed Netherlands Avenue the tracks, flanked by traditional granite setts, survived to become officially 'listed' 30 years later – and were actually extended a few feet when the carriageway was widened!

The death of Mr C. J. Spencer, reported in the month in which the last tram ran, seemed a fitting conclusion to the story of the tramway undertaking whose architect he was. Described as "nobbut a lad" at the time of his appointment, he had lived to see his other protegés, the trolleybuses, assume a major role which few practical men could have foretold at the time of their inception.

Meanwhile, what had become of tramcar No. 104, last seen disappearing from Bankfoot depot on Pickfords' waggon?

In spite of official indifference, preservation moves were afoot. When the normally unsentimental Rolling Stock Engineer failed to persuade the Manager to retain car No. 51, either wholly or partly, Mr Harry Hornby of Bradford Northern Rugby Football Club stepped in to acquire car No. 104 with the intention of mounting it on a short length of track at Odsal Stadium and displaying it, flags, coloured lights and all, on 'Speedway Nights'.

Bureaucracy, intransigence and muddle then intervened. First the car was stripped of its decorations and then of its truck, trolley and electrical equipment. Then, on removal from Bankfoot, the body mysteriously vanished for a week before being traced to Baildon Moor where a local family who had ordered a lower-deck from BCPT for conversion into a holiday home, had been agreeably surprised to receive a double-deck body instead. Tears were shed when the error was rectified, as the best substitute that could be salvaged for them from the wreckage at Bowling Yard was the windowless lower-deck hulk of No. 127. Finally, in mid-August, No. 104 reached Odsal Stadium, where, no

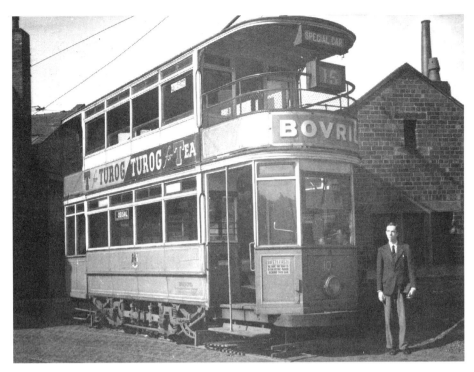

longer usable for its intended role, it served as a rugby scoreboard.

Private plans for the acquisition of No. 219, one of the 'Preston' cars still surviving in Sheffield, were frustrated by a lack of capital and accommodation, and by 1953 the sole ex-BCPT representative in Sheffield was No. 251 in the guise of SCT railgrinder No. 330 (preserved since 1960 at the National Tramway Museum).

By that time the management of Bradford's transport was in the hands of Mr C. T. Humpidge, who was not only a convinced advocate of electric traction but was always receptive to new ideas. Thus, when on 1st March 1953, the author first discussed with Mr J. A. Pitts the concept of acquiring the body of No. 104, persuading BCPT to house it at Thornbury Works and gradually reuniting it with all its missing parts, the enthusiasm of both Mr Humpidge and Mr Harry Hornby was such that within six weeks – 17th April – the body was back in the Works, resting on the old paintshop truck.

The congenial task of assembling all the items needed for the car to be made operational took several years. The Thornbury stores yielded a trolley boom and head; the redundant Works traverser and driving school contributed controllers, motors and brake gear; private collectors donated many small items, and a conventional trolley base was bought from Liverpool.

Unfortunately, Dick Kerr 21E trucks were no longer available in Britain, and through the good offices of the Bradford and Sheffield managers a Brush/Brill type 21E of 6ft 0ins wheelbase, similar to the 6ft 6ins version purchased in 1912 for cars Nos. 210 and 229, was taken from Sheffield snowplough No. 358, re-gauged, dismantled and despatched to Thornbury.

During several months of painstaking work Mr Hubert Robinson and colleagues in the Works renovated and assembled the truck. The car body was repaired, re-wired, mounted upon the restored truck and tested. Great was Mr Robinson's joy when, having jacked the wheels clear of the track by means of the slipper brake, he gently fed power to the motors and the car came to life again.

Following a 1938-style repaint (using a can of blue paint miraculously found in the stores) No. 104 received a trial run up the Works siding on 21st July 1958, just in time for the Diamond Jubilee of the Department two days later.

Thereafter the increasingly famous tramcar was used on many occasions for hugely-popular 'excursions' up and down the siding, drawing power from the trolleybus wires, with a special connection to allow the return current to be transmitted via the negative wire.

Unfortunately, suspicion arose that the special connection was actually earthing the trolleybus installations, thus allowing stray currents to leak back to the Valley Road power station by unorthodox means. The last excursion therefore took place on 14th September 1963 and No. 104 made its final sortie up the siding on 26th September 1966.

With the closure of the trolleybus system in 1972 the power supply vanished, but in anticipation of that event the author, in

---

BRADFORD CORPORATION PASSENGER TRANSPORT DEPARTMENT

NOTICE TO PASSENGERS

ODSAL SERVICE

Commencing Sunday, 7th May, 1950, tramcars on the Odsal service will be substituted by motor buses, Route No. 75. For frequency, see new timetables.

Route and fares will remain as at present, except that the Odsal terminus will be extended to Crawford Avenue. Passengers are requested to note alterations to certain stopping places.

The Horsfall Playing Fields service will be withdrawn.

C. R. Tattam, M.Inst.T.,
General Manager

11, Forster Square,
Bradford. 21st April, 1950.

73422 50.450

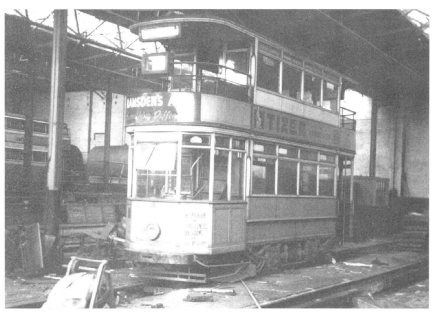

partnership with Mr J. A. Pitts, had, in 1965, suggested to the Corporation Museums Department the idea of establishing an Industrial Museum for the preservation of textile machinery, industrial archaeology (then a new term) – and the tramcar. Happily the idea fell on fertile ground, and following the purchase of Moorside Mills, Eccleshill, in 1970, a special 'Tram and Trolley Shed' was unveiled on 4th March 1975 – the 25th anniversary of the last Thornbury tramcar.

Faded memories of the long-defunct horse trams were revived when a 'Horses at Work' museum was added to the Moorside Mills attractions, thereby creating a need for a replica of Bradford Tramways & Omnibus Company ex-Shipley single-deck horse tram No. 40. Built by W. G. H. Transportation Engineering of Doncaster, the car made its first journeys in April 1992, on 4ft gauge tracks laid in the museum yard

The last survivor: surrounded by the wreckage of other trams, No. 255 was still intact and mobile when photographed on 13th July 1950, but four days later the depot was finally cleared.
Copyright: Mr J. Copland

The skilful restoration of tramcar No. 104 in 1958 enabled the Transport Department to operate an occasional 'service' in the Thornbury Works siding. Pouring rain on 25th April, 1959, provided an authentic atmosphere, even though the tram was not actually travelling to Briggate, Shipley (in fact, it probably never ventured there at any time). The driver was Mr Eric Thornton.
Copyright: The late Mr J. A. Pitts

and comprising rails unearthed from Manchester Road, Queensbury, Duckworth Lane Depot, the 'Far West' and even Blackpool.

The author hopes that one day tramcar No. 104 will also be able to operate under power at the Museum and allow Bradfordians of the 21st century to savour the pleasure once taken for granted by their more fortunate predecessors – the supreme pleasure of riding upon the most noble and character-filled of all vehicles – the Bradford Corporation Tramcar.

TRAMCAR LIVERIES

(1) BRADFORD TRAMWAYS & OMNIBUS COMPANY

(a)   Horse Trams and Steam Trams:–
Nut brown and deep cream with red platform dashes; decorative gilding on brown panels; single gold lining on platforms and staircases; scarlet lining on upper panels; corner posts red and gold; gold fleet numbers.

(b)   Engines: Maroon and cream; orange-brown skirts; double gold lining: fleet number on red oval on skirts.

(2) BRADFORD AND SHELF TRAMWAY COMPANY – Cars and engines

Prussian blue and cream; gold and white lining on blue panels and vermilion lining on cream. Outsize gold fleet numbers on tramcar dashplate but conventional size on engines. In the last few years a chocolate and cream livery was used, and latterly dashplates and staircases were red.

(3) BRADFORD CITY TRAMWAYS

1898:   Prussian blue and ivory; red oxide truck and lifeguards; trolley mast green; trolley boom and beading black; gold and white lining on blue panels; brown and red lining on rocker panels; fine red line on window posts; corner pillars vermilion and gold; fleet numbers gilt shaded in red (square 'Spencer' style).

1917:   Austerity livery of navy grey and white, unlined, with white painted numerals. After 1918 many grey cars were temporarily overpainted in unlined Prussian blue and white, with Clarendon or Spencer numerals.

1919:   Prussian blue and ivory; red oxide truck, lifeguards and roof; trolley boom, beading and fenders black; gold and white lining on blue panels; bright blue lining on rocker panels and side window posts; black lining on corner posts; 'Clarendon' gilt fleet numbers shaded in rose red.

1928:   Ornamental corners on waist-panel gold lining simplified; coloured lining on upper deck side panels and balcony 'tins' abolished.

1930:   Gold lining reduced to single plain line; blue lining on rocker panel reduced to single plain line.

1931:   'Clarendon' numerals superseded by (i) plain Gill Sans with blue edging (ii) unshaded numeral with serifs; (iii) plain 'microscopic' 2 ins numeral; (iv) plain Gill Sans with black edging.

1937:   Blue-black and pale cream

1938:   'Ultramarine' blue-black and pale cream.

1940:   'Chrome yellow' lining replaced gold.

1942:   South Sea blue and primrose; 'chrome' yellow lining on blue; South Sea lining on window posts; black beading, trolley boom and fenders; gold fleet names; fleet numbers as 1931 (iv); red oxide truck, lifeguards and roof; black axle-boxes and coil-springs.

1946/7   One coat repaints without lining or varnish for 23 cars already in South Sea blue livery.

TRAM STANDARDS (poles) Emerald Green; from 1934 pole bases bottle green; pole numerals white.

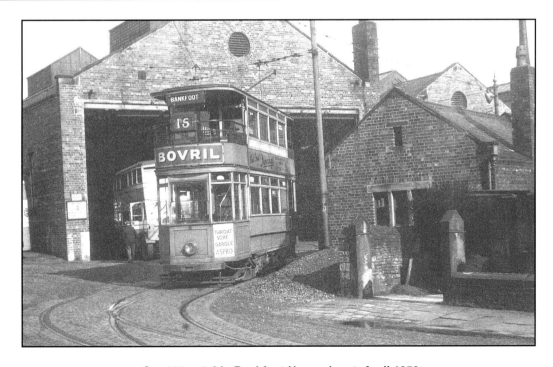

Car 195 outside Bankfoot Upper depot, April 1950

APPENDIX 1A

BRADFORD TRAMWAYS & OMNIBUS COMPANY – TRAMCARS

Fleet No.	Date into Service	Builder	Type	Seats	Withdrawn	Notes
1-6	Jan/Feb 1882	Ashbury/Eades	Horse, open-top		By 1902	
7-10	1882	Ashbury/Eades	Steam, 4-wheel	1882 Top deck knife-board, 1887 2 and 1 garden seats.	– ditto –	Front vestibule only
11-13	?	?	Steam, 4-wheel	1882 Top deck knife board, 1887 2 and 1 garden seats	– ditto –	Front vestibule only
14-15	1884	?	Steam double-deck	24/22 = 46	(b)	Top deck partly open
16-17	1885	Ashbury/Eades	Horse, Vestibuled top deck front	18/16 = 34	c.1890	See car 38
18-19	1885	Ashbury/Eades	Horse, Vestibuled top deck front	18/16 = 34	c.1890	See car 41
20-23	1885	?	Steam, bogie, enclosed	28/26 = 54	By 1902	9-window body
24-25	1887	G.F. Milnes	Steam, bogie, enclosed	30/26 = 56	– ditto –	
26-33	1888	G. F. Milnes	Steam, bogie, enclosed	30/26 = 56	– ditto –	7-window body
34-35	1889	G. F. Milnes	Steam, bogie, enclosed	30/28 = 58	– ditto –	
36-37	1890	?	Horse	16	– ditto –	
38	c.1890	–	Steam, bogie, enclosed	34/33 = 67	– ditto –	Ex-horse cars 16/17 spliced together
39-40	1892	?	Horse, enclosed	18	– ditto –	Ex-Shipley
41	c.1890	?	Steam, bogie, enclosed	34/33 = 67	– ditto –	Ex-horse cars 18/19 spliced together
42-45	1893	G. F. Milnes	Steam, bogie, enclosed	30/28 = 58	– ditto –	
46-47	?	?	Horse, Open charabanc, toastrack	24	– ditto –	Later canopy roof
16-17	1894	B.T.O.C.	Horse, Open charabanc, toastrack			
18-19	1895	? Milnes	Steam, single-ended	28/31 = 59	– ditto –	
48	1901	? Milnes	Steam, single-ended	28/31 = 59	– ditto –	
49-50(a)	1900	(Second hand)	Steam, wide top deck	38/28 = 66	– ditto –	2 and 2 seats, top deck
51-52(a)	1901	(Second hand)	Steam, single-ended	31/28 = 59	– ditto –	

(a)   First licensed in 1900/1901; source unknown but possibly North Staffs. Tramways or Blackburn
(b)   Rebuilt c.1888 as 6-wheel steam trailers

BRADFORD TRAMWAYS & OMNIBUS COMPANY – ENGINES

(Acknowledgments to Messrs F. Hartley and J. Pollard)

Engine No.	W/ No.	Date into Service	Builder	Type
1		July 1882	Kitson	7¼ horizontal bore cylinder, 12 ins stroke) All inspected August 1882
2, 3		August 1882	Kitson	7¼ horizontal bore cylinder, 12 ins stroke) by Maj-Gen Hutchinson
4-6		October 1882	Kitson	7¼ horizontal bore cylinder, 12 ins stroke) Weight 7 tons
7	4?	June 1883	T. Green	Wilkinson patent, vertical boiler. On trial.
8		1884	Kitson	Locomotive type, 8½ cylinders, compound
7(ii)	15	1885	T. Green	Locomotive type
9	20	1885	T. Green	Locomotive type, delivered 20/06/85, compound
10	21	1885	T. Green	Locomotive type, delivered 06/07/85, compound
11	22	1885	T. Green	Locomotive type, delivered 31/07/85, compound
12	77	1887	T. Green	Locomotive type, delivered 28/10/87, compound
13	78	1888	T. Green	Locomotive type, delivered 24/02/88, compound
14	79	1888	T. Green	Locomotive type, delivered 24/04/88, compound
15	88	1888	T. Green	Locomotive type, delivered 14/09/88, compound
16	89	1888	T. Green	Locomotive type, delivered 21/09/88, compound
17	90	1888	T. Green	Locomotive type, delivered 13/10/88, compound
18	91	1888	T. Green	Locomotive type, delivered 21/10/88, compound
19	97	1888	T. Green	Locomotive type, delivered 17/11/88, compound
20	98	1888	T. Green	Locomotive type, delivered 01/12/88, compound
21	99	1888	T. Green	Locomotive type, delivered 13/12/88, compound
22	100	1888	T. Green	Locomotive type, delivered 20/12/88, compound
23	133	1889	T. Green	Locomotive type, compound, delivered 14/04/89
24	134	1889	T. Green	Locomotive type, compound, delivered 03/08/89
25	155	1890	T. Green	Locomotive type, compound, delivered 30/06/90
26	156	1890	T. Green	Locomotive type, compound, delivered 02/08/90
27	165	1891	T. Green	Locomotive type, compound, Burrell condenser, delivered 01/08/91
28	195	1893	T. Green	Locomotive type, compound, Burrell condenser, delivered 29/04/93
29	196	1893	T. Green	Locomotive type, compound, Burrell condenser, delivered 20/05/93
30	197	1893	T. Green	Locomotive type, compound, Burrell condenser, delivered 19/07/93
31	198	1893	T. Green	Locomotive type, compound, Burrell condenser, delivered 01/08/93
32	199	1893	T. Green	Locomotive type, compound, Burrell condenser, delivered 30/08/93
33	202	1893	T. Green	Locomotive type, compound, Burrell condenser, delivered 30/08/93
34	203	1893	T. Green	Locomotive type, Burrell condenser, delivered 18/11/93
35	205	1894	T. Green	Locomotive type, Burrell condenser, delivered 06/07/94
36		1896	B.T.O.C.	Locomotive type, Burrell condenser
37-40		1900	?	* Reputed second-hand ex North Staffs Tramways Company.

The seating capacity of the bogie 'two-deckers' was declared as 58 in 1892, and each car weighed 8 tons fully laden.   Livery: engines maroon, gold and white lining; window frames cream; skirts orange/brown; gold number on oval. Cars: lower panels nut-brown, gold-lined; rest cream lined in vermilion. Corner posts, dashplates and staircases bright red. Oil lighting.
* per Dr Whitcombe. Board of Trade returns include an increase from 35 engines at 30/06/1900 to 38 a year later, but Duncans' Tramway Manual records no change.

B.S.T. & B.T.O.C. : Service braking: steam operated, controlled by two upright levers which were duplicated at each end for running in either direction. One lever controlled expansion and reversing and the other the throttle and brake. By pushing the lever forward the throttle was opened; pulling it back applied the brake on all wheels of the engine and car. Other levers opened or closed the fire door and regulated the damper. The Green engines weighted 12 tons - like all the engines could be driven from either end. The handle of the B.S.T. vacuum brake was mounted halfway along the boiler, so that when running chimney first, the driver had to work the throttle with his left hand, reach back with his right hand for the brake and watch the road over his left shoulder. Running stern-first, his position was reversed.

APPENDIX 1B

BRADFORD & SHELF TRAMWAY COMPANY – TRAMCARS

FLEET NO.	DATE INTO SERVICE	BUILDER	TYPE	SEATS	W/DRAWN	NOTES
1-5	September 1884	Starbuck	Bogie double-decker	30/28 = 58	1902	Top deck middle section originally open
6	March 1885	Starbuck	Bogie double-decker	30/28 = 58	1902	
7-11	March 1885	Starbuck	4-wheel single-decker	18	1886	
12	November 1885	Starbuck	Bogie double-decker	30/28 = 58	1893	
13-14	November 1885	Starbuck	4-wheel single-decker	18	1886	
7	May 1887	?	Bogie double-decker	30/28 = 58	1893	
8, 9, 13	May 1887		Bogie single-decker	40	1902	Rebuilt from six of the 4-wheel cars 7-11, 13-14, New No. 13 became No. 10 in 1891
7, 12	February 1893					
	March 1893	G. F. Milnes	Bogie double-decker	30/28 = 58	1903	To B.C.T. 1902
13	June 1893	Milnes or Ashbury	Bogie double-decker	30/28 = 58	1902	
14	January 1894	G.F. Milnes	Bogie double-decker	30/28 = 58	1903	To B.C.T. 1902

One of the three bogie single-deckers 8, 9 or 10 ex 13 became B.C.T. No. 229, 1903. All had 6 side-windows with a thicker window-post in the centre where the two original bodies had been spliced together and mounted on 3ins channel iron underframes. All had turtle-back roofs and clerestories.

BRADFORD & SHELF TRAMWAY COMPANY – ENGINES

(Acknowledgements to Messrs F. Hartley and J. Pollard)

ENGINE NO.	WORKS NO.	DATE DELIVERED	BUILDER	TYPE	W/DRAWN	NOTES
1*	11/33	25/8/1884	T. Green (Wilkinson)	7½ins cylinder	1887	
2*	11/34	28/8/1884	T. Green (Wilkinson)	7½ ins cylinder	1890	Blackburns condenser, 1890
3*	11/35	04/9/1884	T. Green (Wilkinson)	7½ ins cylinder	1887	
4*	11/36	24/9/1884	T. Green (Wilkinson)	7½ ins cylinder	1887	
5**	13	29/1/1885	T. Green	9ins x 14ins cylinder	1902	
6	14	12/2/1885	T. Green	9ins x 14ins cylinder	1902	
7	15	01/4/1885	T. Green	9ins x 14ins cylinder	1902?	
5	44	10/6/1886	T. Green	9ins x 14ins cylinder	1902	
8**	13?	1886	T. Green	9ins x 14ins cylinder	1902	Ex No. 5?
9	46	23/8/1886	T. Green	9ins x 14ins cylinder	1902	
10	47	17/9/1886	T. Green	9ins x 14ins cylinder	1902	
11		1887	C. Burrell	10ins x 14ins cylinder	1891	Approx 12 tons
1	65	30/07/1887	T. Green	9ins x 14ins cylinder	1902	
3	48	1887	T. Green	9ins x 14ins cylinder	1902	
4	58	26/5/1887	T. Green	9ins x 14ins cylinder	1902	
2***	96	27/2/1890	T. Green	9ins x 14ins cylinder	1902	Blackburns condenser
11	94	1891	T. Green	9ins x 14ins cylinder	1902/3	High-ressure cylinders
12	95	18/1/1893	T. Green	9ins x 14ins cylinder	1902/3	High-pressure cylinders
13	193	25/4/1893	T. Green	9ins x 14ins cylinder	1902/3	High-pressure cylinders
14	206	23/12/1893	T. Green	9ins x 14ins cylinder	1902/3	High-pressure

*   Converted from vertical to horizontal boiler, 1887. All other engines horizontal.

**   A Manning, Wardle engine may have been hired as a temporary replacement for No. 5 in Autumn 1885. No. 5 may have re-entered service as No. 8. Engines 11-14 of 1891-3 had Burrell condensers.

***   Part-exchange for the original No. 2

No. 7 appears to have been exchanged for T. Green Works No. 24 which was delivered 22nd September 1885, and was also numbered 7

Kimberley (South Africa) Tramways Company Nos. 1-4 (Green works Nos. 231/2/3/5) supplied c.1895 are reputed to have been rebuilt from Bradford & Shelf engines (or possibly Bradford Tramways & Omnibus Company), but T. Green records do not confirm this.

APPENDIX 1C

HOLROYD SMITH'S ELECTRIC TRAMCAR, 1892

Body:
Lancaster Carriage & Wagon Company. Seats: 18 inside (9 per side, longitudinal); top deck 12 on reversible seats (4 x 2 and 4 x 1) and 3 on each balcony; total 36. 'The first of its kind that has been built in England.' Overall length 21ft.

Truck:
Easton and Anderson of Erith Ironworks to Holroyd Smith's design. Wheelbase 5ft 10ins. Truck frame: double upper and lower side-plates with vertical and cantilever braces; the top rail to which the body was bolted rested on coiled springs at each side of the axle boxes. Wheels 28ins diameter chilled iron.

Motors and drive:
Each axle driven by a 17½hp motor inclined several degrees from horizontal. A form of differential drive used to minimise friction on sharp curves: both wheels on each axle could turn independently, as one was keyed to the axle and the other to a sleeve which revolved around the axle. A triple-thread 4½ins pitch worm mounted on the end of each armature shaft; the worm-wheels had a 1½ins pitch with 34 teeth, giving a 11:1 ratio and good coasting qualities when power was shut off. Gears fully enclosed in oil, with ball bearings. Drive designed by Mr Anthony Reckenzaun, a 42-year old Austrian who had pioneered the worm-drive on a series-parallel accumulator-powered car in South London; following the Bradford trials he emigrated to Philadelphia but died there only a year later. Each motor had one pair of field magnets but two armatures, each 11ins long and 12¼ins in diameter, thus providing in effect a 4-motor car. The motor winding arrangement permitted three running-speeds:– (1) with all four armatures in series for maximum starting-torque; (2) with two pairs in series for half-speed, attaining 5 mph with 47 passengers aboard, and (3) with all four in parallel for full speed. Power admitted to the motors via a 'resistance switch' probably mounted under the stairs and controlled by 'a wheel resembling a helmsman's wheel on a steamer'. Efficiency of motors and gears 65%.

Brakes:
(1) Wheel brake applied via a handle mounted on a vertical staff outside the platform dash, tightening a chain which applied cast-iron brake shoes to the wheels by means of coupling rods, pressure bars and levers.
(2) Four-shoe track (slipper) brake, actually a wheel-scotch controlled by levers for safe descent of gradients.
(3) Rheostatic brake which in effect reversed the motors, thus feeding power back into the resistances which dissipated it in the form of heat; as the power built up the car slowed, but on reaching a crawling pace the momentum resumed.

Weight:
Truck and equipment 3ton 19cwt 2qr; total weight of car 6ton 9cwt.

Towing gear:
The car appeared to have a coupling arrangement which would allow it to be hauled to Thornbury Depot by a steam engine, for overnight accommodation.

Power supply:
Nominally 305 volts from Bradford Corporation Electricity Department. On a test run with 40 passengers the consumption was about 70 amps maximum.

Current collection:
Originally a primitive form of bow collector at each end of the upper deck, superseded by a trolley boom with fixed (ie rotating but non-swivel) trolley wheel, current being drawn by the 'trailing' trolley while the 'leading' trolley over the driver's head was tied down (failure to ensure this incurred damage to the overhead wires more than once).

Fastest ascent of Cheapside – 11mph. Greatest number of passengers on any journey – 44 (excluding driver and conductor).

BRADFORD CORPORATION TRAMCAR FLEET

"Bradford trams?" said the unobservant observer. "Why, they're all the same!".

"Nay," protested the veteran connoisseur with more enthusiasm than grammar, "There isn't one alike!"

Truth, as usual, lay somewhere in the middle. Although the original batches of cars bought 1898-1904 were basically standard products, most were fundamentally altered and modernised as the years passed. The post-1912 Thornbury-built products underwent a process of continuous evolution and improvement, and together with the older trams were drawn into periodic cycles of whirligig renumbering which, in the end, successfully concealed their age and origin.

For example, in 1930 trams 119, 120 and 121 were all very different beings – a B.C.T.-built vestibuled canopy-top high-speed car, a Milnes open-top car in virtually original condition, and a rebuilt, re-trucked Milnes body with six side-windows, a canopy top and 'temporary glass front', respectively. A line-up of tramcars at football grounds or in city streets revealed intriguing differences in height, vestibule design, truck, location of the side destination box, size and number of windows and so on. Other features such as advertisements occasionally provided the only obvious evidence that two otherwise similar cars had exchanged fleet numbers.

In accordance with the basic rule that fleet numbers must relate to the actual size of the fleet, which never exceeded 258 (including cars awaiting scrapping or being prepared for service), new cars or new bodies took vacant numbers (eg in 1929 No. 181 was followed by Nos. 61, 20, 125, 54 and 2) although exceptionally when 46 Dick Kerr (E.E.) trams were bought in 1919-1921, they were allocated a block of numbers (213-258), thereby displacing existing trams. Other renumberings stemmed from a short-lived desire to group cars of similar origin into a distinctive batch (eg 'Greengates' 64-75 and the pre-Wilkinson B.C.T.-built products 140-164 – but No. 107 escaped). Some trams exchanged numbers and trucks (eg Brush 78 and Milnes 161 in 1912).

The following lists are as accurate and comprehensive as it has been possible to devise.

Cars 1-7 Type: 1898 Brush/Westinghouse

Entered Service 1898

Body: Brush Electrical Engineering Co, Loughborough;
4 camber-arched side windows; direct stairs.

Seating:	29 outside + 22 inside = total 51.
Truck:	Peckham B9 standard cantilever 6ft wheelbase.
Motors:	Two 25hp Westinghouse B49; efficiency over 75%.
Controllers:	Westinghouse type 5915; 4 series, 3 parallel and 5 brake notches.
Brakes:	Hand/wheel, hand/track (slipper) and rheostatic (electric).
Major modifications:	Extended balconies: 4, 5, 7, (1906)
	Bailey tops: 1, 2, 3, 6 (1903/4)
	High Canopy tops, balconies, reversed stairs: 1-4, 6/7, seats 38+22 = 60.
	'Temporary glass fronts': 1, 2, 7 (1924/5)
	Hurst, Nelson truck, Siemens motors: 4 (1914), 5 (1924)
	Dick Kerr 21E truck, DK31 motors: 2, 7 (1924)
	Seating 37+22 = 59 : 5

Cars 8-16   Type : 1898 Brush/westinghouse (as 1-7 but with roller-bearings)

Entered service 1898

Major Modifications:	Extended balconies: 8, 12, 13, 15
	Bailey top: 16
	High Canopy tops, balconies, reversed stairs: 8, 11-14, 16
	High Canopy top, balconies, reversed stairs, platform vestibules (1916): 9
	To Illuminated Car (1911-1929): 10
	'Temporary glass front': 8, 14, 16
	Seating 37+22 = 59 : 8, 12, 13, 15
	Seating 43+22 = 65 : 9
	Seating 38+20 = 60 : 11, 12 (1919), 14
	Hurst, Nelson S4W truck, BTH motors : 15 (1924)
	Dick Kerr 21E truck, DK31 motors 45hp : 8, 14 (1922)
	Hurst, Nelson 21E truck, Siemens motors 40hp : 9, 16
	Hurst, Nelson 21E truck, DK31 motors 45hp : 13 (1919)

Entered service 1899

Cars 17-24   Type 1899 Brush/Westinghouse (as 8-16 but with higher end dashplates)

Major Modifications:	Extended balconies: 18, 19
	Bailey tops: 20-24
	High Canopy tops, balconies, reversed stairs: 17-20, 22-24
	Medium-height ('Windhill') canopy top, balconies, reversed stairs: 21
	Seats 38+22 = 60 all
	'Temporary glass front': 18, 20, 22, 23
	Dick Kerr 21E truck, Siemens 40hp motors: 17
	Dick Kerr 21E truck, DK31 45hp motors: 17 (1922), 18, 19, 20, 23
	Hurst, Nelson 21E truck, Siemens 40hp motors: 21, 24
	Hurst, Nelson 21E truck, DK31 45hp motors: 18 (1926)
	Boving 21E truck, DK31 45hp motors: 22

Entered Service 1899	Cars 25-28	Type: Trailer cars, a shorter version of 17-24
		Body: Brush
		Seating: outside 20 + inside 20 = Total 40
	Major Modifications:	motorised 1900, with two 25hp Westinghouse B49 motors.
		Westinghouse controllers, hand/wheel, hand/track and rheostatic brakes, Blackwell trolley equipment.
		1905: cars 25, 26, 28 Brush AA 6ft wheelbase trucks, two 25hp Westinghouse
	motors, BTH B 18 controllers.	
		Extended balconies, reversed stairs: 25, 26, 28
		To Pay Car (1910-1925) 27
		To School Car (1927-1932) 28
		Seats 33+20 = 53: 25, 26, 28

Entered Service 1900　　Cars 29-53　Type 'White Board cars'

Body: Brush open-top, 4 camber-arched windows, reversed quarter-turn
stairs, semi-open balcony ends

Seating:	29 outside, 22 inside = total 51
	Truck:　Peckham B9 standard cantilever, 6ft wheelbase, plain bearings (as all
subsequent trucks)	
Motors:	Two 'Witting' T52-3 30hp
	Controllers:　　'Witting' type EH
Brakes:	Hand/wheel, hand/track, rheostatic
Major Modifications:	Enclosed balcony ends – all cars
	High canopy tops: 35, 41, 44, 53 (41 was last open-top car to be canopied, 03/25).
	Medium-height ('Windhill') canopy tops: 49, 50, 52
	To Illuminated Car 1925 : 37, 1925-9 : 45, 1929-1937 : 33
	Hurst, Nelson 21E trucks with Siemens 40hp motors: 48, 53
	Hurst, Nelson 21E trucks with DK31 50hp motors: 29
	Brush A truck: 30 (1919)
	Hurst, Nelson S4W truck (1921) 39
	Dick Kerr 21E truck with DK31 50hp motors: 40, 51
	'Temporary glass front', 41, 44, 49
Seating:	37+22 = 59　41? 47, 48 (open top cars)
	38+22=60　35, 41 (1925), 44, 49, 50, 52, 53

Entered Service 1901　　Cars 54-68　Type: 1901 Brush (as 29-53 but with fully-enclosed balcony ends, stronger corner-posts and no 'White Boards')

Major Modifications:	Bailey tops: 54-59, 60/61/63, 65-68
	High canopy top: 61, 62, 64
	Medium-height ('Windhill') canopy top: 55, 67 (1914)
	High canopy top, direct stairs, lengthened platforms, platform vestibules, air/oil
brake: 54 (1916)	
	'Temporary glass front': 55 (1924), 61 (1924)
	Seating: 43+22 = 65 : 54 (1916)
	28+22 = 50 : 54, 55/6/7/8/9/60/1/3/5/6/7/8
	38+22 = 60 : 55 (1919), 62, 64, 67 (1914)
	Boving 21E truck with Siemens 40hp motors: 55
	Hurst, Nelson 21E truck with Siemens 40hp motors: 54
	Dick Kerr 21E truck with DK31 50hp motors: 61

Entered Service 1901-2　　Cars 69-128　Type: 1902 Brush

Body:	Brush open-top, 4 side windows with radiused upper corners and
	ventilating half-lights; reversed quarter-turn stairs.
Seating:	28+22 = 50
Truck:	As 29-53
Motors:	As 29-53
Controllers:	As 29-53
Brakes:	As 29-53
Major modifications:	Bailey tops: 69, 81-3, 90/1/4/7/9, 101-106, 120/1, 123?, 124
	High canopy tops: 70-90, 92-96, 98, 100, 106-119, 121-128
	Dual-gauge trucks and DK19A motors: 72/6/8, 93, 110/1/6/8, 124/7
	High canopy top, direct 180° stairs, lengthened pforms, pform vestibules: 97

Cars 69-128 continued

Air/oil brakes: 73/74/7/9, 80/1/7/8, 92/3/6/8, 111, 128
Seating: 28+22 = 50   Bailey top cars
          36+22 = 58   108 (c1920)
          38+22 = 60   Canopy top cars
Hurst, Nelson 21E truck with Siemens 40hp motors: 70/1/2/3/5/6/7/9,
          80/1/7/8/9, 90/2/3/6/7/8, 100/6/7/8/9, 111/3/5/7/9, 123/5/7/8
Mountain & Gibson truck: 104 (c.1910)
Brush A truck: 76 (c.1905), 78 (1913), 122 (1903)
Brush AA truck: 100 (1905)
Westinghouse air/track brake: 122 (1903-?)
Mechanical 4-shoe track brake (replacing air/oil) 73 (c.1922), 79, 81/7,
          92/3/6/8, 122 (1925)
'Temporary glass front': 71/3/5/6/9, 81/2/4/7, 90/2/3/4/6/8, 100/6/7,
          111/5, 121/5/6/7/8
Note: Car 122 was displayed by Brush at the 1905 Tramways Exhibition as
a demonstration of the durability of their products.

Entered Service 1902-3   **Cars 129-228   Type: Milnes**

Body: G. F. Milnes open-top, 3 side windows with ventilating half-lights
                     (rectangular on 129/130, radiused upper corners on 131-228); direct half-
                     turn stairs.
Seating: 29 outside, 22 inside = total 51
Truck: Brush 'A' 6ft wheelbase (No. 129 Peckham cantilever when new).
Motors: Two 'Witting' T111 35hp
Controllers: BTH B18, 4 series, 4 parallel and 6 brake notches
Brakes: Hand/wheel, hand/track and rheostatic
Major modifications: Fitted with twin trolleys for short-lived Allerton shuttle service, 1902 – 129
                     Bradford Exhibition 'drawing-room car', 1904 – 130
                     Bailey tops (including converted Milnes tops) 133, 141/2, 151/2, 157-160,
                     171/2, 182-4, 186-188, 190-216, 218/9, 221-228; several others (nos unknown).
                     Bottom deck rebuilt with 6 side windows, retaining Bailey top – 141,   171,196
                     High canopy tops and reversed stairs – 88 (ex 144), 152, 176
                     High canopy tops and reversed stairs: lower deck rebuilt with six side
                     windows – 132-136, 138-140, 142/3/8, 149?, 153/5, 157-162, 164-167,
                     172/4/5/7, 181/3/4/7, 208, 217, 221, 242 (ex 210?) = 35 cars.
                     High canopy tops, reversed stairs and lower deck rebuilt with teak frames
                     and six side windows (considered as new bodies) – 156, 188, 198.
                     Used as basis of 'Modern 6-window cars' – ie 30 vestibuled 6-window cars
                     with teak frames, lengthened platforms, direct stairs and high canopies –
                     131, 141?, 147, 151, 163, 171/3, 182/5, 190/1, 193/4/6/7, 200-204, 206/7,
                     209, 210 (ex 163), 211/2, 223/6/7/8.
                     Used as basis of 10 'High 4-window cars' with teak frames, lengthened
                     vestibule platforms, direct stairs and high canopy tops: 129?, 214?, 218?
                     and seven others.
                     Rebuilt to B.C.T. 1914 design with 4 side windows, teak frames, reversed
                     stairs and high canopy tops – 198, 213.
                     Bailey top car (52 seats) reconverted to open top (50 seats) – 192 (c.1917)
                     'Temporary glass fronts': 132-6/8/9, 140/2/3/4/8, 149?, 152/3/5-9, 160-2,
                     164-7, 172/4-7, 181/4/7/8, 198, 217/221.
                     Seats: 28+22 = 50, open top cars 129, 130/7/9, 146, 150, 168/9, 170/8, 189
                              30+22 = 52, all Bailey top cars.
                              32+22 = 54 (by 1929) open top cars 137, 168
                              34+22 = 56 (by 1929) open top car 146
                              35+22 = 57 (by 1929) canopy top cars 155/7, 175, 184
                              36+22 = 58 (by 1929) canopy top cars 139, 142
                              37+22 = 59 (by 1929) canopy top cars 158, 179
                              38+22 = 60 : remaining canopy top cars
                              43+22 = 65 : vestibuled canopy top cars
                     'Floodlighting': teak-framed cars 112 ex 156, 153 ex 198, 188
                     Air/oil brake: 131-135/8, 140/8, 153/5-9, 160/2/4/6/7. 173-5, 181/2/7/8,
                     190-4/6/9, 200/202, 217, 221/6/7, 242 (ex 210?)
                     Mechanical 4-shoe track brake replacing air/oil : 1917 – 193/9; 1919 – 132,
                     148, 156/9, 160, 184, 217, 221; c.1922 – 134, 181/7; 1925/6: remainder.
                     Peckham 'cantilever' trucks (ex Brush cars): 154, 168/9, 176, 181/6, 216/9, 220/4

125

Cars 129-228 continued		Experimental 11ft wheelbase radial truck: 133, 165 (c.1910)
		Experimental Barber 6-wheel radial truck: 224 (1910)
		Brush 21E 6ft 6ins wheelbase truck: 1912 – 157, 160/2, 181/4; 242 (ex 210?); 1921 – 145
		Mountain & Gibson 21E 6ft wheelbase truck, 1911/2: 132, 147/8, 153, 170, 180/7, 201 (203 later), 217 (220 later)
		Conaty & Lycett 6ft wheelbase truck: 217 (1913), 226
		Dual-gauge trucks with DK19A motors: 136, 142/3, 149?, 161, 172/7, 183?, 242 (ex 210?)
		Hurst, Nelson 21E truck and Siemens 40hp motors: 131/2/3/4/5/6/8/9, 140, 142/3/7, 149?, 151/3/5-9, 160/2/3/4/5/6/7, 171/3/4/5/6, 182/5/8, 190/3/4/6/7/8/9, 217/8, 221/8
		Hurst, Nelson 21E truck and DK31 45hp motors: 184
		Hurst, Nelson S4W (ex-Mid-Yorks) truck: 189 (1920)
		Boving 21E truck and Siemens 40hp motors: 161, 172/7, 185
		Dick Kerr 21E truck and DK31 45hp motors (1921/2), 144, 176
		Note: 130 exhibited by Witting Bros Tramways Exhibition, London in July 1902.

Entered Service 30th September 1903   **Car 229**

	Body:	Ex-Bradford & Shelf steam trailer, converted by B.C.T. to a 6-window single-decker with turtle-back clerestory roof.
	Seating:	40, all longitudinal
	Trucks:	Brush type D equal wheel bogies, 33ins wheels
	Motors:	Four 'Witting' T11 (EH2) 20hp
	Controllers:	'Witting' EH9, 5 series, 3 parallel and ? brake notches
	Brakes:	Hand/wheel, hand/track and rheostatic
	Trolley mast (roof mounted):	either Estler or Munro, Willis & Rogers
	Cost of conversion:	£400

Entered Service 1904   **Cars 230-239   Type: Mid-Yorkshire**

	Body:	Ex Mid-Yorkshire Tramways, built 1903 by Hurst, Nelson as open-top, 3 Tudor-arch windows and half-lights, direct quarter-turn stairs and no balconies.
	Seating:	24 outside + 22 inside = total 46
	Truck;	Hurst, Nelson S4W 6ft wheelbase
	Motors:	Two British Thompson-Houston (BTH) 35hp
	Controllers:	BTH type B18, 4-series, 4 parallel and 6 brake notches
	Brakes:	Hand/wheel, hand/track and rheostatic
	Major modifications:	Upper deck dashplates ('tins') increased in height
		Balconies and reversed stairs with extra seating: 37+22 = 59 – cars 230/3/6
		Balconies, top covers and reversed stairs,
		Seating: 37+20 = 57 – car 230; 38+22 = 60 – cars 231/7
		Rebuilt to BCT 4-side window design with canopy top, reversed stairs and seats 38+22 = 60 – car 239
		'Temporary glass front' 239 (November 1925)
		Hurst, Nelson 21E truck with Siemens 40hp motors: 239 (1930)
		'Floodlighting' 239 (June 1933)

Entered Service June 1912   **Cars 210, 229   Type: 1912 BCT**

	Body:	BCT 4-side windows, teak frame, platform vestibules, reversed stairs high canopy top, folding platform doors, driver's pedestal seat.
	Seating:	Upper saloon 28, balconies 10, saloon 22 = total 60
	Truck:	Brush 21E 6ft 6ins wheelbase. Wheels $33^5/_8$ins diameter with full tyres (as all subsequent cars except No. 1)
	Motors:	Two 'Witting' T111, 35hp
	Controllers:	BTH type B18; 4 series, 4 parallel and 6 brake notches.
	Brakes:	Spencer-Dawson air/oil, mechanical wheel brake (for parking), and rheostatic
	Major modifications:	Platform doors and driver's seat removed
		1919 Mechanical track brakes; top deck seats 41 (210) and 43 (229)
		1921 (210) Boving truck, Siemens 40hp motors, (229) Siemens motors and (210/229) DK DB1 controllers
		1930 Upholstered seats, 33+19 = 52, and (229) Hurst, Nelson 21E truck, Siemens 40hp motors

Entered Service May-July 1913   **Cars 240, 241, 243   Type: 1913 BCT**

Body:	BCT 4 side-windows, teak frame, platform vestibules, reversed stairs, high canopy top
Seating:	Upper saloon 28, balconies 10, saloon 22 = total 60
Truck:	Hurst, Nelson 21E 7ft wheelbase
Motors:	Two Siemens 40hp
Controllers:	Dick Kerr type DB1 Form K4, 4 series, 4 parallel and 7 brake notches
Brakes:	Hand/wheel, hand/track and rheostatic
Major modifications:	1915 – BTH/GEC ventilated motors, gear ratio 5.266 to 1 – 241
	1914/5 – Air/oil brake – 240, 243; Trapdoor seats for 3 (new total 63) – all
	c.1925 Mechanical track brakes
	c.1930 Upholstered, 33+19 = 52 seats – all
	1932 'Floodlighting'

Entered Service April-November 1914   Cars 244-249   Type: 5-window cars

Body:	BCT 5 side windows, teak frame, platform vestibules, reversed stairs and high
canopy top – 244-248.	
	As above but lengthened platforms and 180° direct stairs – 249.
Seating:	244-248 upper saloon 32, balconies 10, saloon 26 = total 68
	244 upper saloon 32, balconies 12, saloon 26 = total 70
Truck:	Hurst, Nelson 21E 7ft wheelbase
Motors:	Two Siemens 40hp
Controllers:	Dick Kerr type DB1 K4, 4 series, 4 parallel and 7 brake notches.
Brakes:	Air/oil and rheostatic
Major modifications:	Trapdoor seats for 3 – 244-248: new total 71,
	249: new total 73
	c.1925 Mechanical track brakes – all
	c.1927 Boving 21E truck, Siemens 40hp motors – 247
	1930-5 Upholstered seats, 33+19 (245/7/8/9), 43+19 (246)
	c.1932 'Floodlighting'

Entered Service 1914   **Cars 250-252   Type: 1914 BCT**

	As 240/1/3 except for 180° direct stairs, lengthened platforms and balcony seats for 12, total 62. Air/oil and rheostatic brakes.
Major modifications:	By 1919 – 251/2 seats 43+22 = 65
	In 1920 – 250 seats 36+22 = 58
	By 1930 – 250-2 upholstered, 33 +19 = 52
	By 1922 – mechanical track brakes 251
	By 1925 – mechanical track brakes 250/2
	c.1932 – 'Floodlighting'

Entered Service 1915-1920   **Type: 'Modern Six Window'   Cars 131, 147, 151, 163, 171/3, 182/5, 190/1/3/4/6/7, 199 (ex 91 ex 141?), 200-204, 206/7/9, 210 (ex 161), 211/212,223/6/7/8 (30 cars)**

Body:	Vestibuled 6-window cars built by BCT, nominally on basis of old Milnes 3-window bodies but almost wholly new with teak frames, lengthened platforms, 180° direct stairs and high canopy tops.
Seating:	43+22 = 65
Truck:	Hurst, Nelson 21E 7ft wheelbase (204 Boving 21E)
Motors:	Two 40hp Siemens
Controllers:	Dick Kerr DB1 K4
Brakes:	Air/oil and rheostatic – 131, 173, 182, 190/1/3/4/6, 200/1, 223/6/7
	Hand/wheel, mechanical 4-shoe track and rheostatic: remainder.
Major modifications:	Air/oil brakes converted to mechanical: all
	New medium-height canopy top: 228 (as 136), 1926
	Upholstered seating, 33+19 = 52: 199, 147, 151, 171/3, 182/5, 190/3/4/7, 201/9
	DK31D 'high speed' motors: 151, 190/1/4, 203/4, 227
	Boving 21E truck, DK31D 'high-speed' motors: 201 (1930), 209 (1931), 197 (1932), 202 (1934), 147/163 (1935)
	Hurst, Nelson 21E truck, DK31D 'high speed' motors : 207 (1934)
	Reverted to Siemens 40hp ('slow') motors: 227 (1934), 204 (1935)
	'Floodlighting': probably all except 131, 196

Entered Service 1917-1921	Type: 'High Four Window'	Cars 118 (later 107), 129 (later 159), 158, 160, 163, 164, 179 (later 157), 205 (later 156), 214 (later 155) and 218 (later 154) (10 cars)

	Body:	Built by BCT with Milnes interior furnishings and lower-deck half-lights with radiused upper corners; teak frames, platform vestibules, 180° direct stairs and high canopy tops (158, 160 and 164 second-hand canopies rebuilt to match lengthened platforms but 129/163 inherited unrebuilt (short) canopies).
	Seating:	Wooden, 43+22 = 65 – 129, 205, 214, 218
		40+22 = 62 – 118, 158, 160/3/4, 179
	Truck	Hurst, Nelson 21E – 129, 160, 179, 205
		Boving 21E – 118, 164, 214, 218
		Dick Kerr 21E – 158, 163
	Motors:	DK31A or B 45hp – 158, 163
		Siemens 40hp – remainder
	Controllers:	Dick, Kerr DB1 K4
	Brakes:	Air/oil and rheostatic – 214, 218
		Hand/wheel, hand/track and rheostatic – remainder.
	Major modifications:	Lower (5ft 10ins) canopy top: 118 (date unknown)
		Mechanical hand/track brake: 214, 218 (1925)
		DK31D 'high speed' 60hp motors: 118, 160, 205 (c.1930)
		Hurst, Nelson 21E truck, Siemens motors: 163 (1925), 158 (1930)
		Hurst, Nelson 21E truck, DK31D 'high speed' motors: 179, 218 (1935)
		Boving 21E truck, DK31D 'high speed' motors: 214 (c.1930), 163 (1935)
		Dick Kerr 21E truck, DK31D 'high speed' motors: 118 (c.1938)
		Upholstered seats, 33+19 = 52 – probably all
		'Floodlighting' (c.1930-2) – probably all
		Received truck and fleet number from 'Preston cars' – 118 (107), 158, 164 (see 'Numbers and Renumberings')

s

Entered service between 30th September 1919 and September1928	Cars 64-75, 80, 90, 92 (15 cars)	Type: 'Greengates'

	Body:	Low-height built by BCT; teak frames, platform vestibules, 180° direct stairs
		64-69 standard Wilkinson narrow body and extra-low canopy top
		70-75 Wilkinson wide body, lower deck lower than 64-69 but top deck slightly
	higher	
		80, 90, 92 Wilkinson wide body as 70-75 but frameless plate-glass upper deck
	windows	
	Seating:	Wooden 43 upper deck, 22 saloon = total 65 : 64-69
		Wooden 40 upper deck, 22 saloon = total 62 : 70/1, 73-75
		Wooden 37 upper deck, 22 saloon = 59 : 72
		Upholstered 37 upper deck, 19 saloon = 56 : 80, 90, 92
	Truck:	Boving 21E 7ft wheelbase – 64-69
		Dick Kerr 21E 7ft wheelbase – 70-75, 80, 90, 92
	Motors:	Two Siemens 40hp – 64/5
		Two Dick Kerr DK31 50hp – 66-75
		Two Dick Kerr DK31D 60hp – 80, 90, 92
	Controllers:	Dick Kerr DB1 K4
	Brakes:	Air/oil and rheostatic – 64/5/7/8
		Hand/wheel, mechanical track and rheostatic: 66, 69, 70-75, 80, 90, 92
	Major modifications:	Mechanical track brakes: 65 c.1922, 64/7/8: c.1925
		Hurst, Nelson 21E truck: 65/6/9
		Dick Kerr 31D 60hp motors: all
		Upholstered seats 33+19 = 52: 64-71, 73-75
		Upholstered seats 37+19 = 56: 72
		Upholstered seats 43+19 = 62: 92 (about 1935)
		'Floodlighting': all (1931-3)
		Received truck and fleet number from 'Preston' car: 1936-69 (see 'Numbers and Renumberings')

Entered service between :
20th October 1919
and 9th August 1921

Cars 213-258 (46 cars)   **Type: Preston**

Body:	English Electric; teak frames; galvanised iron panelled vestibules and lower saloon sides; full-width fenders; 180° direct stairs, frameless plate-glass upper deck windows
Seating:	43+22 = 65 – 233-258
	40+22 = 62 (Wilkinson seating arrangement in top saloon) – 213-232
Truck:	Dick Kerr 21E 7ft wheelbase
Motors:	Two Dick Kerr DK31A or B, 45/50hp
Controllers:	Dick Kerr DB1 K4
Brakes:	Hand/wheel, mechanical track brakes, rheostatic
Major modifications:	Upholstered seats, 33 +19 = 52 – 213/6, 221/2/3/5-230, 232/5/9, 240/1/5/7/8/9, 250/2/5
	Upholstered seats, 37+19 = 56 – 231/3, 254
	Upholstered seats, 43+19 = 62 – remainder
	Motors rewound to DK31D ('high speed') 60hp – all
	Boving 21E truck with DK31D ('high speed') 60hp motors – 221 (1938)
	'Floodlighting' – presumably all

Entered Service between :
September 1919
and June 1931

Type: 1919 BCT   **Total 81 cars**

Body:	BCT Wilkinson type, teak frame, platform vestibules, 180° direct stairs (except car 40 reversed).
	Narrow bodies with medium-height (Windhill Bridge) canopy tops (in chronological order): 63, 70 (later 11), 74* (later 39), 21*, 86, 24*, 56, 77*, 58, 50*, 57* (11 cars),
	Wide bodies with medium-height (Windhill Bridge) canopy tops, indicated as 'M', or high canopy tops, indicated as 'H': 52M*, 47M*, 6H*, 97M, 195M, 34H*, 4M, 35H*, 19H*, 95H*, 83M, 102H*, 130M, 13H*, 104M, 12H*, 31M, 3H*, 189H*, 37M, 27M, 26M, 40M, 45M, 43M, 111M, 108M, 119H*, 42M, 48M, 15M, 89H*, 30M, 99H*, 8M, 51M, 196M, 5M, 29M, 79H*, 94H*, 16H*, 103M, 105M, 93M, 109M, 28M, 44M,
49M*, 53M* (50 cars)	
	Intermediate-width bodies with medium-height canopy tops, frameless plate-glass upper deck side windows and plainer interior woodwork: 23, 55, 17, 178, 7, 61, 181, 20, 125, 54, 2, 33, 82, 60 (23 and 55 had flush steel vestibule panels) (14 cars)
	Intermediate-width bodies with medium-height canopy tops, conventional oak-framed sheet-glass upper deck side windows and plainer interior woodwork: 41, 87, 81, 88, 205, 14 (6 cars)
	* indicates top deck inherited from an earlier car
Seating:	Wooden, 40+22 = 62

	Wooden, 40+22 = 62	3, 4, 5, 8, 12, 13, 19, 21, 24, 27, 29, 30, 31, 34, 35, 40/42/43, 45, 47, 50, 52, 57, 58, 70, 77, 83, 86, 94, 99, 102, 111, 130, 189, 195
	Wooden, 37+22 = 59	6, 15, 26, 37, 48, 49, 51, 56, 79, 89, 95, 97, 104, 108, 119
	Wooden, 43+22 = 65	63, 74
	Upholstered, 37+19 = 56	7, 16, 17, 23, 28, 44, 53, 55, 61, 93, 103, 105, 109, 178, 181, 196
	Upholstered, 33+19 = 52	2, 14, 20, 33, 41, 54, 60, 81, 82, 87, 88, 125, 205

Trucks:	Boving 21E 7ft wheelbase: 23, 54, 55, 60, 63, 87, 125, 205
	Hurst, Nelson 7ft wheelbase: 14, 21, 24, 33, 41, 70, 81, 82, 86
	Dick Kerr 21E 7ft wheelbase: remainder
Motors:	Siemens 40hp: 21, 24, 63, 70, 86
	Dick Kerr 31A/B: 45/50hp: 3-6, 8, 12/3/5/9. 26-31, 34/5/7. 40/2/3/4/5/7/8. 50-53, 56-58, 74/7, 83/9, 93/5/7/9, 102/4/8, 111/9, 130, 189, 195
	Dick Kerr 31D 60hp: 2, 7, 14/6/7, 20/3, 33, 41/9, 54/5, 60/1, 81/2/7/8, 103/5/9, 125, 178, 181, 196, 205
	EE31/1 60hp 79, 94
Controllers:	BTH B18: 63 (in 1919 only)
	Dick Kerr DB1 K4: remainder (and 63 after 1919)
Brakes:	Air/oil and rheostatic: 70
	Hand/wheel, mechanical 4-shoe track and rheostatic: remainder
Major modifications:	Hand/wheel, mechanical track and rheostatic brakes: 70 (before 1925)

Type: 1919 BCT continued	'Canopy grids', ie iron wire mesh behind balcony railings, introduced with car 93 and gradually applied to whole fleet.

'Canopy grids', ie iron wire mesh behind balcony railings, introduced with car 93 and gradually applied to whole fleet.
180° direct stairs: 40 (July 1934)
'Floodlighting' (probably introduced with car 82, February 1930) – all cars 1930-3
Upholstered seats, 37+19 = 56: 3, 6, 15, 26, 30/7, 48/9, 51, 79, 89, 103 (1929), 108, 119 (1929)
Upholstered seats, 33+19 = 52: 4/5/8, 12/3/9, 21/7/9, 31/4, 40/2/3/5/7, 50/2/6/7/8, 63, 70/4/7, 83/6, 94/5/7/9, 102/5, 109 (1929), 111, 130, 181 (1948), 189, 195
Upholstered seats, 43+19 = 62: 1933 – 52, 1935 – 23, 48/9, 53, 79; 1936 – 12, 15, 26, 42, 104; 1937 – 55, 119; 1939 – 3; 1943 – 103
Boving 21E truck, Siemens 40hp motors: 1932 – 50
Boving 21E truck DK31D 60hp motors: 1935 – 86
Hurst, Nelson 21E truck, Siemens 40hp motors: 1926 – 56, 77; 1927 – 57/8
Hurst, Nelson 21E truck DK31D 60hp motors: 1935 – 24, 50/6/7/8, 77
Dick Kerr 21E truck, DK31D 60hp motors: 1944 – 77; 1948 – 81; 1949 – 86.
Also all cars which inherited trucks from 'Preston' cars (see 'Numbers and Renumberings').
DK31D 60hp motors – remainder (1927-1931)
(Brush 21E 6ft wheelbase truck, DK31D 60hp motors: 1958 – 104)

Completed 28th February 1927 **Demonstrated 8th March 1927**	**Car 1 – BCT 'Pullman' bogie single-decker, cost £3,992. 1s. 6d.**

BCT Body: Teak frame dropped centre-entrance, separate driver's compartments; folding entrance doors, rubber-edged, unequally leaved, controlled by driver's valve and conductor's emergency valve (G. D. Peters National Pneumatic valve C3620) interlocked to prevent starting before closure – red lamp glowed in cab when open.
Seating: Siddall & Hilton red leather sprung upholstery, intended as 20 (10 per side) longitudinal in each compartment + 33 standing = total 73 (maximum permissible) but altered to 17 per compartment with 36 standing = total 70, on 3 double and 3 single transverse seats and a double longitudinal seat in each corner. **Interior finish:** mahogany panels, birdseye maple ceiling and thick green linoleum floor covering; Pullman-type sliding vents and half drop windows with Rawlings catches. **Radius** of roof dome (horizontal) 3ft 6ins, interior cove radius 10ins. **Driver's compartment:** adjustable seat attached to sliding door, with foot pedestal. **Exterior finish:** panels and window posts mahogany finished in natural grain; ivory roof; black trolley and fenders: underframe, bogies, lifeguards and beadings (probably horizontal beadings only) red oxide. Gold fleet numbers and lettering.
Saloon and cab doors sliding to right within hollow bulkheads. Separate external opening door in each cab.
Lighting: Four diffusing bulbs with glass covers in each saloon; one similar in central vestibule; 3 in each destination box; 2 in each numeral box; one rear red signal lamp – total 20 in 4 banks of 5 x 110v = 550 volts dc.
Conductor's bells: Faraday single-stroke bell pushes, 500v d.c.
Roof access: fold-up steps on central door-frame.
Destinations: ECO roller-blinds, usually 'Town Hall Square' screens only.
Bogies: BCT design; 8ins x 3½ins rolled steel sections with 4ins x 3ins section sub-frame to carry motors; Woodhead bogie bolster springing, Ferodo and rubber cushioned; axles $3^{25}/_{32}$ins diameter, of 40ton high-tensile steel. Wheelbase 4ft 6ins, distance between bogie centres 19ft; wheel diameter 26ins. Connecting rods with Skefco ball-bearings in dustproof cases. **Motors:** two English Electric type 30K 106A 63hp, plain series winding, weight 1,340lb each. **Drive:** by propeller shaft mounted on two Spicer joints to a Bostock phosphor-bronze worm gear on driving (outer) axle, 5.75:1 reduction ratio. **Axle-boxes:** plain bearings with Armstrong oiler pads, side-thrust taken by phosphor-bronze washer between wheel and axlebox. **Brakes:** (i) air/track (4 shoes per bogie), straight air-brake by Consolidated Brake & Engineering Company (G. D. Peters), Revell compressor driven by Bull 2¼hp motor, (ii) mechanical through hand-brake handle to two brake-drums on each inner axle, Ferodo-lined shoes, (iii) rheostatic. Eight sanders controlled by Bowden cable.
Controllers: English Electric DK type L (as K type but with field-shunt on final notch, ie running notches 4 (full series), 7 (full parallel) and 8 (field shunt); probably 6 brake-notches.
Lifeguards: Standard BCT (Tidswell) at each end, and continuous detachable side-guards.
Total weight: (estimated before construction) 9½ tons
Length: saloons (interior) 13ft 3ins, overall interior 35ft 6ins; body exterior 38ft 3ins, over roof 38ft 10ins, over fenders 39ft 3¾ins; trolley 18ft 6ins, each bogie 8ft 2ins.
Width: interior 6ft 4½ins, cab 6ft 3⁵/₈ins, gangway 1ft 11⁵/₈ins minimum; interior doorways 2ft 3ins; central entrances 4ft 6ins (doors closed), 4ft (doors open); single seats 1ft 6ins, double seats 2ft 10ins, corner seats 2ft 9ins x 10½ins; width over side panels 6ft 10ins, maximum width over cant rails (roof) 7ft.
Height: clear interior 7ft 2ins; rail to underside of dropped centre frame 6ins; each step 10ins; rail to saloon floor surface 3ft 0¼ins; rail to roof top 10ft 4¾ins; roof thickness 2½ins.
Designed to negotiate a 29ft radius curve 'with ease'.

---

* Details derived from *Tramway & Railway World*, 1927, and BCT drawing 2826/2, 17th December 1927. Where slight differences occur, the BCT (ie later) version is used.

APPENDIX 1E

BRADFORD CORPORATION TRAMCARS: NUMBERS AND RENUMBERINGS

Fleet No.	FIRST Type	Into service	(First)	SECOND Type	Into Service	(Second)	THIRD Type	Into Service	(Third)	FOURTH Type	Into Service	(Fourth)
1	1898 Brush	July 1898	Renumbered 16 1927	'Pullman'	March 1927	Scrapped April 1931						
2	1898 Brush	July 1898	Withdrawn 1928	1919 BCT	Dec 1929	Renumbered 213 May 1939						
3	1898 Brush	July 1898	Withdrawn 1925	1919 BCT	June 1925	Renumbered 218 May 1939						
4	1898 Brush	July 1898	Withdrawn 1922	1919 BCT	Dec 1923	Renumbered 226 May 1939						
5	1898 Brush	July 1898	Withdrawn 1926	1919 BCT	Apl 1927	Renumbered 230 May 1939						
6	1898 Brush	July 1898	Withdrawn 1922	1919 BCT	June 1923	Renumbered 231 May 1939						
7	1898 Brush	July 1898	Withdrawn Aug 1928	1919 BCT	May 1929	Renumbered 233 May 1939						
8	1898 Brush	Aug1898	Withdrawn Dec 1925	1919 BCT	Dec 1926	Renumbered 240 May 1939						
9	1898 Brush	Aug 1898	Withdrawn May 1930									
10	1898 Brush	Aug 1898	Withdrawn 1921	Milnes	Ex 145	Withdrawn 1931						
11	1898 Brush	Aug 1898	Withdrawn 1922	1919 BCT	Ex 70	Renumbered 247 Aug 1936						
12	1898 Brush	Aug 1898	Withdrawn 1924	1919 BCT	Apl 1925	Renumbered 244 May 1939						
13	1898 Brush	Aug 1898	To plough S18 1925	1919 BCT	Jan 1925	Renumbered 245 May 1939						
14	1898 Brush	Aug 1898	Withdrawn Aug 1929	1919 BCT	June 1931	Renumbered 227 Oct 1935						
15	1898 Brush	Aug 1898	Withdrawn 1926	1919 BCT	July 1926	Renumbered 253 May 1939						
16	1898 Brush	Aug 1898	Withdrawn 1926	1898 Brush	Ex 1	Withdrawn 1927	1919 BCT	Dec 1927	Renumbered 254 May 1939			
17	1899 Brush	1899	Withdrawn 1923	1902 Brush	Ex 71	Withdrawn 1928	1919 BCT	March 1929	Renumbered 117 Mar 1949			
18	1899 Brush	1899	Withdrawn June 1930									
19	1899 Brush	1899	Withdrawn 1923	1919 BCT	Jan 1924	Renumbered 119 Mar 1949						
20	1899 Brush	1899	Withdrawn early 1929	1919 BCT	Aug 1929	Renumbered 120 Mar 1949						
21	1899 Brush	1899	Withdrawn 1921	1919 BCT	Aug 1921	Renumbered 248 July 1936						
22	1899 Brush	1899	Withdrawn Oct 1929									
23	1899 Brush	1899	Withdrawn early 1928	1919 BCT	Jan 1929	Renumbered 123 Mar 1949						
24	1899 Brush	1899	Withdrawn 1921	1919 BCT	July 1921	Withdrawn Jan 1947						
25	'Trailer'	1899	Withdrawn Feb 1931									
26	'Trailer'	1899	To 'School car' c.1924	1919 BCT	Sept 1925	Withdrawn Apl 1948	'White Board'	Ex 32	Withdrawn 1925	1919 BCT	Sept 1925	Renumbered 127 Mar 1949 (4th)
27	'Trailer'	1899	To Pay Car 1910	Mid-Yorks	Ex 237	Withdrawn 1919						
28	'Trailer'	1899	To School Car 1927	1919 BCT	Feb 1928	Renumbered 128 Mar 1949						
29	'White Board'	1900	Withdrawn 1926	1919 BCT	May 1927	Renumbered 129 Mar 1949						
30	'White Board'	1900	Withdrawn 1920	Mid Yorks	Ex 232	Withdrawn 1926	1919 BCT	Aug 1926	Withdrawn Dec 1949			
31	'White Board'	1900	Withdrawn 1919	Mid Yorks	Ex 236	Withdrawn 1923	1919 BCT	Apl 1925	Withdrawn Oct 1948			
32	'White Board'	1900	Renumbered 27 1920	Mid Yorks (Teak Frame)	Ex 219	Withdrawn June 1935						
33	'White Board'	1900	To illuminated Car 1929	1919 BCT	Jan 1930	Renumbered 252 Oct 1935						
34	'White Board'	1900	Withdrawn 1922	1919 BCT	Aug 1923	Renumbered 134 Mar 1949						
35	'White Board'	1900	Withdrawn 1923	1919 BCT	Dec 1923	Renumbered 135 Mar 1949						
36	'White Board'	1900	Withdrawn 1922	1902 Brush	Ex 72	Withdrawn Aug 1931						
37	'White Board'	1900	Renumbered 45 July 1925	1919 BCT	July 1925	Renumbered 137 Mar 1949						
38	'White Board'	1900	Withdrawn 1923	1901 Brush	Ex 73	Withdrawn 1930						
39	'White Board'	1900	To snow plough 17 1923	1919 BCT	Ex 74	Renumbered 228 July 1936						
40	'White Board'	1900	Withdrawn Apl 1925	1919 BCT	Nov 1925	Renumbered 140 Mar 1949						
41	'White Board'	1900	Withdrawn Apl 1929	1919 BCT	May 1930	Renumbered 250 Oct 1935						
42	'White Board'	1900	Withdrawn 1925	1919 BCT	Mar 1926	Renumbered 142 Mar 1949						
43	'White Board'	1900	Withdrawn 1925	1919 BCT	Dec 1925	Renumbered 143 March 1949						
44	'White Board'	1900	Withdrawn early 1928	1919 BCT	Apl 1928	Renumbered 144 Mar 1949						
45	'White Board'	1900	Withdrawn 1925	'White Board'	Ex 37	Withdrawn Aug 1925	1919 BCT	Dec 1925	Renumbered 145 Mar 1949			
46	'White Board'	1900	Withdrawn 1919	Milnes	Ex 146	Withdrawn 1931						
47	'White Board'	1900	Withdrawn 1920	1901 Brush	Ex 62	Withdrawn 1922	1919 BCT	Feb 1923	Withdrawn Jan 1947			

Fleet No.	First Type	First Into service	First event	Second Type	Second Into Service	Second event	Third Type	Third Into Service	Third event	Later events
48	'White Board'	1900	Withdrawn 1926	1919 BCT	June 1926	Renumbered 148 Mar 1949				
49	'White Board'	1900	Withdrawn 1928	1919 BCT	May 1928	Renumbered 149 Mar 1949				
50	'White Board'	1900	Withdrawn 1921	1919 BCT	Mar 1922	Withdrawn Sept 1947				
51	'White Board'	1900	Withdrawn 1926	1919 BCT	Jan 1927	Withdrawn May 1950				
52	'White Board'	1900	Withdrawn 1921	1919 BCT	Aug 1922	Withdrawn May 1950				
53	'White Board'	1900	Withdrawn 1919	1901 Brush	Ex 61	Renumbered early 1928	1919 BCT	Oct 1928	Withdrawn June 1949	
54	1901 Brush	1901	Withdrawn early 1929	1919 BCT	Nov 1929	Renumbered 255 Oct 1935				
55	1901 Brush	1901	Withdrawn May 1928	1919 BCT	Jan 1929	Withdrawn Aug 1949				
56	1901 Brush	1901	To snowplough S14 1921	1919 BCT	Dec 1921	Withdrawn Nov 1949				
57	1901 Brush	1901	Withdrawn 1919	1901 Brush	Ex 67	Withdrawn 1922	1919 BCT	July 1922	Withdrawn Nov 1949	
58	1901 Brush	1901	Withdrawn 1919	1901 Brush	Ex 83	Withdrawn 1921	1919 BCT	Feb 1922	Renumbered 241 June 1938	
59	1901 Brush	1901	Withdrawn 1919	1901 Brush	Ex 69	Renumbered 83 1920	1902 Brush	Ex 108	Withdrawn July 1930	
60	1901 Brush	1901	Withdrawn 1920	1902 Brush	Ex 121	Withdrawn Apr 1929	1919 BCT	Mar 1930	Renumbered 249 Oct 1935	
61	1901 Brush	1901	Renumbered 53, 1920	1902 Brush	Ex 107	Withdrawn Aug 1928	1901 Brush	July 1929	Withdrawn May 1950	
62	1901 Brush	1901	Withdrawn 1918	1901 Brush	Ex 66	Renumbered 47, 1920		Ex 70	Withdrawn Dec 1929	
63	1901 Brush	1901	Withdrawn 1919	1919 BCT	Sept 1919	Renumbered 223 Dec 1936				
64	1901 Brush	1901	Withdrawn 1919	'Greengates'	30 Sept 1919	Withdrawn May 1939				
65	1901 Brush	1901	Renumbered 227 1919	'Greengates'	Oct 1919	Withdrawn May 1939				
66	1901 Brush	1901	Renumbered 62 1919	'Greengates'	Oct 1919	Withdrawn May 1939				
67	1901 Brush	1901	Renumbered 57 1919	'Greengates'	Oct 1919	Withdrawn June 1934				
68	1901 Brush	Aug 1901	Renumbered 83 1919	'Greengates'	Nov 1919	Withdrawn May 1939				
69	1901 Brush	1901	Renumbered 59 1919	'Greengates'	Nov 1919	Renumbered 222 Dec 1936				
70	1902 Brush	1901	Renumbered 62 1920	1919 BCT	Feb 1921	Renumbered 11 1923	'Greengates'	March 1924	Withdrawn May 1950	
71	1902 Brush	1901	Renumberd 17 1923	'Greengates'	Mar 1924	Withdrawn Apr 1948				
72	1902 Brush	1901	Withdrawn 1916	Milnes	Ex 151	Renumbered 170 1920	Milnes	Ex 170	Renumbered 103 1921	1902 Brush 'Greengates', Ex 128, May 1924; Renumbered 36 1923 (4th); Withdrawn Dec 1949 (5th)
73	1902 Brush	1901	Renumbered 38 1923	'Greengates'	June 1924	Withdrawn June 1949				
74	1902 Brush	1901	Withdrawn 1919	1919 BCT	May 1921	Renumbered 39 1923	'Greengates'	July 1924	Withdrawn Dec 1949	
75	1902 Brush	1901	Renumbered 180 1923	'Greengates'	Sept 1924	Withdrawn June 1949				
76	1902 Brush	1901	Renumbered 142 1914	Milnes	Jan 1922	Renumbered 114 1921				
77	1902 Brush	1901	Withdrawn 1921	1919 BCT	Ex 161	Withdrawn May 1950	1902 Brush	Ex 114	Withdrawn 1932	
78	1902 Brush	1901	Renumbered 161 1912	Milnes	June 1927	To Railgrinder 1932				
79	1902 Brush	1901	Withdrawn 1927	1919 BCT	Ex 127	Withdrawn May 1950				
80	1902 Brush	1901	Withdrawn 1920	1902 Brush	Oct 1930	Withdrawn 1927	'Greengates'	Aug 1928	Withdrawn May 1950	
81	1902 Brush	1901	Withdrawn June 1929	1919 BCT	Feb 1930	Withdrawn May 1950				
82	1902 Brush	1901	Withdrawn Apr 1929	1919 BCT	Ex 68	Withdrawn May 1950				
83	1902 Brush	1901	Withdrawn 1919	1901 Brush		Renumbered 229 Oct 1935	1902 Brush	June 1921	Withdrawn 1921	1919 BCT, Feb 1924, Withdrawn Sept 1948 (4th)
84	1902 Brush	1901	Withdrawn June 1930	1902 Brush	Ex 126	Renumbered 58 1920				
85	1902 Brush	1901	Withdrawn 1919	Milnes	Ex 143	Withdrawn 1930				
86	1902 Brush	1901	Withdrawn 1918	1919 BCT	July 1930	Renumbered 117 1921	1919 BCT	Dec 1930	Withdrawn May 1950	
87	1902 Brush	1901	Withdrawn Apr 1929	Milnes	Ex 144	Renumbered 235 Oct 1935				
88	1902 Brush	1901	Withdrawn Feb 1918	1919 BCT	July 1926	Withdrawn July 1929			Withdrawn Oct 1949	
89	1902 Brush	1901	Withdrawn Apr 1926	'Greengates'	Aug 1928	Withdrawn May 1948				
90	1902 Brush	1901	Withdrawn Dec 1927	Milnes		Withdrawn June 1949				
91	1902 Brush	1901	Withdrawn 1914/1916	'Greengates'	Ex 141	? Renumbered 199 1919				
92	1902 Brush	1901	Withdrawn early 1928	1919 BCT	Sept 1928	Withdrawn June 1949	1902 Brush	Ex 115	Withdrawn 1930	
93	1902 Brush	1901	Burnt out Oct 1926	1919 BCT	Dec 1927	Withdrawn May 1949				
94	1902 Brush	1901	Withdrawn 1927	1919 BCT	June 1927	Withdrawn Oct 1948				
95	1902 Brush	1901	Withdrawn 1923	1919 BCT	Jan 1924	Withdrawn Aug 1945				
96	1902 Brush	1901	Withdrawn Dec 1929							
97	1902 Brush	1901	Withdrawn 1923	1919 BCT	June 1923	Withdrawn Aug 1948				

No.	Builder	Year	Note	Body	Ex	Body	Ex/Date	Note	Body	Ex/Date	Note (final)
98	1902 Brush	1901	Withdrawn 1932						1919 BCT	Oct 1926	Withdrawn May 1948 (4th)
99	1902 Brush	1901	Withdrawn 1915								
100	1902 Brush	1902	Withdrawn Jan 1930								
101	1902 Brush	1902	Withdrawn 1921								
102	1902 Brush	1902	Withdrawn 1921	Milnes	Ex 164	1919 BCT	Aug 1924	Withdrawn 1934	1919 BCT	Mar 1925	Withdrawn May 1950 (4th)
103	1902 Brush	1902	Withdrawn 1921	1902 Brush	Ex 136	1919 BCT	Nov 1927	Withdrawn 1923			
104	1902 Brush	1902	To plough 16 1920	Milnes	Ex 72	1902 Brush	Ex 117	Withdrawn early 1927	High 4-window	Ex 118	Withdrawn Nov 1949 (4th)
105	1902 Brush	1902	To plough 13 1920	Milnes	Ex 215	1919 BCT	Nov 1927	Withdrawn early 1927			
106	1902 Brush	1902	Withdrawn Dec 1930	Milnes	Ex 220			To plough 8 1920			
107	1902 Brush	1902	Renumbered 61 1920	Milnes	Ex 225	Milnes	Ex 123	Withdrawn 1925			
108	1902 Brush	1902	Renumbered 59 1921	Milnes	Ex 154	1919 BCT	Ex 224	Withdrawn May 1950			
109	1902 Brush	1902	Withdrawn June 1926	1919 BCT	Jan 1928			Withdrawn Feb 1935			
110	1902 Brush	1902	Renumbered 136 1912	Milnes	Ex 136	High 4-window	Mar 1926	Withdrawn Dec 1949			
111	1902 Brush	1902	Withdrawn June 1925	1919 BCT	Jan 1926	1919 BCT		Withdrawn Feb 1935			
112	1902 Brush	1902	Withdrawn 1921	Milnes (Teak Frame)	Ex 156	Milnes		Withdrawn July 1938			
113	1902 Brush	1902	To plough 15 1919	Modern 6-window	Ex 163			Withdrawn Nov 1933			
114	1902 Brush	1902	Renumbered 76 1921	Milnes	Ex 76	Milnes		Withdrawn 1929			
115	1902 Brush	1902	Renumbered 91 1921	Milnes	Ex 142	Milnes		Withdrawn Mar 1932			
116	1902 Brush	1902	Withdrawn 1914; to 183 1919?	Milnes	Ex 149?	1919 BCT	Ex 17	Withdrawn 1932			
117	1902 Brush	1902	Renumbered 104 1920	High 4-window	Ex 86	Milnes	Ex 160	Renumbered 107 1920			
118	1902 Brush	1902	Withdrawn 1919	1919 BCT	Nov 1920	1919 BCT	Ex 19	Withdrawn June 1944			
119	1902 Brush	1902	Withdrawn 1926	Milnes	Mar 1926	1919 BCT	Ex 20	Withdrawn Aug 1931			
120	1902 Brush	1902	Withdrawn 1916	Milnes	Ex 150			Withdrawn June 1933			
121	1902 Brush	1902	Renumbered 60 1921	Milnes	Ex 153			Withdrawn 1931			
122	1902 Brush	1902	Withdrawn 1919	Milnes	Ex 152	1919 BCT	Ex 23	To plough July 1933			
123	1902 Brush	1902	Renumbered 99 1921	Milnes	Ex 155			Withdrawn Dec 1929			
124	1902 Brush	1902	?Withdrawn 1914	1919 BCT	Ex 149?	Preston	Ex 221	Renumbered 221 May 1938			
125	1902 Brush	1902	Withdrawn Feb 1929	Milnes	Oct 1929			To plough June 1933			
126	1902 Brush	1902	Renumbered 85 1919	Modern 6-window	Ex 217	1919 BCT	Ex 27	Withdrawn Feb 1935			
127	1902 Brush	1902	Renumbered 80 1921	High 4-window	Ex 221	1919 BCT	Ex 28	Withdrawn Sept 1935			
128	1902 Brush	1902	Renumbered 72 1921	1919 BCT	Ex 223	Milnes	Ex 159	Renumbered 159 1921			
129	Milnes	1902	Withdrawn 1918	Modern 6-window	Sept 1920			Withdrawn July 1949	1919 BCT	Ex 29	Withdrawn June 1949 (4th)
130	Milnes	1902	Withdrawn 1923		Jan 1925			Withdrawn Nov 1935			
131	Milnes	1902	Withdrawn 1915		May 1915			Withdrawn May 1950			
132	Milnes	1902	Withdrawn Jan 1935					Withdrawn Oct 1949			
133	Milnes	1902	To plough July 1933					Renumbered 102 1921			
134	Milnes	1902	Withdrawn Jan 1935	1919 BCT	Ex 34			Withdrawn May 1949			
135	Milnes	1902	To plough Nov 1933	1919 BCT	Ex 35	1902 Brush		Withdrawn Aug 1935			
136	Milnes	1902	Renumbered 110 1912	1902 Brush	Ex 110	1919 BCT	Ex 228	Withdrawn Aug 1935			
137	Milnes	1902	Withdrawn Aug 1931	1919 BCT	Ex 37			Renumbered 99 1919			
138	Milnes	1902	Withdrawn 1932					Withdrawn Nov 1935			
139	Milnes	1902	To plough July 1933					Burnt out Oct 1926			
140	Milnes	1902	Renumbered 186 1919	1913 BCT	Ex 240	1919 BCT	Ex 40	Withdrawn May 1935			
141	Milnes	1902	Renumbered 91 1919	1913 BCT	Ex 241	Milnes	Ex 242	Withdrawn May 1935	1915 BCT	Ex 213	Withdrawn Feb 1937 (4th)
142	Milnes	1902	Renumbered 76 1914	1902 Brush	Ex 76			renumbered 115 1921	1919 BCT	Ex 42	Withdrawn May 1950 (5th)
143	Milnes	1902	Renumbered 86 1919	1913 BCT	Ex 243	1919 BCT	Ex 43	Withdrawn Mar 1950			
144	Milnes	1902	Renumbered 88 1919	5-window	Ex 244	5-window	Ex 44	Withdrawn July 1949			
145	Milnes	1902	Renumbered 10 1919	5-window	Ex 245	5-window	Ex 45	Withdrawn Mar 1950			
146	Milnes	1902	Renumbered 46 1919	5-window	Ex 246	5-window		Withdrawn Apr 1935			
147	Milnes	1902	Renumbered 192 1919	5-window	Ex 247	5-window		Withdrawn May 1935			
148	Milnes	1902	Renumbered 178 1919	5-window	Ex 248	5-window	Ex 48	Withdrawn May 1935			
149	Milnes	1902	Renumbered 116 or 124?	5-window	Ex 249	5-window	Ex 49	Withdrawn July 1935			
150	Milnes	1902	Renumbered 120 1919	1914 BCT	Ex 250	1919 BCT		Withdrawn Feb 1937			
151	Milnes	1902	Renumbered 72 1919	1914 BCT	Ex 251	1919 BCT		Withdrawn Feb 1937			
152	Milnes	1902	Renumbered 122 1919	1914 BCT	Ex 252	1919 BCT		Withdrawn Oct 1936			
153	Milnes	1902	Renumbered 121 1921	Milnes/BCT	Ex 198			Withdrawn June 1935			

Fleet No.	FIRST Type	FIRST Into service		SECOND Type	SECOND Into Service		THIRD Type	THIRD Into Service		(4th)
154	Milnes	1902	Renumbered 108 1921	High 4-window	Ex 218	Withdrawn Mar 1939				
155	Milnes	1902	Renumbered 123 1921	High 4-window	Ex 214	Withdrawn May 1939				
156	Milnes	1902	Renumbered 112 1921	High 4-window	Ex 205	Withdrawn Oct 1935				
157	Milnes	1902	Renumbered 179 1920	High 4-window	Ex 179	Withdrawn Apr 1939				
158	Milnes	1902	Renumbered 169 1921	High 4-window	July 1921	Renumbered 239 Dec 1936				
159	Milnes	1902	Renumbered 129 1921	High 4-window	Ex 129	Withdrawn June 1935				
160	Milnes	1902	Renumbered 118 1921	High 4-window	Oct 1921	Withdrawn May 1939				
161	Milnes	1902	Renumbered 78 1912	1902 Brush	Ex 78	Withdrawn 1919	Ex? Modern 6-window	Mar 1920	Renumbered 210 1921	1912 BCT / Ex 210 / Withdrawn Mar 1937 (4th)
162	Milnes	1902	Renumbered 205 1921	1912 BCT	Ex 229	Withdrawn Aug 1935				
163	Milnes	1902	Renumbered 113 1919	High 4-window	May1919	Withdrawn July 1938				
164	Milnes	1902	Renumbered 101 1921	High 4-window	June 1921	Renumbered 232 Dec 1936				
165	Milnes	1903	Withdrawn Oct 1929							
166	Milnes	1903	Withdrawn 1934							
167	Milnes	1903	Withdrawn 1933							
168	Milnes	1903	Withdrawn Aug 1931							
169	Milnes	1903	Withdrawn 1919	Milnes	Ex 158	Withdrawn Mar 1935				
170	Milnes	1903	Renumbered 72 1920	Modern 6-window	Ex 72	Withdrawn Aug 1935				
171	Milnes	1903	Withdrawn 1919	Modern 6-window	Jan 1920	Withdrawn July 1938				
172	Milnes	1903	Withdrawn Mar 1935							
173	Milnes	1903	Withdrawn 1914	Modern 6-window	Feb 1915	Withdrawn Feb 1937				
174	Milnes	1903	Withdrawn 1934							
175	Milnes	1903	Withdrawn 1933							
176	Milnes	1903	Withdrawn Aug 1929							
177	Milnes	1903	Withdrawn Feb 1935							
178	Milnes	1903	Withdrawn 1919	Milnes	Ex 148	Withdrawn June 1928	1919 BCT	May 1929	Withdrawn June 1949	
179	Milnes	1903	Withdrawn 1919	High 4-window	Dec 1920	Renumbered 157 1920	Milnes	Ex 157	Withdrawn 1932	
180	Milnes	1903	Withdrawn 1923	1902 Brush	Ex 75	Withdrawn June 1930				
181	Milnes	1903	Withdrawn Feb 1929	1919 BCT	July 1929	Withdrawn June 1949				
182	Milnes	1903	Withdrawn 1915	Modern 6-window	Apr 1916	Withdrawn Aug 1935				
183	Milnes	1903	Withdrawn 1920	Modern 6-window	Ex 227	Withdrawn June 1935				
184	Milnes	1903	Withdrawn 1933							
185	Milnes	1903	Withdrawn 1916	Modern 6-window	Apr 1917	Withdrawn Feb 1937				
186	Milnes	1903	Withdrawn 1919	Milnes	Ex 140	Withdrawn 1934				
187	Milnes	1903	Withdrawn July 1930							
188	Milnes	1903	Withdrawn 1914	Milnes (Teak Frame)	June 1914	Withdrawn July 1935				
189	Milnes	1903	To Towing Car 1925	1919 BCT	June 1925	Withdrawn June 1949				
190	Milnes	1903	Withdrawn 1914	Modern 6-window	Feb 1915	Withdrawn Oct 1935				
191	Milnes	1903	Withdrawn 1915	Modern 6-window	June 1915	Withdrawn Aug 1935				
192	Milnes	1903	Withdrawn 1919	Modern 6-window	Ex 147	Withdrawn May 1939				
193	Milnes	1903	Withdrawn 1917	Modern 6-window	May 1917	Withdrawn July 1938				
194	Milnes	1903	Withdrawn 1919	Modern 6-window	Apr 1919	Withdrawn May 1939				
195	Milnes	1903	Withdrawn 1922	1919 BCT	July 1923	Withdrawn May 1950				
196	Milnes	1903	Withdrawn 1919	Modern 6-window	1919	Burnt out Oct 1926	1919 BCT	June 1927	Withdrawn Mar 1950	
197	Milnes	1903	Withdrawn 1917	Modern 6-window	Feb 1918	Withdrawn July 1937	Milnes	Ex 226	Withdrawn June 1938	
198	Milnes	1903	Withdrawn 1913	Milnes/BCT	July 1913	Renumbered 153 1920				
199	Milnes	1903	To plough 1917	Modern 6-window	Ex 91?	Withdrawn July 1938				
200	Milnes	1903	Withdrawn 1915	Modern 6-window	May 1915	Withdrawn Jan 1935				
201	Milnes	1903	Withdrawn 1918	Modern 6-window	July 1919	Withdrawn May 1939				
202	Milnes	1903	Withdrawn 1915	Modern 6-window	Apr 1915	Withdrawn July 1938				
203	Milnes	1903	Withdrawn 1919	Modern 6-window	May 1920	Withdrawn Oct 1935				

No.	Builder	Date		Body/Type	Date		Builder	Date	Date	Withdrawn		Fate
204	Milnes	1903	Withdrawn 1919	Modern 6-window	March 1920	Withdrawn July 1938	Milnes	Ex 162	1919 BCT	Withdrawn Aug 1929	Jan 1931	Renumbered 225 Oct 1935 (4th)
205	Milnes	1903	Withdrawn c1917	High 4-window	June 1917	Renumbered 156 1921	Modern 6-window	Ex 161		Withdrawn July 1938		
206	Milnes	1903	Withdrawn 1915	Modern 6-window	July 1915	Withdrawn Nov 1936						
207	Milnes	1903	Withdrawn 1915	Modern 6-window	Aug 1915	Withdrawn July 1938						
208	Milnes	1903	Withdrawn 1930	Modern 6-window	Jan 1916	Withdrawn May 1939						
209	Milnes	1903	Withdrawn 1915	1912 BCT	June 1912	Renumbered 161 1921						
210	Milnes	1903	Withdrawn July 1907	Modern 6-window	Sept 1915	Withdrawn July 1938				Sheffield 325 Oct 1942		
211	Milnes	1903	Withdrawn 1915	Modern 6-window	Jan 1916	Withdrawn Nov 1936						
212	Milnes	1903	Withdrawn 1915	1914 BCT	May 1916	Renumbered 142 1921						
213	Milnes	1903	Withdrawn 1914/5	High 4-window	Mar 1918	Renumbered 155 1920	Preston	Feb 1921	1919 BCT	Withdrawn May 1939	Ex 2	Withdrawn May 1949 (4th)
214	Milnes	1903	Withdrawn 1915	Preston	Feb 1921	Sheffield 332 Dec 1942	Preston	Feb 1921		Sheffield 333 Dec 1942		
215	Milnes	1903	Renumbered 104 1920	Preston	Feb 1921	Sheffield 328 Dec 1942						
216	Milnes	1903	To plough 1920	High 4-window	Mar 1921	Sheffield 334 Dec 1942						
217	Milnes	1903	Renumbered 126 1919	Mid-Yks (Teak Frame)	Ex 239	Renumbered 154 1920	Preston	Mar 1921	1919 BCT	Withdrawn May 1939	Ex 3	Withdrawn Feb 1950 (4th)
218	Milnes	1903	Withdrawn 1918	Preston	Mar 1921	Renumbered 32 1920	Preston	Mar 1921		Withdrawn May 1950		
219	Milnes	1903	To plough 1915	Mid-Yorks		Withdrawn Aug 1945						
220	Milnes	1903	Renumbered 105 1920	Preston	June 1921	Renumbered 125 May 1938	1919 BCT	Ex 125		Withdrawn May 1950		
221	Milnes	1903	Renumbered 127 1921	Mid-Yorks	Ex 234	Withdrawn Oct 1921	Preston	June 1921	Greengates	Withdrawn Dec 1936	Ex 69	Withdrawn May 1948 (4th)
222	Milnes	1903	Withdrawn 1919	Modern 6-window	Mar 1915	Renumbered 128 1920	Preston	June 1921	1919 BCT	Withdrawn Dec 1936	Ex 63	Withdrawn Oct 1948 (4th)
223	Milnes	1903	Withdrawn 1915	Preston	June 1921	Withdrawn Sept 1945						
224	Milnes	1903	Renumbered 107 1920	Preston	July 1921	Withdrawn Oct 1935	1919 BCT	Ex 205	1919 BCT	Withdrawn May 1950	Ex 4	Withdrawn 1949 (4th)
225	Milnes	1903	Renumbered 107 1920	Modern 6-window	June 1920	Renumbered 198 1921	Preston	July 1921	1919 BCT	Withdrawn Apr 1939	July 1921	Withdrawn Oct 1935 (4th)
226	Milnes	1903	Withdrawn 1920	Modern 6-window	1920	Renumbered 183 1920	1901 Brush	Ex 65	1919 BCT	Withdrawn 1920	Ex 14	Withdrawn Mar 1950 (5th)
227	Milnes	1903	Withdrawn 1920	Modern 6-window								
228	Milnes	1903	Withdrawn 1916	Modern 6-window	May 1916	Renumbered 136 1921	Preston	July 1921	1919 BCT	Withdrawn July 1936	Ex 82	Withdrawn May 1950 (4th)
229	1919 BCT	Ex 39	Withdrawn June 1948	Single-decker	June 1912	Renumbered 162 1921	Preston	Aug 1921	1919 BCT	Withdrawn Oct 1935	Ex 5	Withdrawn June 1949 (4th)
230	Mid-Yorks	Sept 1903	Withdrawn c1907	Mid-Yorks	Ex 238	Withdrawn Feb 1920	Preston	Aug 1921		Withdrawn Apr 1939		
231	Mid-Yorks	1904	Withdrawn 1919	Mid-Yorks	Aug 1921	Withdrawn May 1939	1919 BCT	Ex 6		Withdrawn Sept 1945		
232	Mid-Yorks	1904	Withdrawn 1920	Mid-Yorks	Ex 233	Renumbered 30 1921	Preston	Aug 1921		Withdrawn Dec 1936		
233	Mid-Yorks	1904	Withdrawn 1919	Preston	Oct 1919	Withdrawn May 1939	1919 BCT	Ex 7		Withdrawn Aug 1949		
234	Mid-Yorks	1904	Renumbered 232 1919	Preston	Oct 1919	Withdrawn June 1944			High 4-window		Ex 164	Withdrawn Dec 1944 (4th)
235	Mid-Yorks	1904	Renumbered 222 July 1919	Preston	Oct 1919	Withdrawn Oct 1935						
236	Mid-Yorks	1904	Withdrawn 1919	Preston	Oct 1919	Withdrawn Aug 1945	1919 BCT	Ex 87		Withdrawn Mar 1950		
237	Mid-Yorks	1904	Renumbered 31 1919	Preston	Nov 1919	Sheffield 329 Dec 1942						
238	Mid-Yorks	1904	Renumbered 27 1919	Preston	Nov 1919	Withdrawn Aug 1945						
239	Mid-Yorks	1904	Renumbered 230 1919	Rebuilt teak frame	Sept 1913	Renumbered 219 1919	Preston	Nov 1919	High 4-window	Withdrawn Dec 1936	Ex 158	Withdrawn May 1948 (4th)
240	1913 BCT	May 1913	Withdrawn 1913	Preston	Nov 1919	Withdrawn May 1939	1919 BCT	Ex 8		Withdrawn June 1949		
241	1913 BCT	June 1913	Renumbered 140 1919	Preston	Nov 1919	Withdrawn June 1938	1919 BCT	Ex 58		Withdrawn Aug 1948		
242	Milnes 6-window	Apr 1912	Renumbered 141 1919	Preston	Nov 1919	Sheffield 327 Nov 1942						
243	1913 BCT	July 1913	Renumbered 142 1919	Preston	Dec 1919	Sheffield 326 Nov 1942						
244	5-window	Apr 1914	Renumbered 143 1919	Preston	Dec 1919	Withdrawn May 1939	1919 BCT	Ex 12		Withdrawn Oct 1948		
245	5-window	Apr 1914	Renumbered 144 1919	Preston	Dec 1919	Withdrawn May 1939	1919 BCT	Ex 13		Withdrawn Aug 1945		
246	5-window	Apr 1914	Renumbered 145 May 1919	Preston	Dec 1919	Withdrawn May 1942	1919 BCT	Ex 11		Withdrawn May 1950		
247	5-window	May 1914	Renumbered 146 May 1919	Preston	Dec 1919	Withdrawn July 1936	1919 BCT	Ex 21		Withdrawn May 1950		
248	5-window	Aug 1914	Renumbered 147 May 1919	Preston	Jan 1920	Withdrawn June 1936	1919 BCT	Ex 60		Withdrawn Dec 1949		
249	5-window	Nov 1914	Renumbered 148 May 1919	Preston	Jan 1920	Withdrawn Oct 1935	1919 BCT	Ex 41		Withdrawn June 1949		
250	1914 BCT	Dec 1914	Renumbered 149 May 1919	Preston	Jan 1920	Withdrawn Oct 1935						
251	1914 BCT	Dec 1914	Renumbered 150 May 1919	Preston	Mar 1920	Sheffield 330 Dec 1942						
252	1914 BCT	Dec 1914	Renumbered 151 May 1919	Preston	Mar 1920	Withdrawn Oct 1935						
253	Preston	Mar 1920	Renumbered 152 May 1919	Preston	Ex 15	Withdrawn June 1949	1919 BCT	Ex 33	1919 BCT	Withdrawn Aug 1949		
254	Preston	Apr 1920	Withdrawn May 1939	1919 BCT	Ex 16	Withdrawn Feb 1949						
255	Preston	Apr 1920	Withdrawn May 1939	1919 BCT	Ex 54	Withdrawn May 1950						
256	Preston	Apr 1920	Withdrawn Oct 1935	1919 BCT								
257	Preston	May 1920	Sheffield 331 Dec 1942									
258	Preston	Apr 1920	Withdrawn Sep 1945									

SUMMARY OF BCT-BUILT BODIES (Teak Frame)

(1) Older cars rebuilt to BCT 4-window design (213 and 239)	2
(2) Older car rebuilt with teak underframe and vestibules (9)	1
(3) Older cars rebuilt as open-platform 6-window cars (156/188/198)	3
(4) 1912-1915 4 and 5-window cars	14
(5) Vestibuled 'Modern 6-window cars	30
(6) 'High 4-window' cars	10
(7) 'Greengates' and 1919 type BCT cars	96
(8) 'Pullman' single-decker (No. 1)	1
	157

SUMMARY OF WORKS CARS 1909-1933

In 1909 2 snowploughs, 14 Salt trucks, assisted by 30 tramcars with snowplough attachments

In 1912 2 snowploughs, 9 salt trucks, 2 stores trucks, 2 ballast tipper trucks, 2 goods waggons

In 1914 2 snowploughs, 9 salt trucks, 1 stores trucks, 3 ballast tipper trucks

In 1920 Also 1 aircraft truck, presumably Phoenix Works car 11, previously used for carrying aircraft parts

In 1925 18 snowploughs and 10 ballast tipper trucks. One of the ploughs (number unknown) was ex car 219

In 1926 18 snowploughs and 8 ballast tipper trucks, and (driving) school car (ex 26, burnt out Oct 1926)

March 1933 10 snowploughs and 2 ballast tipper trucks, 1 stores waggon, 1 railgrinder

WORKS CARS : NUMBERS AND RENUMBERINGS

No.	FIRST Function	Into Service		SECOND Function	Into Service		THIRD Snowplough		Into Service
1	Box car used as snowplough	?	Withdrawn 1933	Snowplough Ex S.15	Oct 1933	Withdrawn Dec 1947			
2	Box car used as snow plough	?	Withdrawn 1933	Snowplough Ex car 126	Nov 1933	Withdrawn June 1949			
3	Works car	?	?	Snowplough Ex Milnes 149?	1915?	Withdrawn 1933	Ex car 123	Nov 1933	Withdrawn June 1949
4	Water car/crane	?	?	Snowplough Ex a Milnes car	1915?	Withdrawn 1933	Ex car 133	Nov 1933	Withdrawn May 1950
5	P/way tippler	c1905	Withdrawn 1933?	Snowplough ex Milnes 139?	July 1933	Withdrawn Apr 1939			
6	Works truck	c1905	Withdrawn 1933?	Snowplough ExS.13	Dec 1933	Withdrawn May 1950			
7	Works truck	c1905	Withdrawn ?	Snowplough ex S.14	1933	Withdrawn 1933	Ex?	Dec 1933	Withdrawn Jan 1945
8	P/way tippler	1917	Withdrawn 1933	Snowplough Ex Milnes 225	1920	Withdrawn 1933	Ex 135	Dec 1933	Withdrawn Apr 1939
9	Snowplough Ex Milnes 199	?	Withdrawn ?						
10	?	?	Withdrawn ?	Snowplough ex Railgrinder	Jan 1933	Withdrawn June 1949			
11	Ex stores truck	1920	Withdrawn 1933	Railgrinder	c1920	Withdrawn June 1949	(trolley ex Phoenix, cabs ex railless lorries)		
S.12	Snowplough Ex Milnes 216	1920	Renumbered S.6 1933						
S.13	Snowplough Ex Brush 105	1921	Renumbered S.7 1933						
S.14	Snowplough Ex Brush 56	1919	Renumbered S.1 1933						
S.15	Snowplough Ex Brush 113	1920/1	Withdrawn 1933						
S.16	Snowplough Ex Brush 104	1923	Withdrawn 1928						
S.17	Snowplough Ex Brush 39	1925	Withdrawn 1933						
S.18	Snowplough Ex Brush 13		Withdrawn 1933						

APPENDIX 2A
HORSE AND STEAM TRAM SERVICES – OPENING AND CLOSING DATES

Type of propulsion	Opened	Closed
Horse		
Rawson Square to Lister Park	2 February 1882	31 January 1902
Rawson Square turning-circle	19 September 1887	31 January 1902
Extension to Frizinghall	26 January 1885	5 December 1888
Saltaire Road (Fox Corner to Rosse Hotel)	3 August 1882	2 May 1883
– ditto –	7 March 1884	13 February 1885
– ditto –	May 1887	September 1887
– ditto –	(Intermittently until June 1890)	
Saltaire to Frizinghall (boundary)	26 August 1888	9 October 1891
Steam (BTOC)		
Leeds Road (Bridge Street-Thornhill Terrace)	3 August 1882	26 February 1902
– ditto – extended to Rushton Road	17/18 July 1885	26 February 1902
– ditto – extended to Thornbury Depot	Early 1888	26 February 1902
Bridge Street to Four Lane Ends	21? September 1882	31 January 1902
Leeds Road to Four Lane Ends (through)	30 October 1882	31 January 1902
Extension from Four Lane Ends to Allerton (Chapel Lane)	19 November 1887	5 June 1902
Forster Square to Undercliffe	10 October 1888	21 May 1902
Forster Square to 'Cock & Bottle' (only)	22 May 1902	26 May 1902
Forster Square to Frizinghall	6 December 1888	2 February 1902
Undercliffe to Frizinghall (through)	6 December 1888	2 February 1902
Undercliffe to Saltaire (through)	31 March 1893	2 February 1902
Cheapside closed for electrification		2 February 1902
North Parade replaced Cheapside	3 February 1902	
Rawson Square to Saltaire ceased		13 April 1902
Norfolk Street to Dudley Hill	31 July 1893	14 May 1902
– extended to Fairfield Street	11 October 1893	20 May 1902
– extended to Tong Cemetery	2 March 1894	20 May 1902
Steam (BST)		
Town Hall to Bank Foot (Rooley Lane)	6 September 1884	31 January 1902
– extended to Buttershaw Mills	11 June 1886	1 April 1903
– extended to Shelf (Bottomley's Arms)	27 July 1886	31 January 1903
– cut back to Furnace Inn	1 February 1903	1 April 1903
Town Hall to Wyke (Temperance Hall)	24 January 1893	2 May 1902

Route name in CAPITALS	Inspected	Opened	Closed	Length* Miles Yards
BOLTON ROAD ROUTES				
	20 July 1898 E			
BOLTON (City Boundary)	29 July 1898 T	30 July 1898	29 May 1934	1m 1425
Extended to ECCLESHILL	21 February 1899	21 February 1899	29 May 1934	736
Branch line to FIVE LANE ENDS	10 September 1901	10 September 1901	7 September 1931(A)	862
Extended to IDLE	10 September 1901	10 September 1901	21 March 1931	1621
Ext. to THACKLEY (Victoria Street)	10 September 1901	10 September 1901	29 March 1930	1m 1724
Ext. to THACKLEY (City Boundary)		1 July 1904	29 March 1930	1106
Ext. to NAB WOOD				
(See CIRCULAR ROUTE)		(1 July 1904)	(January 1915)	- -
GREAT HORTON ROUTES				
HORTON BANK TOP	23 August 1898	27 August 1898	5 November 1949	2m1324
Laisteridge Ln/PARK AVENUE	23 August 1898	19 November 1898	5 November 1949	1195
SOUTHFIELD LANE shortworking	-	Oct/Nov 1899	c.1946	- -
Extended to Tyrrel Street	19 December 1899	19 December 1899	5 November 1949	281
Extended to QUEENSBURY	2 August 1901 E	5 November 1949		(To boundary) 1581
	(15 Aug 1901 T)			(Queensbury UD) 1340
Branch Line to LITTLE HORTON	31 July 1902	1 August 1902	7 January 1945	1367
Extended to WIBSEY	9 Oct 1907	9 Oct 1907	7 January 1945	1653
WHITE HORSE shortworking		1921	5 November 1949	- -
LIDGET GREEN ROUTE				
LIDGET GREEN	(30 August 1900 E			
	(7 September 1900 T	31 Aug 1900	11 December 1934	(From New Inn) 1m1066
WHETLEY HILL ROUTE				
Westgate to DUCKWORTH LANE	1 November 1900	2 November 1900	1 October 1935	1m1120
Extended to Sunbridge Road	31 January 1902	13 March 1902		-(Godwin St) 136
Cut back to Westgate	-	14 March 1903	-	
Re-extended to Sunbridge Road	-	?22 June 1903	1 October 1935	
LEEDS ROAD ROUTES				
Thornbury to STANNINGLEY	1 November 1900	16 November 1900	18 October 1942	Tyrrel St to Thornhill Pl) 1m1583
City to THORNBURY	22 April 1902	27 February 1902	4 March 1950	Thornhill Pl to boundary 876
Trial run to LEEDS		22 January 1907	-	Calverley UD 664
Experimental service to LEEDS		22 April 1907	?25 May 1907	Farsley UD 1m 144
				Pudsey UD 15
Tram 124 full-time LEEDS service	-	23 September 1907	?10th May 1908	
Jointly-operated LEEDS service	-	7 June 1909	31 March 1918	
New Hall Ings terminus	-	July 1927	4 March 1950	87
THORNTON ROAD ROUTES				
Four Lane Ends to THORNTON	18 December 1900 E	18 December 1900	20 November 1934 (B)	2m 1203
City to FOUR LANE ENDS	20 December 1900 T	1 February 1902	20 November 1934 (B)	1m 1276
Branch to ALLERTON (Druids Arms)	31 January 1902	6 June 1902	30 November 1929	
Extended to ALLERTON (Ivy Lane)	24 October 1902	24 Oct 1902	30 November 1929	2m 312
Extended to ALLERTON (Prune Park Lane)	12 October 1904	12 October 1904	30 November 1929	
MANCHESTER Rd ROUTES				
City to BANKFOOT (Red Lion)	31 January 1902	1 February 1902	6 May 1950	1m 1575
Extended to ODSAL		1902	6 May 1950	
Extended to WYKE	Trial 29 April 1902	3 May 1902	11 June 1944	2m 143
Branch line to King's Head	3 July 1903	29 May 1903	19 February 1935	1528
Extended to FURNACE INN	3 July 1903	early June 1903	19 February 1935	1549

APPENDIX 2B				
BRADFORD CITY TRAMWAYS – OPENING AND CLOSING DATES				
Route name in CAPITALS	**Inspected**	**Opened**	**Closed**	**Length* Miles Yards**
Extended to SHELF		2 September 1903	19 February 1935	Shelf UD 1326
Diverted via Nelson St/Croft St.		21 January 1904	6 May 1950	426
Branch to BOWLING OLD LANE	31 March 1904	1 April 1904	13 December 1947	1085
Extended to BAILIFF BRIDGE	13 March 1913	17 March 1913	10 June 1944	(To boundary 1m 19
				(Hipperholme UD 780
				(Clifton parish 26
Re-extended to				
HORSFALL PLAYING FIELDS		11 September 1939	6 May 1950	(About 860)
MANNINGHAM LANE ROUTES				
Penny Bank to PARK GATES		8 March 1902	6 May 1939	1511
Forster Square to Penny Bank	22 April 1902	28 March 1902	6 May 1939	(a) 1064
Park Gates to FRIZINGHALL	22 April 1902	28 March 1902	6 May 1939	1532
	18 February 1902 E			
Frizinghall to BRANCH Hotel	1 July 1902 T	5 May 1902	6 May 1939	Shipley UD 967
	18 February 1902 E			
BRANCH to SALTAIRE	1 July 1902 T	17 May 1902	6 May 1939	Shipley UD 1487
(Branch line to NORTH PARK RD)				
(via St Mary's Road)		29 May 1902	7 April 1935	700
(RAWSON SQUARE to NORTH PARK		?4 June 1902	May 1915	(d) 220
(RD, via St Mary's Road)				
North Park Road to HEATON	23 December 1902	24 December 1902	7 April 1935	1347
(Saltaire to Nab Wood				
(See CIRCULAR ROUTE)		(1 July 1904)	(January 1915)	(b) Shipley UD (1195)
BRANCH to BAILDON BRIDGE				
(see Mid-Yorkshire)		(30 April 1904)	(4 February 1936)	(b) Shipley UD (1319)
('Exhibition' track, North				
(Park Road (from Oak Lane)		4 May 1904	22 April 1939	474
(to St Mary's Road				
Nab Wood to BINGLEY (Ann St)	29 Jan 1914	3 Feb 1914	6 May 1939	Bingley UD 1m 1071
CIRCULAR ROUTE extended				
to Cottingley Bar		3 February 1914	January 1915	- -
Ann Street to BINGLEY (Post Office)	8 October 1914	25 August 1914	6 May 1939	Bingley UD 417
Post Office to CROSSFLATTS	8 October 1914	13 October 1914	6 May 1939	(c) Bingley UD 1604
WAKEFIELD ROAD ROUTES				
Norfolk Street to DUDLEY HILL		15 May 1902	5 July 1938	2m 134
Dudley Hill to Fairfield Sreet	31 July 1902	5 July 1902	5 July 1938	1050
Fairfield Street to TONG CEMETERY	31 July 1902	2 August 1902	5 July 1938	1069
Tong Cemetery to DRIGHLINGTON	3 July 1903	30 June 1903	8 August 1933	(To boundary 1m 347
				(Drigh. UD 1109
Siding in Sticker Lane		Summer 1903	5 July 1938	98
Tong Cemetery to BIRKENSHAW	30 September 1903 Trial	30 September 1903	29 October 1935	To boundary 179
				Hunsworth UD 1224
				(Birkenshaw UD 1012
Sticker Lane siding extended		1909 (part) & March 1928	1938	82
CHURCH BANK ROUTES				
Leeds Road bottom to	(Temporary	27 or		
'Cock & Bottle' via Harris Street	Service)	28 May 1902	(One day only)	-
Harris Street		10 June 1902	23 July 1949	551
East Parade, Humboldt St.		10 June 1902	14 November 1948	351
Forster Square to Peel Park Gates		10 June 1902	7 April 1935 (C)	Well Street 248
				Otley Road 1007
Peel Park to UNDERCLIFFE		28 June 1902	7 April 1935 (C)	Otley Road 1087
Diversion via Church Bank	15 December 1903	19 December 1903	23 July 1949	453
Cock & Bottle to BRADFORD MOOR	15 December 1903	30 January 1904	23 July 1949	1m 990
Undercliffe to GREENGATES	12 October 1904	14 October 1904	11 November 1928	1m 428
UNDERCLIFFE re-opened		11 September 1939	17 July 1948	

APPENDIX 2B
BRADFORD CITY TRAMWAYS – OPENING AND CLOSING DATES

Route name in CAPITALS	Inspected	Opened	Closed	Length* Miles Yards
MID-YORKSHIRE SERVICES				
(NAB WOOD to THACKLEY (BOUNDARY (Windhill)	23 July 1903	23 July 1903	30 April 1904	2m 1244
(BRANCH Hotel to (BAILDON BRIDGE	27 November 1903	14 November 1903	30 April 1904	1319
Forster Square-NAB WOOD (via Branch & Shipley)		1 May 1904	30 June 1904	(Listed elsewhere)
Forster Square-BAILDON BRIDGE (via Branch & Shipley)		1 May 1904	4 February 1936	(Listed elsewhere)
Forster Square-THACKLEY BOUNDARY, Windhill (via Branch & Shipley)		1 May 1904	30 June 1904	(Listed elsewhere)
CIRCULAR ROUTE from Forster Square to Shipley (via Bolton, Thackley Windhill, Shipley and Branch) (and vice-versa)		1 July 1904	1905	(Connecting track from Victoria Street, Thackley, to Shipley/Thackley 1106 boundary)
CIRCULAR ROUTE extended to NAB WOOD (clockwise cars travelled direct without passing through Shipley centre)		21 April 1905	2 February 1914	(Listed elsewhere)
CIRCULAR ROUTE extended to Cottingley Bar		3 February 1914	January 1915	(Listed elsewhere)
Circular Route replaced by Forster Square to NAB WOOD (via Bolton, Thackley and Shipley)		January 1915	25 September 1927	(Listed elsewhere)
NAB WOOD cut back to SALTAIRE		26 September 1927	29 March 1930	(Listed elsewhere)
MISCELLANEOUS				
John Street (Westgate to Rawson Square)		13 December 1905	By March 1936 but still usable until May 1939	260
			Total	**58m 1710 yds**

NOTES

(E = Electrical T= Track)
A   A few peak-hour cars 21 November
B   One daily (weekday) journey retained.

* Correct Nov 1928

(a)   includes the whole of the Forster Square layout.
(b)   length included in Mid-Yorkshire figures
(c)   total route length Forster Square to Crossflatts including ForsterSquare layout 7 miles 288 yards.
(d)   North Parade and Rawson Square

APPENDIX 3A – ROUTE COLOURS

ROUTE COLOURS – were introduced 1911-1914 and superseded after 1919 by roller-blind destination and route-number indicators.

Bolton Road:	Green – Idle
	Red – Eccleshill
	Yellow and Green – Thackley
Church Bank:	Green – Undercliffe
	Red – Greengates
	Yellow – Bradford Moor
Leeds Road:	Green – Stanningley
	Red – Thornbury
	White – Leeds
Manchester Road:	Green – Odsal
	Red – Bailiff Bridge and Wyke
	Yellow – Shelf
	White – Bowling Old Lane
Manningham Lane:	Green – Saltaire
	Green and Yellow – Nab Wood
	Red and Yellow – Bingley and Crossflatts
	Red – Baildon Bridge
	Yellow – Heaton
Sunbridge Road:	Green – Allerton
	Red – Thornton
	White – Four Lane Ends
	Yellow – Duckworth Lane
Tyrrel Street:	Green – Lidget Green
	Red – Queensbury
	White – Southfield Lane
	Yellow – Wibsey
Wakefield Road:	Green – Drighlington
	Red – Birkenshaw
	Yellow – Tong Cemetery
	White – Dudley Hill

NB. Circular Route cars displayed placards hung over the dashplate

APPENDIX 3B – ROUTE NUMBERS

As Chapter 10, with the following observations:

Route Number

2	Also WHITE HORSE (GREAT HORTON) from 1921
5	Also FAIRWEATHER GREEN and (1928-30) SCHOOL GREEN
6	Used for SCHOOL GREEN from 1930
12	Also FURNACE INN (occasional workings) until 1935; used for PUDSEY LANE END from 1938.
13	Also occasional journeys to Shirley Manor
14	Also peak-hour and late-night journeys to LOW MOOR
15	Also BANKFOOT and (from 1939) HORSFALL PLAYING FIELDS
16	Used for KILLINGHALL ROAD from 1933
18	Also occasional journeys to WESTGATE HILL
25	Also NAB WOOD via Manningham Lane
27	Also BRANCH from 1936
28	Also NORTH PARK ROAD via St Mary's Road (late night), and Buxton Street (works specials)
32	Also shortworkings to SALTAIRE (Depot), BRIGGATE, THACKLEY and TOWN GATE.

KILLINGHALL RD (a)
CITY
BRADFORD MOOR
HEATON
NORTH PARK ROAD
PARK GATES
FRIZINGHALL
BRANCH
BAILDON BRIDGE
SALTAIRE
BINGLEY
CITY
SPECIAL CAR
(Blank)
CROSSFLATTS
UNDERCLIFFE
GREENGATES (b)
NAB WOOD
THACKLEY (b)
BRIGGATE (b)
TOWN GATE (b)
IDLE (b)
FIVE LANE ENDS
ECCLESHILL
VALLEY PARADE
DEPOT ONLY
PARK AVENUE (c)
CITY
WYKE
BAILIFF BRIDGE
BANKFOOT
ODSAL
HORSFALL PLAYING FIELDS (d)
LOW MOOR
SHELF
FURNACE INN
BOWLING OLD LANE
THORNBURY
PUDSEY LANE END (e)
STANNINGLEY
CITY
DEPOT ONLY
DUDLEY HILL
BIRKENSHAW
DRIGHLINGTON
WESTGATE HILL
TONG CEMETERY
(Blank)
SPECIAL CAR
LITTLE HORTON
WIBSEY
SOUTHFIELD LANE
WHITE HORSE
(GREAT HORTON)
HORTON BANK TOP
QUEENSBURY
LIDGET GREEN
CITY
ALLERTON (b)
SQUIRE LANE (f)
FOUR LANE ENDS
FAIRWEATHER GREEN
SCHOOL GREEN (g)
THORNTON
DUCKWORTH LANE
PARK AVENUE
VALLEY PARADE
RAWSON SQUARE

NOTES

(a)   added 23rd December 1931
(b)   probable location of names deleted before October 1931
(c)   probable division between the 'Town Hall Square' and 'Forster Square' sets of blinds: not all cars carried a complete blind in view of its extreme length.
(d)   added 1940
(e)   added 5th April 1938
(f)   added about 1925
(g)   added 1928

Dimensions: screens 2ft 7⅝ins wide; names 2ft 4ins wide (max) with letters 4ins high.

SIDE DESTINATION SCREENS: as above but excluding CITY (not displayed) and HORSFALL PLAYING FIELDS (too long) and including

(BRADFORD MOOR   (CROSSFLATTS
(& HEATON   (& UNDERCLIFFE

(BINGLEY   (SALTAIRE
(& UNDERCLIFFE   (& UNDERCLIFFE

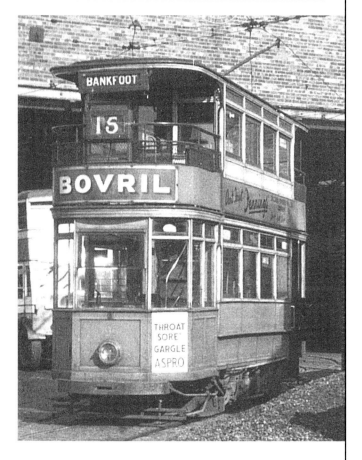

Appropriately displaying 'Bankfoot, 15', car No. 195 was photographed entering Carrbottom Road from the upper part of Bankfoot Depot in April 1950, by the late Mr R. F. Mack

APPENDIX 4

WEIGHTS AND MEASURES

(From BCT and City Engineer's drawings and records, 1887-1950, and actual measurements 1943-1997)

Steam cars:
Bogie wheelbase 4ft 6ins; distance between bogie centres 11ft 7ins.

Electric car truck:
Brush 21E, March 1912, wheelbase 6ft 6ins, height on full tyres 2ft 3□ins, distance between spring posts 5ft 5□ins, axle length 5ft 11□ins

WEIGHTS	Tons	cwt	qr	lb
Peckham truck with Westinghouse equipment	4	9	0	14
Hurst Nelson 21E truck without equipment	2	9	2	14
Witting, Westinghouse and BTH motors – each		15	-	-
Dick Kerr 31 motors – each		13	2	-
Siemens motors – each	1	0	1	10
– ditto – with gears and gear cases	1	2	2	21
Cole, Marchent & Morley air/oil brake		9	2	12
Mechanical 4-shoe iron track brake		8	-	-
Car 125, 'low deck' (open top) Brush body on Peckham truck, 1913	8	3	0	14
Car 140, open top Milnes body on Brush truck, 1913	8	13	3	-
Car 152, 'old top' (Bailey top), Milnes body on Peckham truck	9	13	0	14
Car 119, unvestibuled Brush body, 'oak top' (canopy top), Peckham truck, 1913	9	4	-	-
Car 165, unvestibuled 6 window Milnes body, canopy top and 11ft wheelbase radial truck	11	6	3	14
Vestibuled car (probably 'Modern 6 window') on Mountain & Gibson truck	11	-	-	-
BCT-built car 241, vestibuled, top cover, Hurst Nelson truck, Siemens motors, 1915	11	1	0	14
Car 241 as above but BTH/GEC ventilated motors, 1915, unladen	10	17	0	14
Car 241 as above but BTH/GEC ventilated motors, 1915, laden	12	16	0	23
BCT-built 5-window car 244, 1914, unladen	12	6	1	14

Car 80, weighed on Bowling weighbridge, 1918:

Brush unvestibuled lower deck, 22 seats	4	3	0	23
Oak canopy topy, 38 seats	1	9	0	7
Hurst Nelson 21E truck, Siemens motors,				
Cole, Marchent & Morley air/oil brake	5	4	2	12
Trolley base, pole and head		2	1	14
Total	10	19	1	0

	Tons	cwt	qr	lb
Car 9, vestibuled Brush body, oak canopy top, 65 seats, Hurst Nelson truck, Siemens motors	11	4	-	-
Car 241, 1920, Preston (EE) car, unladen	12	17	1	0
laden	16	15	-	-
BCT 1919-type car, high canopy top, 1921, unladen	11	7	-	-
laden	15	5	-	-

Miscellaneous:

Height from rail to centre of gravity – Preston car	– unladen 4ft 7ins
– BCT vestibuled car, high canopy	– unladen 4ft 9ins
	– laden 5ft 4□ins

Truck widths: Peckham 6ft 6ins, Hurst Nelson/Boving 6ft 9ins, Dick Kerr 7ft 0ins
Window glass: Lower deck □ins polished plate
          Upper deck 26oz sheet
Electricity units per car mile, 1924:–

BCT built cars	1.863d
Preston cars	2.108d

Depot allocation:

Thornbury	100 (approx)	Horton Bank Top	24
Bankfoot	47	Bolton	16
Bowling	34	Fairweather Green	4
Saltaire	30	Lidget Green	4
Duckworth Lane	28		287 (approx)

APPENDIX 4 (Continued)

KNOWN DIMENSIONS

LENGTH CAR TYPE	LOWER SALOON OVER PILLARS	EACH PLATFORM	LENGTH OVER PLATFORMS	TOTAL LENGTH OVER COLLISION FENDERS	TOTAL LENGTH OVER CANOPY ROOF
BRUSH	16ft 0ins	5ft 3ins			
MILNES	16ft 0ins				
1912 BCT 5 window	16ft 0ins	5ft 4ins	26ft 8ins	27ft 6ins	27ft 0ins
244-248 5-window	18ft 8ins	5ft 4ins	29ft 4ins	30ft 4ins	
249	18ft 8ins	5ft 10ins	30ft 4ins	31ft 8ins	
250-252 1914	16ft 0ins	5ft 10ins	27ft 8ins	29ft 0ins	28ft 0ins
1919 BCT	16ft 0ins	6ft 0ins	28ft 0ins	29ft 0ins	28ft 3ins

HEIGHT – Interior					
	Brush	6ft 6ins			
Lower deck:	Milnes	7ft 3ins	Upper deck:	High canopy	6ft 0½ins
	1912 BCT	6ft 6ins		Medium canopy	5ft 7⅝ins
	1919 BCT	6ft 2ins		1919 Greengates	5ft 6ins
	1919 Greengates	6ft 2ins		1924/8 Greengates	5ft 8ins
	1924/8 Greengates	6ft 0ins			

HEIGHT – Overall, rail to top of trolley base

Brush canopy top car, Peckham truck 1910   16ft 8ins
Brush canopy top car, dual-gauge truck 1910   17ft 0ins
BCT 1912 type, on full tyres   16ft 5⅛ins
Measurements taken in 1916 with varying tyre depths:–
    Open-top 'White Board' cars   – No. 38: 13ft 10ins;   No. 36: 14ft 3½ins
                Milnes cars   – No. 150: 14ft 7ins;   No. 170: 14ft 9ins
                Mid-Yorkshire   –   No. 238: 14ft 9ins
    Bailey top Brush car   –   No. 94: 15ft 10ins
                Milnes cars 141, 215, 218: 15ft 9ins; 222: 15ft 10ins; 152: 15ft 11ins 216: 16ft 0½ins
    High canopy top: Milnes 6 window   160: 16ft 3½ins;   181: 16ft 4ins
                'Modern 6 window'   202: 16ft 4ins
                1914 BCT   251: 15ft 11ins
'Preston' car, full tyres, 1921: rail to roof 15ft 5ins (+6ins for trolley = 15ft 11ins)
1919 High canopy type (6 window?) rail to roof 16ft 5ins (+6ins for trolley = 16ft 11ins)
BCT 1919 type with medium canopy top   15ft 11ins
BCT 1919 type with high canopy top   presumably   16ft 3ins
Greengates (all types)   presumably   15ft 0ins

WIDTH – Lower deck

	Over Solebars	Interior (Maximum)	Over Pillars	Over Rubbing Strip
Brush	5ft 9ins		6ft 6ins	6ft 6ins
Milnes	5ft 8¼ins			6ft 6½ins
BCT 1912 type	5ft 8¼ins	6ft 0ins	6ft 5½ins	6ft 8ins
(BCT post-1919 (narrow type	5ft 10ins	6ft 0ins	6ft 3⅝ins	6ft 7⅝ins
(BCT post-1919 wide type	5ft 10ins	6ft 3ins	6ft 6⅝ins	6ft 10⅝ins
(BCT post-1919 (intermediate (type	5ft 10ins	6ft 0¼ins	6ft 3⅞ins	6ft 7⅞ins
Dick Kerr cars	6ft 3ins		6ft 7ins	6ft 11ins

WIDTH – Upper deck	Interior	Over pillars	Over roof	
Bailey tops			6ft 2½ins	
BCT oak canopy top	6ft 3¾ins	6ft 8½ins	6ft 11½ins	